Garcian Meditations

Speculative Realism

Series Editor: Graham Harman

Since its first appearance at a London colloquium in 2007, the Speculative Realism movement has taken continental philosophy by storm. Opposing the formerly ubiquitous modern dogma that philosophy can speak only of the human-world relation rather than the world itself, Speculative Realism defends the autonomy of the world from human access, but in a spirit of imaginative audacity.

Editorial Advisory Board

Jane Bennett
Levi Bryant
Patricia Clough
Mark Fisher
Iain Hamilton Grant
Myra Hird
Adrian Johnston
Eileen A. Joy

Books available

Onto-Cartography: An Ontology of Machines and Media by Levi R. Bryant
Form and Object: A Treatise on Things by Tristan Garcia, translated by Mark Allan Ohm and Jon Cogburn
Adventures in Transcendental Materialism: Dialogues with Contemporary Thinkers by Adrian Johnston
The End of Phenomenology: Metaphysics and the New Realism by Tom Sparrow
Fields of Sense: A New Realist Ontology by Markus Gabriel
Quentin Meillassoux: Philosophy in the Making Second Edition by Graham Harman
Assemblage Theory by Manuel DeLanda
Romantic Realities: Speculative Realism and British Romanticism by Evan Gottlieb
Garcian Meditations: The Dialectics of Persistence in Form and Object by Jon Cogburn

Forthcoming titles

A Speculative Empiricism: Revisiting Whitehead by Didier Debaise, translated by Tomas Weber
After Quietism: Analytic Philosophies of Immanence and the New Metaphysics by Jon Cogburn
Infrastructure by Graham Harman

Visit the Speculative Realism website at:
edinburghuniversitypress.com/series/specr

Garcian Meditations

The Dialectics of Persistence in *Form and Object*

Jon Cogburn

EDINBURGH
University Press

For Ian Crystal (1966–2012)

Edinburgh University Press is one of the leading university presses in the UK. We publish academic books and journals in our selected subject areas across the humanities and social sciences, combining cutting-edge scholarship with high editorial and production values to produce academic works of lasting importance. For more information visit our website: www.edinburghuniversitypress.com

Edinburgh University Press Ltd
The Tun – Holyrood Road
12(2f) Jackson's Entry
Edinburgh EH8 8PJ

Typeset in 11/13 Adobe Sabon by
Servis Filmsetting Ltd, Stockport, Cheshire,
printed and bound in Great Britain by
CPI Group (UK) Ltd, Croydon CR0 4YY

A CIP record for this book is available from the British Library

ISBN 978 1 4744 1591 0 (hardback)
ISBN 978 1 4744 1592 7 (webready PDF)
ISBN 978 1 4744 1594 1 (paperback)
ISBN 978 1 4744 1593 4 (epub)

Contents

Acknowledgements

I must first thank Emily Beck Cogburn for conversations and proofreading. My greatest joy is the extent to which everything we do is collaborative.

It's not possible to thank Lee Braver, Tristan Garcia, Graham Harman, Paul Livingston, and Graham Priest enough for the amount of inspiration I get from their work. I hope that this is clear enough from the nature of my engagement in what follows. Perhaps less immediately clear is my debt to figures such as Gustav Bergmann, Jonathan Bennett, Roderick Chisholm, Saul Kripke, David Lewis, and P. F. Strawson, who did so much to deliver analytic philosophy from its dreary and self-defeating period of neo-Kantian anti-metaphysics. Two of my central conceits in what follows are (1) that the speculative realism event is an analogous moment in continental philosophy, one from which analytic philosophers might learn much, and (2) that *Form and Object* secures Garcia's place among metaphysics' mighty dead and living. Garcia is recognisably a continental philosopher, as most of us reckon these things; nonetheless, he is doing excellent analytic metaphysics. A fair-minded reader who takes the time to peruse my assorted endnotes will find this not implausible.

I would also like to thank Graham Harman and Carol Macdonald for encouragement and input, Philip (Andy) McLean for research assistance, conversations, and formatting help, Jeffrey Roland for checking the logical material in Chapters 3 and 5 and suggesting improvements in the exposition, as well as the participants of two classes on Garcia at Louisiana State University for their patience and conversation, in the latter regard in particular: Landin Bencaz, Katie Benton, Neal Caire, Delores Cowie, James Davis, Ron Dupuis, William Franklin, Ronnie Grant, Connor Leblanc, Jill Levraea, Eli Minor, Dylan O'Brien, Justin Owen, and Marylynn Smitherman.

I should also thank my friends and colleagues Marco Altamirano, Joel Andrepont, Chris Blakley, Graham Bounds, Levi Bryant, Debbie Goldgaber, Neal Hebert, Caroline and Joshua Heller, Mark Ohm, François Raffoul, Jeffrey Roland, Gregory Schufreider, Abigail and Christopher RayAlexander, James Rocha, Mark Silcox, and Tom Sparrow for metaphysical discussions; and Heller and Ohm in particular for permission to use co-written material. The description of Graham Harman's relationship to Heidegger in Chapter 1 comes from Mark Ohm's and my 'Actual Properties of Imaginative Things: Notes Towards an Object-Oriented Literary Theory', published in *Speculations*. The description of Russell's paradox in Chapter 3 comes from Joshua Heller's and my unpublished 'The Bearable Inconsistency of Being: Badiou Beyond the Limits of Thought', and much of the discussion of 'no-matter-what' in Chapter 4 was presented with Mark Ohm at the 2013 Notre Dame Translating Realism conference. Some of that discussion found its way into our Translator's Introduction to *Form and Object*, and this creates some Matthew and Luke style overlap between that text and Chapter 4 (with our original talk playing the role of the lost Q Gospel).

Series Editor's Preface

Like many important intellectual movements, Speculative Realism (SR) has faced attacks from multiple and even opposite directions. The abrasive webmaster of analytic philosophy has depicted it – inaccurately – as just another a mainstream continental philosophy. Meanwhile, continental philosophy itself has shown no affection for Speculative Realism, usually presenting its trademark critique of 'correlationism' as a straw man or red herring even as the group continues to wallow in correlationist dogma. Finally, Speculative Realism has even been assaulted from within by one of its co-founders, who emerges from seclusion every year or two with wild insulting remarks about those who have remained in the fold.

As one would expect, the remaining Speculative Realists have defended themselves vigorously against such attacks. A less expected form of support has come from the analytic philosopher Jon Cogburn of Louisiana State University, who has consistently defended this basically continental trend on the merits of its arguments alone. While I have never had the pleasure of meeting Cogburn, I remain grateful to him for explaining the virtues of Speculative Realism despite the heavy price he has paid for doing so: the blows of the powerful webmaster, a borderline pornographic attack by a sour and idle courtier, and the usual online sabotage of young nihilists. What does an analytic philosopher like Cogburn see in Speculative Realism that makes it worth his time to endure such astonishing abuse? The book now before you is the answer to that question.

In Spring 2011, Cogburn taught what was surely the first graduate seminar on Speculative Realism to be offered in the United States. But his first contact with Edinburgh University Press and its Speculative Realism series came through his role as co-translator of Tristan Garcia's landmark *Form and Object: A Treatise on Things*. First published in French less than five years ago, the book appeared in English as quickly as 2014 only thanks to the rapid and backbreaking labor of Cogburn and Mark Allan Ohm, also of Louisiana State University. Never previously a translator, Cogburn worked so closely with Ohm on this project out of conviction that *Form and Object* is a crucial book not just for continental philosophy, but for any attempt whatsoever to move past the analytic/continental divide. Indeed, it is Cogburn's view that 'Garcia's vision of the flat, formal plane of equality is one of the most audacious gambits in the history of metaphysics.' The reference here is to Garcia's introduction of the 'no-matter-what' or *n'importe quoi*: the notion of 'any entity whatever', stripped of the qualities that differentiate it from all others. Not only does Garcia proclaim allegiance to a 'flat ontology' that treats all things equally. More than this, he gives us an ontology flatter than those of Alexius Meinong or Bruno Latour, since even these thinkers add restricting conditions to what may be counted as an object. But there is more to *Form and Object* than this radical equality of beings, since the second half of Garcia's book reflects brilliantly and wisely on a number of highly concrete philosophical topics. Among them, Cogburn seems especially interested in Garcia's accounts of 'value', 'gender', and 'event'. Yet he also makes the more far-reaching case that Garcia's later chapters amount to a historically important adaptation of Hegel's dialectic to the needs of a basically non-Hegelian philosophy.

More generally, Cogburn has written one of the best 'bridge' books between contemporary analytic and continental philosophy. Even a casual observer will notice that metaphysics has become popular again in both analytic and continental philosophy, after many decades in which metaphysics was viewed by both schools as Lucifer incarnate. Cogburn notes an important difference in motivation between these two separate revivals of metaphysics. As he sees it, the new continental metaphysics arises as soon as we reject phenomenology's supposition that the transcendental subject is something different in kind from other objects. In his own words: 'Once classic phenomenology is reinterpreted as metaphysics of the subject, which itself is an object among other objects in the world, then classic phenomenology can be mined in a guerilla fashion to help us understand non-human objects.' Cogburn sees the issue as playing out rather differently in analytic philosophy: 'If continental philosophers found the royal road to philosophy to lay through the characterisation of the human subject, early analytic philosophers found it in the characterisation of human language.' Yet the distinction between approaches based on 'consciousness' and 'language' is not as large as it might first appear; the analytic and the continental thinker can easily meet on the joint ruins of these two basically anthropocentric traditions. For instance, 'Garcia's discussion of events and time in Book II of *Form and Object* (discussed in Chapter 8 below) is itself a fantastic piece of analytic philosophy, building on earlier analytic thinkers' work.'

One of the most thrilling gestures of Cogburn's book is his attempt to read the variant positions of Speculative Realism as different efforts to address 'what [the analytic philosopher] Graham Priest calls inclosure paradoxes, paradoxes that arguably arise whenever philosophers think deeply enough about totality'. In his book *Realist Magic*, Timothy Morton had already drawn on Priest's work for the purposes of Object-Oriented Ontology; I later did so as well in the final chapter of *Bells and Whistles*, though with somewhat less enthusiasm. Yet Cogburn pushes the dialogue with Priest to a level of greater intensity, considering the inclosure paradoxes as the very material of philosophy, and as inherently offering four different paths towards solution. While Cogburn links my own tacit solution to the inclosure paradox with that of Bertrand Russell, he deftly links Garcia with Priest. One way he does so is with reference to my book *Quentin Meillassoux: Philosophy in the Making*, published in 2011 as the inaugural work of this series. There I argued that there are two separate ways of escaping the correlationist view that we cannot know thought or world in isolation, but only in their primordial relation or rapport. That is to say, correlationism can mean either of two different things: (1) the human–world relation is the only relation to which we have direct access, and therefore it mediates all of our thinking; (2) all knowledge is finite, unable to grasp reality directly as it really is. As the title of his book *After Finitude* indicates, Meillassoux's gesture is to reject (2), thereby regaining knowledge of the absolute, with the cost that he retains the modern privilege of the human subject as a full half of all reality. By contrast, object-oriented philosophy rejects (1), accepting Kantian finitude while complaining instead that it should have been extended to all relations, including those between inanimate objects as well.

But now Cogburn adds a fascinating twist to the argument: 'On the interpretation of Garcia that I've developed thus far, he joins Graham Priest in rejecting *both* (1) and (2), with the price to pay being the cost of characterising reality as a contradictory whole.'

Cogburn is lucid as a thinker and equally lucid as a writer. His natural gifts as a teacher come through in his various anecdotes about the contribution of his students to the arguments in this book. In roughly eight or nine months he has written this wonderful volume, which should take the dialogue between Speculative Realism and analytic philosophy to a new level, and should also jump-start the analytic reception of Garcia. This is a book that no one but Cogburn could have written. Only his unique combination of intellectual talents, and his unique vantage point on various conflicting philosophical trends, could have enabled the arguments found in the pages below. This book gives me a stronger sense than ever of Cogburn's irreplaceable intellectual persona and his fearlessness in speaking what he takes to be the truth, no matter the philosophical or political fallout.

Graham Harman
Dubuque, Iowa
January 2016

Preface

The Preface to the first edition of Immanuel Kant's *Critique of Pure Reason* contains an interesting meditation on literary finitude:

> The Abbé Terrasson says that if a book's size is measured not only by (a) the number of pages but also by (b) the time needed to understand it, then it can be said of many a book that it would have been much (b) shorter if it weren't so (a) short.[1]

And while it may seem the pinnacle of exegetical perversity to apply this point to a 400-page plus (170,401 words in English translation) doorstop such as Tristan Garcia's *Form and Object*, the fact that it does apply is a testament to the depth and expanse of his vision.

My task is twofold. First, I hope that the addition of 80,000 or so words to Garcia's will help readers learn, criticise, and apply his insights and perspectives. Mark Ohm and I decided to translate *Form and Object* because we were (and remain) convinced that it is a genuine philosophical event in the sense of being both important and radically novel. Garcia has reconfigured the dialectical space gifted us by the Western philosophical tradition's mighty dead. Not only has he, as Quentin Meillassoux notes on the cover blurb of his book, single-handedly revived encyclopedic metaphysics, but he has done so in a way that yields non-trivial contributions to ongoing debates in both analytic and continental philosophy. But, as all good readers of Badiou's *Being and Event* know, fidelity to the event requires hard work. Despite, and because of, the radical novelty, one must patiently reconsider the event's antecedents in order to make sense of its consequences. And, as Kant and the good Abbé realised, it is precisely such antecedents that systematic philosophers such as Garcia have to skimp on in order for their books to fit inside the bicycle bags of the rest of us. As a result, much of my task in this book is to provide more background context about the philosophical debates in which Garcia intervenes.

Fortunately, the major joints of Garcia's system *can* be presented in terms of traditional oppositions, particularly those concerning substance and process, analysis and dialectic, simple and whole, and discovery and creation. In each case, Garcia further develops his account of what reality is like such that both sides of the opposite in question are rejected. While there is a more than superficial resemblance between Garcia's technique and Hegel's dialectic, we shall see that Garcia is correct to stress the ways in which he radically departs from the Hegelian paradigm. For Garcia, dialectical tension is not a reliable motor of conceptual, historical, and physical change. Rather, he believes that the kind of strains seen by Hegelians as contradictions that force transitions are in fact often what enable objects to persist; thus this book's title.

Any sufficiently rich system of philosophy has distinct points of entry. One can fashion Garcia in the mode of Hegel's *Logic*, beginning by trying to discern what is in common to all things by seeing what is left when all determinations that serve to differentiate them are removed. While Hegel adduces his initial trinity of Being, Nothingness, and Becoming in this manner, Garcia is led to no-matter-what/matter, thing, and world, with instances of each latter categories containing instances of the previous ones, and things constituted merely as differentiators between that which they contain and that which contains them. Then Garcia considers de-determined things to characterise objects and the universes that contain them, after which he introduces the notion of intensity to provide the rich set of regional ontologies given in Book II.

Reading Garcia closely alongside Hegel is a defensible exegetical route, but it risks obfuscating Garcia's deeper philosophical motivations. This is why, rather than presenting Garcia in terms of the methodological homology with Hegel, Chapter 1 begins by explaining his radical rejection of any form of reductionism. In the broadest possible sense, to say that some discourse, such as chemistry, reduces to another, like physics, is to say that all of the events explained via chemistry can be adequately explained via physics. But for Garcia, what makes an object an object is precisely its resistance to such reduction. To say a chemical molecule is an object is thus to deny that it is merely the atoms that compose it (in Garcia's terminology, the molecule 'comprehends' the atoms), and to deny that it can be explained away with the relational structures (such as cultural institutions involved with science) that contain it. For Garcia, what makes an object an object is that it differentiates that which comprehends it from that which it comprehends.

In Chapters 2 and 3, I contrast Garcia's model of objects as differentiators with other canonical theories in the new continental metaphysics, showing how a defining feature is the manner in which metaphysicians can be interpreted as responding to a paradox concerning metaphysical explanation. This allows us to foreground what I call Garcia's paradoxico-metaphysics, and also allows us to see clearly how Garcia's achievement should be interpreted alongside related meta-metaphysical developments by Graham Harman and Graham Priest, as well as other recent speculative philosophers such as Alain Badiou, Markus Gabriel, and Paul Livingston. In addition, it allows us to begin to appreciate the fact that Garcia is contributing to contemporary analytic metaphyics. After clarifying one of Garcia's major terms of art, 'no-matter-what' in Chapter 4 (and in the process deriving a new argument for the existence of the empty set), Chapter 5 begins a more detailed examination of Garcia's system. I start by considering Graham Harman's claim that Garcia's characterisation of an object in terms of its difference from that which it comprehends and from what comprehends it ends up having the object depend on these very things. Changing any of the comprehended or comprehending things would change the precise difference in question, resulting in a different object. Worse, since the object is comprehended by all of the relations that it has to every other object, we seem to have that the object's identity is a function of everything in the universe, a position which easily veers into the (British) Hegelian affirmation that there is only one thing. Discussing Garcia allows me to pose this problem in a novel way, via what I call the Putnam/Parmenides argument. And it is precisely to rebut this argument, as I show in Chapter 6, that Garcia's triad of matter/thing/world comes in. For Garcia, the de-determined object, the entity qua thing, works as a solitary anchor, differentiating the object from those objects it comprehends and those that comprehend it. In this manner, Garcia's Janus-faced ontology is neither relational (since each entity is simultaneously a solitary thing) nor atomistic (since these things are merely differentiators between matter/no-matter-what and world).

From here, there are just a few more steps towards an interpretation of Garcia as an analytic speculative realist.[2] Once Garcia's theory of entities is better understood, we are in a place to critically evaluate the Kantian-sounding claims he makes with respect to the universe, scales, and limits. Then, just as the de-determined world of the thing must be buttressed by the world of the object, the extensive world of (n)either/(n)or must be buttressed by an account of the intensive world of more and less, a world I present in Chapter 8. This buttressing provides the material used in the anti-reductionist regional ontologies of Book II, some of which are discussed in Chapters 9 and 10.

I have found the following table to help with teaching this book alongside *Form and Object*. The left-hand column gives the sections of Garcia's book and the right-hand column gives the relevant chapter number and section title of this one. I've tried as much as possible to make the order of reading the same, so that this book works as both a sympathetic critical study and a reader's guide. Often, the relevant section of my book helps readers interpret the following sections (on the left-hand side) of Garcia's book.

I should note that there is *a lot* of interesting and important philosophy in *Form and Object* that will not be discussed in what follows. Garcia's anti-Heideggerian accounts of nothingness (*FO* 46–50) and the question of being (*FO* 108–11) as well as his critique of Lewisian views of possibility and necessity (*FO* 89–93) from Book I are not mentioned.[3] A reader who just reads this book will have no idea of Book II's anti-Derridean account of representation (Book II, Chapter VII), Garcia's attempts to avoid both naturalism and relativism with respect to humanity (Book II, Chapters VI), culture, history, and economics (Book II, Chapters IX–XI), his rich theory of rules and art (Book II, Chapter VIII), or his formally interesting account of classes (Book II, Chapter XIII). It simply was not possible to begin to do justice to all of these in the space to which I've limited myself. On the other hand, I do think that my general attempt to lay bare the mechanisms at work in Garcia's thinking will also help readers with respect to these sections. And I do hope that no one will say of the following that it would have been much longer if it weren't so long.

Table of correspondences between *Form and Object* and *Garcian Meditations*

Table (continued)

Form and Object	Garcian Meditations
Part III: Being and Comprehending	
I. Being is Being Comprehended	Chapter 7: Relativism versus Absolutism
	Chapter 7: Objective Matter
II. That which is a Thing, That which a Thing is	—
III. The Two Senses	—
IV. In Things: Matter	—
V. Outside Things: Form	—
Book II: Objectively	
Chapter I: Universe	—
Chapter II: Objects and Events	Chapter 8: Events (Presence)
Chapter III: Time	Chapter 8: Time (Intensive Presence)
Chapter IV: Living Things	Chapter 8: Life (Intensive Difference)
Chapter V: Animals	—
Chapter VI: Humans	—
Chapter VII: Representations	—
Chapter VIII: Art and Rules	—
Chapter IX: Culture	—
Chapter X: History	—
Chapter XI: Economy of Objects	—
Chapter XII: Values	Chapter 9: Beauty (Intensive Identity)
	Chapter 9: Truth (Intensive Comprehension)
	Chapter 9: Goodness
Chapter XIII: Classes	—
Chapter XIV: Genders	Chapter 10: Gender
Chapter XV: Ages of Life	Chapter 10: Adolescence
Chapter XVI: Death	Chapter 10: Death
Coda: Formally, Objectively	—
The Chance and the Price	—

Notes

1. Kant, *Critique of Pure Reason*, p. xix.
2. Which in no way is meant to preclude other interpretations. Part of the greatness of systematic philosophers from Plato onward is the manner in which they serve as productive machines for inconsistent and philosophically valuable interpretations. One of the pleasures of writing this book has been conversations with Christopher RayAlexander, who interprets (with no less plausibility and equal philosophical interest) Garcia as primarily in conversation with Heidegger, Lacan, and Žižek.

3. Here and elsewhere, quotations from *Form and Object* are taken from Mark Ohm's and my translation (Edinburgh University Press, 2014) and are indicated by *FO* followed by the page reference.

Introduction: Tristan Garcia among the Cave Dwellers

The astute reader of this book's Preface will have noted the strange fact that my first three chapters are all paired with Garcia's rather short (16-page) Introduction. This is the result of Garcia's decision not to follow the example of Hegel with respect to Introductions. In some ways, my first three chapters are an attempt at the Introduction Hegel would have written, were he the author of *Form and Object*.

But in my own Introduction, I want to do something slightly different from Garcia and Hegel. I wish to give a sense of the historical and dialectical background for Garcia's affirmation of realism, something Garcia himself is a little bit equivocal about.

> Does this treatise present a defence of 'realism', since it considers things rather than our access to these things? If one thinks that reality consists merely of possible, impossible, imaginary, or virtual kinds of things, then I think we can answer negatively. No preference is given here to any one special kind of thing, since each kind is neither better nor worse than another kind. *Real* things do not matter to us here. Real *things* matter to us – and, for this reason, other kinds of things as well. (*FO* 4)

Articulating the sense in which Garcia nonetheless *is* a realist requires quite a bit of backing up. Here we sketch a Whig history of realism and its discontents from Plato to the positivists and beyond.[1] The reader will hopefully get a sense not only of Garcia's position in dialectical space, but also a sense of what is at stake.

So let us begin by backtracking a few millennia. In Book VII of Plato's *Republic*, Socrates presents one of the founding myths of Western philosophy, a story concerning the sad fate of impoverished creatures who live 'in a sort of subterranean cavern with a long entrance open to the light on its entire width'. Socrates enjoins his indefatigably willing interlocutor Glaucon, Son of Ariston, to:

> Conceive them as having their legs and necks fettered from childhood, so that they remain in the same spot, able to look forward only, and prevented by the fetters from turning their heads. Picture further the light from a fire burning higher up and a distance behind them, and between the fire and the prisoners and above them a road along which a low wall has been built, as the exhibitors of puppet shows have partitions before the men themselves, above which they show the puppets . . . See also, then, men carrying past the wall implements of all kinds that rise above the wall, and human images and shapes of animals as well, wrought in stone and wood and every material, some of these bearers presumably speaking and others silent.[2]

For Socrates, the plight of these chained wretches is to serve as a metaphor for the uneducated who have no insight into the causes of their perceptions and beliefs, and hence no ability to reliably align their beliefs with the true or their actions with the good.

Socrates' story raises the question of the extent to which Socratic education is actually even possible. Perhaps the cave dwellers' condition just is humanity's. Something is going on in the great outdoors, but we are imprisoned by fetters of our own perceptual and conceptual limitation. The philosophical sceptic finds thoughts such as these dispositive, and denies that we can have knowledge about the world outside the cave, that is, the world as it is in itself apart from our parochial capacity to make sense of it.[3] Socrates, on the other hand, was considerably more sanguine about the prospect of escape, and he contemplated the possibility of a prisoner unfettering himself and walking into the light, slowly acclimatising, realising that the world outside the cave is more real, even to the point where the former cave dweller can gaze at the sun itself.

In a weird twist surely meant to reference Socrates' own destiny at the hands of his fellow Athenians, Plato has Socrates describe the desolate fate of the escapee upon returning to the cave:

> Now if he should be required to contend with these perpetual prisoners in 'evaluating' these shadows while his vision was still dim and before his eyes were accustomed to the dark – and this time required for habituation would not be very short – would he not provoke laughter, and would it not be said of him that he had returned from his journey aloft

with his eyes ruined and that it was not worthwhile even to attempt the ascent? And if it were possible to lay hands on and to kill the man who tried to release them and lead them up, would they not kill him?[4]

Here the philosophical sceptic is interjected into the story as a criminal. In Socrates' telling, the returned escapee's killers agree that there is a world outside the cave, yet deny that anyone can have knowledge of it.

The history of Western philosophy is to some extent a history of permutations of Plato's myth. For example, instead of thinking that the attempt to escape the prison led to blindness, the other prisoners might kill the Socratic hero because they think that he is not telling the truth. Perhaps the hero was simply deluded about even having left the cave, and the shadow play we perceive is not really a shadow play because it is *all there is*. And perhaps it is incoherent to attempt to educate oneself about the causes of all there is, because such causes would themselves be part of all there is. If this is correct, then both the sceptic *and* the escapee are mistaken. Both agree that there is more to the world than what one can see on the cave wall. The only difference is that the escapee thinks that she possesses knowledge about this transcendent world.

Contemporary philosophy contains many distinct positions that roughly correspond to the non-sceptical murderers. So-called 'philosophers of immanence'[5] refuse to philosophise about such 'transcendent' (defined in various ways below) entities as a non-perceptual ground of our perceptions. Weirdly, immanence so described is consistent with both Berkeleyan Idealism, the position that all that exists are perceptions and minds containing them, and Naive Realism, the position that non-perceptual matter exists, but that it exists exactly the way we perceive it to be (so, for example, colour properties are as much properties of things considered in themselves independently of people as are those things' capacity to reflect light).

At first glance, we've exhausted all of the options for characters suggested by the myth of the cave: the sceptic, the immanentist, and the (sophisticated) realist. Consider:

	Knowledge of . . .	No knowledge of . . .
Transcendent realm	(sophisticated) realist	sceptic
Merely immanent realm	immanentist	

Of course things are not quite so simple, for four reasons. First, we very rarely think about the world as a whole, and the ability to think of different aspects of the world gives rise to the ability to be a realist about one kind of thing (say, mathematical objects) and a sceptic about other kinds of things (say, facts that would make moral claims true). This being said, just as our discourses include mathematical and moral talk, they also include talk about totality. The question of whether everything exists and whether we can have knowledge of it is just as meaningful as the question of whether numbers exist and we can have knowledge of them. So division of reality according to the different discourses by which we talk about it (for example, pure and applied mathematics, moral deliberation) doesn't obviate the need to consider whether some form of *global* realism, scepticism, or immanentism is defensible.

Second, we have yet to define 'transcendent', and for good reasons! There are *lots* of ways to flesh out the cave story depending upon what one means by this term. For example, in a recent historical survey of metaphysics, A. W. Moore notes that the transcendent/immanent distinction has been used to mark at least eight different boundaries:

- what is inaccessible (to us) through experience and what is accessible (to us) through experience,
- what is unknowable (by us) and what is knowable (by us),
- what is supernatural and what is natural,
- what is atemporal and what is temporal,
- what is abstract and what is concrete,
- what is infinite and what is finite,
- what bespeaks unity, totality, and/or identity and what bespeaks plurality, partiality, and/or difference, and
- what we cannot make sense of and what we can.[6]

So there are at least as many varieties of the realist/sceptic/immanentist trichotomy as there are varieties of the distinction between the transcendent and the immanent.

And, third, we haven't even begun to split hairs with respect to what is required with respect to an affirmation of *the existence of* something (such as a transcendent realm) or what it is to have or lack *knowledge* of some kind of thing. Many of the contributions to the 'realism debates' that raged in analytic (and have since expanded to continental) philosophy during the closing years of the previous century[7] concluded that there are distinct ways that one can be a realist with respect to different discourses. For example, commitment to the existence of properties such as 'tastes good' might not require holding that if two people disagree about instances of these properties, one of them is wrong, while commitment to mathematical properties such as 'is an odd number' does seem to require this. In this sense, most of us might be said to be *more* realist about mathematics. But now we must again multiply the number of varieties of our realist/immanentist/sceptic trichotomy, this time by the number of gradations with respect to how strong one's realism might be.

With respect to Tristan Garcia's project, our final complication is the most pressing. We can imagine a *fourth* character in Plato's cave. Let us call this persona the quietist. The quietist witnesses the realist's announcement of her supposed return from outside of the cave as well as the sceptic and immanentist planning her murder. Initially the quietist responds by putting her hands over her ears and saying loudly 'La! La! La! La! La!' but she can't help but to still hear the realist berating the cave dwellers and she moreover knows that after the sceptic and the immanentist dispatch the realist to the Platonic afterworld, they themselves will be at each other's throats. So the quietist tries to convince the other cave dwellers to murder all three of the troublemakers.

The quietist's key philosophical manoeuvre is the articulation of a theory of meaning that entails that the realist, sceptic, and immanentist are all uttering nonsense when they try to state their positions. And if, as Winston Churchill reputedly said, the British and Americans are two great peoples divided by a common language, the two great twentieth-century philosophical schools, logical positivism and phenomenology, were divided by a common quietism. Both schools further radicalised the Kantian thesis that we can only have knowledge of the truth of propositions that are in some manner appropriately rooted in sensory experience into the position that propositions not so rooted actually *lack meaning*. Clearly, this 'strong' correlationism (so labelled by Quentin Meillassoux)[8] entails that the realist's claims about what it might be like outside the cave are simply meaningless. And it's not too hard to see how the sceptic's claim that something outside the cave exists, but that we cannot know anything about it, would likewise be meaningless. If we can't know *anything* about it, then for the quietist, we can't claim with the sceptic that it exists. And, in this manner, the quietist also prevents the immanentist from declaiming that the outside of the cave doesn't exist. Again, for the quietist, *any* claim about an outside is meaningless and not to be uttered.

To be clear, the quietist isn't against all philosophy. Once all possible metaphysics is banished, once we have bracketed all issues concerning how things actually are independently of how they seem to us, we might still arrogate to ourselves the task of clarifying, elucidating, systematising, and rationalising how things seem. Positivists and phenomenologists go about this task in characteristically different ways, but it is at root the same project. In addition, quietists are not immune from the philosophical two-step, where you first say something and then you take it back.[9] Quietists can play to the crowd, claiming to respect the common sense of the person in the cave when she says that one of the shadows on the wall really is a thing itself. This can be true, *loosely speaking*; but such phrases are to be distinguished from the syntactically identical assertions in the mouths of realists or sceptics. Moreover, traditional quietists such as positivists and phenomenologists will attempt to in a sense return to the things themselves by in some way constructing such things via our conditions of access to them.

Although he nowhere uses the term 'quietism' (or French cognates), Tristan Garcia actually poses his whole project as a rejection of it.

> The twentieth century – to which this treatise in some way proposes to bid adieu – was a period of theorising our methodological *access* to things, rather than theorising about *things* as such. For example, our theories of methodological access talked about formal language and ordinary language; the phenomenology of consciousness and the phenomenology of perception; the opening of being; the structure of the unconscious and the structure of myths; normativity and the processes of subjectivation; self-reflection and critical consciousness. (*FO* 3)

While Garcia sees his own project as part of the swing of the pendulum against quietistic strictures, he also presents a positive reason for why the pendulum should so swing. In terms of our cast of characters fighting it out in the cave, though quietists want to recapitulate something like a person on the street's naive realist variety of immanentism, they in fact in the end always tend towards the idealist variety. To see this, note how for Garcia there is an important asymmetry between the realist's order of explanation and that of the quietist trying to recover common sense.

> Third, we must understand that by initially thinking about things [with the realist] we are not prevented from conceiving of our thought, language, and knowledge as things equal to things thought, said, and known. On the other hand, by initially thinking about our relations to things, we systematically fail to accomplish our original goal, the things themselves; this way of thinking loses its objective en route and falls short of its target. Its sole objective is to give a descriptive account of our methods of aiming at things through consciousness, language, representation, or action. But by thinking about things, we make no promises that we cannot keep, whereas a second-order thought about our thought about things, for example, promises an access to things that it ultimately denies the existence of. To the extent that philosophies of access exchange objects for conditions of their enunciation, things become estranged from their own composition as objects. (*FO* 3–4)

Garcia thinks that quietism systematically fails to recapitulate the common sense of the quietist's fellow cave dwellers, and hence tends towards idealism.

But it would be a mistake merely to lump Garcia with realists against sceptics, immanentists, and quietists. Rather, global anti-realists (of any of the sorts we have been considering) are typically moved by the thought that realism is self-defeating for one of two reasons. From Berkeley (and more canonically in some continental circles, Fichte) we have the 'master argument'[10] to the conclusion that we are not justified in thinking transcendent entities exist. The argument typically starts by asking us to attempt to conceive of a genuinely transcendent object. But if genuinely transcendent objects are precisely those objects that can't be conceived by us, then we can't conceive of them. Our inability to conceive of them is a measure of their very transcendence. But if it is incoherent to claim that they can be conceived, then what possible reason could we have for taking them to exist? Evidence for existence always involves some conception of what the kind of thing in question is, but this is precisely what we can't get with genuinely transcendent objects. Far better to either hold they don't exist or at least prescind from them.

For someone moved by Berkeley/Fichte-type arguments, the

myth of the cave is a very bad metaphor. What are we supposed to be conceiving when we think of the cave's outside? We conceive of the escapee as perceiving a world just like the one we perceive. But then if what we *really* perceive is analogous to the perceptions of cave dwellers, the escapee really hasn't escaped in any meaningful way. Thus immanence, either the Berkeleyan idealistic view that all that exists are minds and their perceptions or the naive realist view that reality is just as it seems. Or the quietism that attempts to prohibit discussion, one way or the other (but that, according to Garcia, inevitably tends towards idealism).

The second argument against the realist is Kantian in provenance.[11] The realist claims to have knowledge about the totality of everything. But to have knowledge of a totality requires having knowledge of the things in which that totality is embedded. That is, to think of totality as a thing is to think of it as one more thing contained in totality! But then the supposed totality that the realist originally had knowledge of isn't really total. So we must give up on the pretence that we can have knowledge about the totality of everything. Note that this argument, if valid, tells against idealism as well as realism, for both are totalising metaphysical views. This is the neo-Kantian push to quietism.

Until very recently in the history of Western philosophy, the task of the realist included disarming both the Berkeley/Fichte and Kant/Russell-type arguments. But, very recently, a motley group of logicians, philosophers of language, and reconstructed German idealists have countenanced a different path. Dialetheists note that the anti-realist always generates a contradiction when putting forward such arguments, and then tries to show that her favoured retraction from realism returns consistency. But might the contradictions themselves be true ones? Perhaps at the limits of the conceivable we discover states of affairs simultaneously conceivable and inconceivable? Perhaps problematic totalities both are and are not members of themselves. Amending a term from Paul Livingston's *The Politics of Logic*, we will here call any position that affirms such a contradiction an instance of paradoxico-metaphysics.

Garcia forges a distinctive road into paradoxico-metaphysics. Metaphysics aims to give a maximally general account of what reality is like such that we encounter the phenomena that we do. But what if we encounter phenomena such as the Berkeley/Fichte and Kant/Russell arguments that seem to entail that metaphysics is impossible? Then the task of metaphysics is to give a maximally general account of what reality is like such that metaphysics is impossible. If the project sounds paradoxical, that is because it is. But if reality is paradoxical, such is our fate.

Notes

1. On the necessity of Whig histories in contexts such as this, see Robert Brandom's *Reason in Philosophy: Animating Ideas*.
2. Plato, *The Republic*, pp. 748–9.
3. For the most charitable construal of this tradition in English, see Peter Unger's *Ignorance: A Defense of Skepticism*.
4. Plato, *The Republic*, p. 749.
5. For attempts to read recent French phenomenology in terms of this distinction, see both John Mullarky's *Post-Continental Philosophy* and Ian James's *The New French Philosophy*.
6. Moore, *The Evolution of Modern Metaphysics*, pp. 9–11.
7. For a wonderful overview of these debates in analytic philosophy, see Stuart Brock and Edwin Mares's *Realism and Anti-Realism*. For a sympathetic reading of the continental tradition as a history of increasing anti-realism, see Lee Braver's *A Thing of this World: A History of Continental Anti-Realism*. For a critique of the continental tradition along just these lines, see Richard Sebold's *Continental Anti-Realism: A Critique*.
8. See Meillassoux's *After Finitude* and especially the discussion of various types of correlationism in Graham Harman's *Quentin Meillassoux: Philosophy in the Making*.
9. Cf. Meillassoux's discussion of semantic doubling in *After Finitude* and especially Josh Heller's and my 'Meillassoux's Dilemma'.
10. See the section on the master argument in Lisa Downing's *Stanford Encyclopedia of Philosophy* article on Berkeley. Harman (*Quentin Meillassoux: Philosophy in the Making*) and I both think that the Kantian arguments concerning totality are by far the more important ones. For my critique of the Berkeley/Fichte argument, see 'Moore's Paradox as an Argument Against Anti-Realism'. In this article I show that the same reasoning used by Berkeley and Fichte entails that there are no true disbelieved propositions, and show exactly where all such arguments go wrong by misconstruing the inferential role of assumptions hypothetically assumed.
11. For a canonical presentation, see the discussion of 'Kant's fifth antinomy' in Graham Priest's *Beyond the Limits of Thought*.

Neither Substance Nor Process I: Anti-Reductionism

In the Introduction, I sought to situate Garcia within the history of philosophical realism. Now, here and in Chapter 3, I will place his ideas in the context of one of the most interesting schools in recent continental philosophy, Graham Harman's object-oriented ontology. Garcia himself notes the connection.

> Our project finds common ground among those who are developing an 'object-oriented metaphysics', abandoning what Graham Harman calls 'philosophies of access', and who are interested in a 'flat ontology' of things. (*FO* 4)

Not only is there significant overlap between Garcia and Harman, but Harman's 'Object-Oriented France' was, as far as I know, the first English-language article on Garcia. The overlap between Harman and Garcia is invaluable with respect to breaking through the hermeneutic circle posed by systematic philosophers. Some of Harman's words give better voice to the horizon against which Garcia operates than Garcia's own. In what follows I freely avail myself of them. And, more importantly, the disagreements between Harman and Garcia are not the narcissism of small differences, but rather end up ramifying out into fundamental issues that face anyone interested in metaphysics.

In *Form and Object*'s Introduction, Garcia claims that the 'theoretical compass' of the entire book is 'the conviction that *no thing is reducible to nothing*', and states that this conviction encompasses two key claims.

> Such a proposition means both that no thing can be absolutely reduced to nothingness – because that thing is dead, past, false, imaginary,

nonexistent, or contradictory, for example – and that no thing is absolutely reducible to any other thing. (*FO* 8)

We can label the proposition's first meaning *ontological liberality*, which can be summarised with the Garcian catchphrase: to be is to be determined. In a sense to be explained, Garcia is ontologically committed to the being[1] of the widest possible panoply of kinds of objects, including fictional objects, non-existent objects, impossible objects, and contradictory objects. However, even though he is committed to the being of non-existent objects, this isn't to say that he is committed to *the existence of* all these kinds of things. Thus, even if we agree with Garcia that to be is to be determined, without significant further explication it is of course not immediately clear what is being affirmed.

To begin to understand Garcia's affirmation of ontological liberality, we must make sense of the second meaning of the claim that no thing is reducible to nothing (that nothing is absolutely reducible to any other thing). We can label this thesis Garcia's *radical anti-reductionism*. For Garcia, if we could explain a putative kind of thing (say, chemical compounds) entirely in terms of another kind of thing (say, subatomic particles composing the compounds and the fundamental forces to which they are subject), then there would be no reason to be ontologically committed to chemical compounds any more. All that would really be there would be the subatomic particles and fundamental forces. If this is right, then the more reductionism fails, the more kinds of things there are.

However, Garcia's ontological liberality is not merely the affirmation that various subject matters of our discourse all *are* in the sense that they cannot be fully explained in terms of other kinds of entities. For Garcia's liberality is a liberality of *things*, as attested by the first two paragraphs of *Form and Object*. Consider this fragment of the second.

> In Western philosophical traditions, things were often ordered according to essences, substrata, qualities, predicates, *quidditas* and *quodditas*, being and beings. Precluding anything from being equally 'something', neither more nor less than any other thing, thus becomes a rather delicate task. We live in this world of things, where a cutting of acacia, a gene, a computer-generated image, a transplantable hand, a musical sample, a trademarked name, or a sexual service are comparable things. (*FO* 1)

For reasons to be explained in Chapters 5 and 6 of this book, one of Garcia's fundamental commitments is that the way in which we compare *objects* forces us also to think of these objects as de-determined *things* lacking properties. And for Garcia there is a univocal sense in which each thing is. This is actually an extraordinary claim. Is it really the case that a cutting of acacia, a gene, an image, a piece of music, a name, and a sexual service all *are* in exactly the same way? For Garcia, their differences disappear once we conceive of them under the formal mode of things. Qua things, each stands alone before the same indifferent tribunal, a world that itself stands before nothing. Qua things, all there is to say is that each contains matter and is contained in the world. And Thomas Mann's magic mountain is neither more nor less a thing than the bottle of Tabasco sauce on my desk.

But affirming this ontological liberality with respect to objects/things requires Garcia to supplement his radical anti-reductionism with a countervailing set of arguments that shows that there are no exceptions to the empire of things. That is, if anti-reductionism restores the dignity of being to objects/things, then Garcia's countervailing arguments might be viewed as removing the dignity of all those entities that Garcia labels 'more than things', that is entities such as gods, monsters, and philosophers, which we might take to be yet not be mere things. In this manner, Garcia completes the above paragraph with just this injunction.

> Some resist, considering themselves, thought, consciousness, sentient beings, personhood, or gods as exceptions to the flat system of interchangeable things. A waste of time and effort. For the more one excludes this or that from the world of things, the more and better one makes something of them, such that things have this terrifying structure: to subtract one of them is to add it in turn to the count. (*FO* 1)

In this chapter we will consider both moments: Garcia's anti-reductionism and the countervailing arguments.

Neither Undermining Nor Overmining

One of the many remarkably novelistic discussions in *Form and Object* occurs near the end of Book I. Right in the middle of one of the most abstract discussions in the book (Garcia's attempted dissolution of the 'problem of being'), Garcia compares the phenomenology of looking at a painting with Proust's description of viewing a sleeping beloved.

> Before me is a picture, a painting, framed and at the centre of a museum. I try looking at this landscape, this scene, this composition. But as soon as I look carefully at the painting – if I no longer consider the room of the museum that the work belongs to – I am no longer very certain of truly seeing it. I am seized by doubt. I plunge into the painting. I examine a mass of significant or seemingly insignificant details – distant characters, scattered objects, movements, layers, shades, and so on. By examining the varnish, I perceive coloured matter and its tiny waves on the surface of the canvas. I follow the brushstrokes. I approach an area where there is a subtle overlapping of an almost transparent sienna and Bismarck red, and so on, but in so doing I have lost sight of the object as such.
>
> I wanted the thing, but only ever had *that which enters into the thing*. This is comparable to watching the sleeping beloved, like Proust's narrator, contemplating her closer in order to penetrate her mystery, until discovering what she is in herself. In her skin, through her breath, beneath her closed eyes, her expanding and contracting chest, her freckles, her curled lip, her untied hair. I want the lover herself, and yet I have only found what was in her, what was the awaited person. Her? I have lost her. Dissolved as a thing, she has slipped through my fingers. I have lost her appearance, her profile, and her unity. (*FO* 128–9)

When we get too close to the painting, the painting itself disappears and we find ourselves lost in a world of paint splotches, varnish, brushstrokes, the push-pull of contrasting colours, and various textural contrasts. While it is often worthwhile, indeed necessary, to get so lost (how can this dried-out, protruding blob of paint, linseed oil, and varnish possibly turn into the satiny shimmer of Lady Agnew's dress merely by me taking two steps backwards?), we still learn from such forays that in some sense, the painting cannot itself be the sum of its various splotches.

But then what else is the painting? Theorists of art distance themselves from the painting's constituents, attempting to further divine its meaning by considering the various historical, ideological, economic, ethno-biological, psychological, sociological, and other contexts in which the painting occurs.

I can survey its effects, its consequences, and its posterity. But I also have the opportunity to situate the painting within my singular history, to obtain control over its accidental relationship with what I have experienced up to now. It is possible for me to place the painting in many contexts, with many conditions, and always ask the *meaning* of the painting. (*FO* 129)

But then the opposite danger arises, and the painting becomes a mere placeholder for whatever meaning it is supposed to illustrate given the historical and interpretive framework I am bringing to bear on it. Again, the painting itself seems to disappear. The phenomenological conclusion:

As soon as I look carefully at this thing, the painting or the lover, I realise that I always apprehend this thing as split; either I grasp what is the painting, what is the lover, or I grasp what this painting is, what my lover is. I no longer see the thing, but only see either that which is the thing or that which the thing is. (*FO* 130)

And Garcia's condition with respect to his lover is for him the human condition with respect to everything. Our explanations of an object's parts or the relations that the object enters into always leave something out.

This conceit is precisely what is in common among object-oriented ontologists such as Ian Bogost, Levi Bryant, Graham Harman, Tristan Garcia, Timothy Morton, and the author of this book. Harman calls such downward reductive explanatory strategies, where objects are explained in terms of the behaviour of their constituents, 'undermining',and explores the role that such explanations can play in degrading the ontological status of objects.[2]

The first critical response to objects asserts that they are not fundamental. All of the dogs, candles, and snowflakes we observe are built of something more basic, and this deeper reality is the proper subject matter for philosophy. As the surf pounded the shores of Anatolia, Thales proposed water as the first principle of everything. Later came Anaximenes, for whom air rather than water was the root of the world. It is slightly more complicated with Empedocles, for whom things are composed not of one but of four separate elements: air, earth, fire, and water, joined and divorced through the forces of love and hate. And finally with Democritus, atoms of different shapes and sizes serve as the root element of all larger things. In present-day materialism one speaks instead of quarks or infinitesimal strings. In all such cases, the critical method is the same: what seems at first like an autonomous object is really just a motley aggregate built of smaller pieces. Only what is basic can be real.[3]

Rejecting the explanatory presumption of undermining is old hat to many philosophers working in both continental and analytic anti-reductionist traditions.

What is distinctive about object-oriented ontologists is that they simultaneously endorse a parallel critique of what Harman calls 'overmining', which Harman and Garcia take to be the mirror image of undermining. Here is Harman again:

> A different way of dismissing objects as the chief *dramatis personae* of philosophy is to reduce them upward rather than downward. Instead of saying that objects are too shallow to be real, it is said that they are too deep. On this view the object is a useless hypothesis, a *je ne sais quoi* in the bad sense. Rather than being undermined from beneath, the object is overmined from above. On this view, objects are important only insofar as they are manifested to the mind, or are part of some concrete event that affects other objects as well.[4]

If the pre-Socratics are the patron saints of undermining, then the British Empiricists, with their attempt to see objects as mere bundles of perceptible properties, are the patron saints of overmining. Much contemporary continental philosophy can only be seen as heir to this tradition, as overmining occurs whenever the nineteenth-century 'hermeneutics of suspicion' (for example, Nietzsche, Marx, Freud) are married to phenomenology[5] in attempts to explain aspects of non-human reality such as atoms, quarks, numbers, and divinities in terms of relational networks such as discursive practices, social norms, class struggles, Freudian mechanisms, power, phallo-logocentrism, and so on. Overmining explanations are almost always instances of Meillassoux's correlationism, since the very being of some putatively non-human phenomenon is tied to provincial human practices.

Let us be absolutely clear here. The object-oriented ontologist is *not* urging people to stop providing undermining and overmining explanations. Nor is she saying that such explanations never yield important truths about objects. Successful undermining explanations tell us about the behaviour of objects' constituents and how these relate to the behaviour of the object and other objects at the same scale as those constituents. Successful overmining explanations tell us much about how objects relate to other objects, including human ones. The epistemic project of object-oriented ontology concerns how and when such explanations are successful, and when they wrongly shade into reductionism. The militant anti-reductionism of the object-oriented ontologists is not merely epistemic, though. The metaphysical task is to characterise objects such that it is a part of their being to resist complete characterisation by undermining and overmining.

A Worry about (Anti-)Reductionism

Unfortunately, one of the most frustrating things about anti-reductionist thinking in continental philosophy generally, and about Garcia's book in particular, is that there is so little overlap with the enormous amount of writing about reductionism (and related notions such as supervenience, grounding, and fundamentality) by analytic metaphysicians and philosophers of science and mind. The most Garcia writes about reductionism proper is in the beginning of Chapter II, where his description of key aspects of his system is already under way. This is especially worrisome, given the manner in which late twentieth-century analytic philosophy of mind serves as a particularly grim cautionary tale for all would be anti-reductionists.[6] That generation took for themselves the overriding goal of in some manner accounting for facets of human mental life (paradigmatically sensory experience, belief, and desires) in a way that is consistent with a world-view that rejects the supernatural and gives metaphysical priority to the world as described by physicists.

The initial null hypothesis for the naturalist was that mental properties such as being in pain were *identical with* physical properties such as brains being in certain states, and that it would be unproblematic to characterise the relevant brain states in a language that only made reference to the organisation of the matter composing the brain. But in the canonical article 'What Psychological States are Not', Ned Block and Jerry Fodor discussed robots, evolutionary theory, and actual brain science to argue that the physical states that co-occur with our mental life are 'wildly disjunctive' in the sense that it is extremely unlikely that we would be able to characterise all and only the brain states that reliably co-occur with a given mental state such as possessing a desire. When philosophers say that mental properties are 'multiply realisable' they are affirming that different instances of the same type of mental state (such as believing) might co-occur with radically different types of physical states. For an extreme example of this, consider the *Star Trek* episode in which Spock's mind melds with a silicon-based life form, which is radically physically different from a human body/brain yet manages to still think. If Block and Fodor are correct, then the actual world, with octopi brains and radical differences among human brains, is more like the world of *Star Trek* than we had previously thought. The *multiple realisability* of the mental with respect to the physical was thus taken to be the major problem for physicalism about the mental.

Fodor and Block's article quickly set the research program for most analytic philosophy of mind. The end goal was to come up with a form of 'non-reductive physicalism' that accommodated the manner in which psychology was irreducible to biology (which was assumed to be reducible to chemistry, which was in turn reducible to physics) without departing from the metaphysical naturalism of the original view. The overriding dominance of the strange identification of thinking with *computation* during those three decades can only be understood as an attempt to understand mind as simultaneously purely physical (as digital computers are) yet not such that our theory of mind is reducible to physics.

While many insights were gained along the way, the major conceit of the whole program proved to be chimerical. The claim that psychology does not reduce to physics only makes sense via contrast with examples of *successful* reduction. Only if one could point to the way that, say, chemistry *is* reducible to physics, could one then proceed to clearly characterise the distinct relation that psychology has to it. And the failure cuts both ways! One could, like Mark Wilson in 'What is This Thing Called Pain', conclude that since the irreducibility of chemistry to physics does not entail that chemicals are non-physical, the Fodorian worry about the mind was fundamentally misplaced. Or, like Graham Harman and Tristan Garcia, one might conclude from the generalised failure of reductionist programs that naturalism should not be the default position of contemporary philosophy.

Unfortunately, during the same period that philosophers of mind were constructing their sandcastles, philosophers of physics were showing that the very models of reduction presupposed by the philosophers of mind did not apply *anywhere*. For example, by the account of reduction that fits with the deductive-nomological account of scientific theories, one theory is reducible to another if an axiomatisation of the former can be logically derived from the latter. An axiomatisation is a translation of the laws of the theory into the formal language of first-order logic. The derivations would just be in the normal logic that philosophy professors teach undergraduates.

And for people who don't know very much science, but do know some logic, this seems like a promising characterisation of the manner in which fundamental physics helps to explain chemical interactions. So the thought would then be that the multiple realisability of psychological states vis-à-vis physical ones prevents any such derivation, but some relaxed formal relation (to be worked out with the help of modal logicians and metaphysicians) such as supervenience (roughly, occurrences of two type-distinct psychological states will never be correlated with type-identical physical states; so one and the same type of brain state cannot be sometimes desire and sometimes belief) still guarantees that psychological states are merely physical. And functionalist/computationalist accounts of psychological states will show both that psychology is a genuine science, axiomatisable like chemistry and physics, and exactly how the supervenient psychological states are physically realised.

But from a philosophy of science perspective, nearly every aspect of this program is false. Multiple realisability occurs within physics proper, so it cannot differentiate so-called 'special sciences' such as psychology from physics. As Mark Wilson first showed in 'What is This Thing Called Pain', the criteria for existence in physics are of necessity so extraordinarily liberal that if 'temperature' counts as a 'physical property' then so does 'pain'. Most significantly, scientific theories are not sets of sentences that can be axiomatised into logical systems. Application of physics, even in simple textbook examples, requires learning to instance creative practical capacities, for example with respect to discerning fruitful mathematical approximations, and there is no principled way to characterise the meaning of the true sentences that are a part of the theory apart from such applications. As a result, there is no reason to think that there is an algorithm either to discover *or even check* correct explanations of chemical phenomena using the resources of physics. And from this it follows that axiomatisation fails, since axiomatisation guarantees the existence of an algorithm to check derivations.[7] But then it's both entirely unclear what is being affirmed by the claim that psychology does not reduce to physics and entirely unclear why we should take philosophical theories (modelled after false views of scientific theories as sets of sentences) such as functionalism or the computational theory of mind at all seriously.

At first glance, this seems to pose a very serious problem for Garcia, who says nothing about exactly what he means by reduction. Indeed, analytic philosophers will no doubt first ask exactly which models of reduction are meant to be denied. Could his entire edifice fail because he is only rejecting a particularly naive form of reduction that nobody would accept anyhow? Is his work analogous to the unflattering way I have portrayed much late twentieth-century philosophy of mind?

Consider the bewildering final paragraph of Raphael Van Riel and Robert Van Gulick's *Stanford Encyclopedia of Philosophy* entry on reductionism.

> Reduction has been conceived of as a relation that primarily holds between theories, properties, substances, concepts, or events. It has been described as an explanatory relation that can be cashed out in terms of derivation, and it could be tied to mechanistic or ontological dependence, supervenience and identity. It has been argued that theory-reduction is prior to ontological reduction; and it has been argued that ontological reduction is more fundamental than theory reduction. Reduction has been couched in structuralist, empiricist and functionalist frameworks, and it has been one of the core notions of theories defending one form or another of scientific unification. Most philosophers have abandoned this latter view.

It is thus *very* important to note the disanalogy between object-oriented ontologists such as Garcia and Harman and our hapless late twentieth-century analytic philosophers of mind. First, Garcia is *not* a physicalist; as a result (unlike the non-reductive physicalist in the philosophy of mind) he need not contrast supposed successful cases of reduction within the physical sciences and failures to reduce the human sciences to the physical ones. Second, in the context of the whole system, one does get a sense of what Garcia is rejecting when he talks about reductionism. Anyone familiar both with the reduction literature and *Form and Object* will see that several formal models of reduction of the types discussed in the *Stanford Encyclopedia* article possess the characteristics Garcia is attacking. But then it is enough for Garcia that all such models fail to have applications, which is precisely what philosophy of science in the twentieth century established! Third, it is worth exploring whether other ontological dependence relations such as varieties of supervenience, grounding, or relative fundamentality are inconsistent with Garcia's general picture. But to consider these kinds of issues we need first to be generally clear about what his picture is.

Even though one does begin to get a decent feel for Garcia's enemy as one works through the book, it is still unfortunate that he never *explicitly* says very much about what exactly he is rejecting when he rejects reductionism. On the mere 36 times in the text when he uses some French cognate of the word, he is either denouncing it or elucidating properties of his system that he takes to follow from the rejection. For example,

> §11 Reductionism reduces what things are to what composes these things. Physicalist or materialist reductionism reduces things to the matter that composes them. Evolutionary or naturalist reductionism reduces a living organism to the evolutionary processes of which the living organism is a result.
>
> Other types of reductionism capture the chain of being from the other direction, and reduce a thing to what it is, that is, to what it is in. Social reductionism reduces a social element to its function in the social whole. Historical reductionism reduces a historical event to the history within which it obtains its place.
>
> Reductionism consists in refusing to consider the irreducibility of that which is a thing to that which it is.
>
> The cost of reductionism is the concept of a compact point. (*FO* 118)

Here Garcia connects the rejection of the explanatory hubris of undermining and overmining with his technical notion of compactness (explained below in Chapters 3 and 5), but he does nothing to explain exactly what is wrong with undermining and overmining.

This kind of hermeneutic circle always confronts the exegete of systematic philosophers such as Kant, Hegel, Sellars, Garcia, and Harman. In the case of reductionism in Garcia's work, one doesn't really get a view of what exactly is being avoided until one is conversant with much of the system. But we need to understand what he means by reductionism to understand that very system. Here I will provide a general take, without supporting quotes. What follows does not presuppose familiarity with Garcia's entire system, but readers with such familiarity will recognise my general account as correct.

Garcia and Harman's principal anti-reductionist claim is first and foremost about the limits of predictive explanation. Good undermining and overmining explanations help us to predict the way given systems will evolve. For example, my intuitive understanding of human psychology grants me knowledge that it is not a good idea to pester one of my colleagues about modal logic when he is scowling. Asking him questions during scowling periods reliably fails to yield help. A complete undermining explanation would yield the best possible ability of someone who knew my colleague's constituent parts and the parts of the universe at roughly the same physical scale to predict his behaviour. The physicalist takes the appropriate scale to be the level of the fundamental particles and forces of physics. The overminer is the mirror image of this. For example, a Marxist who explains religious belief in terms of how it legitimates oppressive power predicts that, all else being equal, religious belief will be greater in more unjust societies and lesser in more just societies.

The anti-reductionist's claim cannot merely be that every combination of undermining and overmining will fail to perfectly predict the future course of the universe. For that failure could just hold in virtue of some patterns of events being determined *probabilistically*, that is with some percentage short of 100's likelihood they will come to pass. Such failure is consistent with a statistical undermining/overmining explanation that correctly predicts all of the probabilistic states of the universe, and that correctly predicts the outcomes of all systems that are set up deterministically.

Garcia and Harman should be seen as affirming the more radical claim that, when applied outside of some constrained area, undermining or overmining explanations will have *systematic* failings. They will reliably predict *incorrectly* across some domains, often make no predictions at all (either probabilistically or deterministically) over wide domains, and often contradict the predictions of other explanations which are successful in their domains. So at best, we are confronted with a variety of conflicting over- and undermining explanations across the sciences and humanities, many successful as far as they go. The object-oriented ontologist's rejection of reductionism is in part her taking as a primary metaphysical explanandum that predictive explanations are radically non-unifiable. But since the goal of metaphysics is to provide a unified explanation for reality, this entails that, *pace* over two millennia of philosophical theorising, neither undermining nor overmining are the royal roads to metaphysics.

It should be very clear that typical overmining explanations fail to be universalisable. Consider our cartoon Marxist, for whom *all* expressed beliefs and desires are to be understood merely in terms of the role that those beliefs play in supporting oppressive class relations.[8] Those of us who think that our important beliefs are part of our attempts to understand the world via exploration, experience, and rational assessment are all just fooling ourselves, and there is no reason to take seriously the reasons we adduce for our beliefs once the (cartoon) Marxist unmasks what is really going on behind the façade. But what about the cartoon Marxist's own Marxist beliefs? If *all* beliefs are in need of being so unmasked, then the Marxist beliefs must be included. But then by the Marxist's own logic, Marxism itself is just an ideology that need not be taken seriously. So clearly these kinds of overmining explanations of human belief and desire cannot be universalised to cover *all* human beliefs and desires. There are significant and systematic lacunae where the explanation must fail.

I am not sure if there are any analogously quick self-reflexive arguments against the universality of undermining explanations. However, what I noted earlier about discussions of reductionism in the philosophy of science holds here. Raphael Van Riel and Robert Van Gulick end their piece by noting that most philosophers have abandoned the quest for the unification of science. Members of the so-called 'Stanford School' of the philosophy of science (Nancy Cartwright, John Dupré, Ian Hacking, Peter Galison, and Patrick Suppes)[9] have assiduously critiqued such ideas as the universalisability of laws, unity of scientific methods, privileging of some sciences such as physics as more fundamental than others, the view that causation is only really real at the scales described by the sciences of the very, very small, and the view that all correct scientific explanations must be jointly consistent. With respect to undermining, object-oriented philosophers such as Garcia and Harman can be thought of as developing a realist metaphysics in which the basic correctness of the Stanford School critique is taken for granted.[10]

However, we must also consider whether the kind of self-reflexive argument applied against the Marxist above applies to the object-oriented philosopher. If the critique of under- and over-mining is supposed to show us that such successful explanations are always radically partial and that there is no easy method that gives us a royal road to understanding, what does this entail for metaphysics? The task of metaphysics is traditionally taken to be to provide a unified explanation of how things hang together in the broadest possible sense. But for the radical anti-reductionist, we can't come up with such a *scientific* explanation. But what extra resources do metaphysicians plausibly bring to the table over and above over- and undermining? Any at all? Then why think metaphysics is possible?

What I have called 'paradoxico-metaphysics' results from a characteristic kind of answer to such self-referential challenges. I begin my discussion of it proper in the next chapter. Here I want to close out our discussion of anti-reductionism by noting that for Harman it is not enough to negatively reject the unity of certain types of explanations. We also must accommodate our experiences of the weird. Consider this representative passage from a recent interview:

> David earlier used the term *masterpieces* in reference to architecture, and this is a word that I think needs to be taken more seriously, even in philosophy. Whatever it is that constitutes a masterpiece in any field, though it may often involve elegance and economy, more likely there needs to be a certain strangeness, a weirdness. The weird is an object that cannot be adequately described, not just something deviant and eccentric. Harold Bloom discusses this in connection with literature. He tells us that he's read Milton's *Paradise Lost* countless times, but the more he reads it, the stranger it becomes – like science fiction, even though it doesn't try to sound like science fiction. A masterpiece has an inassimilable strangeness that makes us return to it repeatedly.[11]

Part of the philosophical interest of art for Harman is that the weirdness of masterpieces brings into focus the weirdness of the surrounding world. Our experience of the weird is a direct experience of a world that resists its own under- and overmining. For Harman, any metaphysics that fails to accommodate this is a failure. We will see that this pushes Harman to the belief that aesthetics is first philosophy, while Garcia is pushed to the embrace of contradiction.

Finally, we must stress again that neither Harman nor Garcia think that undermining and overmining explanations always fail. Consider this proposition of Garcia's, from the same section as the anti-reductionist quote given above:

> §12 That which is a thing does not determine that which this thing is; but that which is a thing prevents this thing from being *no-matter-what*. A composition thing thus and not otherwise cannot be all and its opposite. And one cannot determine what this thing is from what composes this thing. (*FO* 118)

'That which is a thing does not determine that which this thing is' is Garcia's way of saying that the objects that compose something (and more broadly objects of the same scale of those parts and the forces that act on them) don't explain all of the relations the object itself enters into. He discusses a piece of slate in the Introduction to *Form and Object* to make just this point.

> Yet, *that in which this slate is* can never be inferred from *everything that is in this slate.* From everything which composes it, I will not obtain the slate's location in the world, the relations in which it inscribes itself, the fact that it is now in my hand, the function of a weapon that it can exercise if someone attacks me, its place in the landscape or in the series of slate pieces scattered alongside this valley. That which it is, this unique thing which exists in the world, and I hold in my hand, is outside itself. The slate can in fact enter into the composition of the side of a mountain, a roof, or a collection of rocks. As a whole, it then becomes a part of another thing, and it is no longer a question of *that which is in the slate,* but of *that in which this slate is.* (*FO* 12–13)

But that doesn't mean for Garcia that the slate's constituents are irrelevant to the relations the slate enters into. Garcia's claim that 'that which is a thing prevents this thing from being *no-matter-what*' is his way of asserting that an object's constituents limit the role the object can play. This tracks many forms of scientific explanation in the manner theorised by the Stanford School. In very highly idealised (frictionless planes, point masses, only two bodies, no other forces, infinite elasticisty, and so on) thought experiments, some systems can be described such that there is a unique way that the system will evolve. Mathematically inclined humans have a good facility at discerning bits of reality where the idealisations don't hold but where the same kinds of description (along with a lot of creative applied mathematics) allow us to predict what will happen with respect to some phenomena within narrow margins of error. But predicting what will happen within a margin of error is really just narrowing down the possibilities of how various things might evolve.

But this is in no ways entails reductionism. Harman makes this more explicit than Garcia.

> The problem lies in assuming that the two balls in collision do not also objectify each other, as if humans faced a world of still unperceived depths but inanimate objects exhausted one another's reality upon the slightest contact. Ball Number One may be shiny and hot to the touch. Ball Number Two will of course be utterly insensitive to these properties. And yet the shininess is somehow present for the beam of light that skids off the surface of the shiny ball and is deflected off into the galaxy. And the heat of the ball is overwhelming for the loose speck of ice that dissolves instantly upon touching it. In other words, even inanimate objects are caught up in something like a 'hermeneutic circle'. No object ever sucks all the juice out of another object.[12]

For both Harman and Garcia, the manner in which objects contain within themselves a kind of radical novelty governing how they interact with different things is an essential commitment of anti-reductionism. Of course metaphysics needs to accommodate the fact that we can develop good undermining theories that predict within margins of error how the pool ball will travel across the table when hit. But to conclude from that that there is a theory that might in principle predict the behaviour of the ball under all stimuli (including my possible decision concerning whether to throw it across the yard and all of the possible idealised and fictional scenarios to which novel writers and physicists might subject it) is an act of hubris.

Garcia's picture of entities as differentiating that which they contain from that which contains them is thus a metaphysical confirmation of the manner in which the world teaches us epistemic humility. Continuing the previously quoted passage, Garcia writes,

A number of things are in this black slate. The black slate on its own can enter into the composition of a number of other things. Therefore, the black slate is not in itself. It is not a substance on which various qualities are predicated – for example, its weight or its colour. No more is it an ephemeral entity, not existing in itself, constructed by my thought, senses, or action, from events or becomings (some variation in the matter's density, some effects of geological transformation, a trajectory of luminous rays). No, the black slate is a relation, inscribed in the world, between the being that enters the world and the being that goes outside it, and that enters in turn into another thing (into the soil, landscape, classes of other objects, my perception, or the world in general).

A thing is nothing other than the difference [differentiation][13] between *that which is in this thing* and *that in which this thing is.* (FO 13)

If the only book Harman had written were *Tool-Being*, then one could take Garcia's system as a development of Harman's, perhaps in the sense in which one can read Deleuze as a student of Gilbert Simondon. But there is much more to the story.

The Speculative Turn and the Autonomy of Objects

Before explicating Garcia's ontological liberality, I want to further situate him with respect to object-oriented philosophy by sketching a little bit of a Whig history of Speculative Realism and object-oriented ontology.[14] Doing this will allow us to see in the next two chapters how Garcia's paradoxico-metaphysics is not just an eccentric view, but rather a principled response to philosophical problems that are both deep and wide.

Harman's 1999 essay 'A Fresh Look at *Zuhandenheit*', republished in *Towards Speculative Realism*, can be seen as the first cast of the die that would lead both to Speculative Realism and its object-oriented wing.[15] The main idea, developed at length in his 2002 book *Tool-Being*, is that the standard account of Heidegger's famed tool analysis contains two related mistakes. For Heidegger, *Zuhandenheit*/readiness-to-hand names human (and possibly animal) pre-linguistic[16] understanding of the valuative, modal, and relational properties of objects, an understanding grounded in our ability to differentiate between the appropriate and inappropriate uses of objects within their holistic context. For the Heideggerian philosopher of mind and language, linguistic and conceptual understanding (*Vorhandenheit*/objective presence) is parasitic on this prior understanding. Heidegger justifiably takes this to be a radical inversion of Cartesian representationalist philosophy of mind. On the Cartesian view, our understanding of things is held in virtue of mental copies of those things, and in virtue of this understanding we are able to manipulate parts of the world. In the Heideggerian inversion, our understanding is a function of the ability to manipulate objects for their appropriate uses. My understanding of a screwdriver is much more a function of the peculiar way one holds and turns a screwdriver and the world of projects in which the screwdriver is brought to bear. For Heidegger, mental representations are actually a function of these abilities.

The tendency among many Heidegger scholars, however, is to take this anti-Cartesian philosophy of mind not to be a consequence of the tool analysis, but rather to exhaust its entirety. Here *Zuhandenheit* simply is the modal serviceability of objects in the world for correct human manipulation and *Vorhandenheit* is the manner in which humans are able to picture and represent such objects as abstracted from their serviceability. Linguistically articulable conceptuality is thus radically *privative* for Heidegger, as abstracting away from modal facets of things in order to think of them qua things is a kind of privation.

Harman examines this notion of privativity in Heidegger and argues that the reading of Heidegger as an anti-representationalist is radically incomplete. First, such a reading ignores the fact that human practical engagement with the world is equally privative! When I pre-linguistically understand the Tupperware container in terms of the uses to which it should be put, I am equally abstracting away from all sorts of properties of the container. Harman shows that Heidegger's discussion of 'withdrawal' applies both to the way (some) practical, modal properties disappear when we intellectualise *and* to the properties that disappear when we take something as some kind of thing via practical comportment. My correct use of a tennis ball only actualises a fragment of the ball's potential with respect to other possible causal interactions.

Harman's second point, the genesis of his speculative realist break from correlationist anthropocentrism, is that there is nothing unique about human beings in this regard. Just as another human might isolate a distinct set of properties of the container from those that become manifest when I interact with it, so too would a dog, match, ray of light, and neutrino. For all of these things too, the container presents a different face, actualising different properties as others withdraw. Harman is not trying to undermine Heideggerian theories of perception and understanding. His point is rather that the *Zuhandenheit/Vorhandenheit* reversal is not merely a model of understanding, but a model of the interaction of any two objects.

As noted above, Garcia's picture of entities as differentiators between that which they contain and that which contains them does the same work as Harman's thesis of the radical withdrawal of objects. In particular, both pictures illustrate the radical irreducibility of entities. Entities cannot be over- and undermined precisely because that which makes them entities is their difference from the way they present themselves to other entities. However, in his post *Tool-Being* work, Harman has added another fundamental distinction to his initial division into that of the withdrawn objects and the properties manifested when they interact. In 2005's *Guerrilla Metaphysics*, Harman presents a novel reading of Edmund Husserl that is just as significant as his earlier take on Heidegger in *Tool-Being*. Harman begins with Husserl's insight that we do not perceive objects as mere bundles of qualities. Then, analogously to his externalisation of Heidegger, Harman goes on to argue that objects themselves are not mere bundles of qualities for each other. And for Harman these sensual objects are not created merely when humans and the world interact, but when any two real objects interact. In a further development of Husserl, Harman argues that we must also posit real qualities of objects when we explain how sensual qualities arise from interaction. Importantly, the real properties for Harman are themselves in some sense emergent. It is not the case that real objects prior to their interaction possess a set of dispositional properties of the sort described by scientists, properties that uniquely determine how the object interacts with other objects, determining which sensual properties arise.[17]

> The relation between an object and its own real qualities (we called this essence) is a relation produced by outside entities. This is not the relativist thesis according to which nothing is real, hidden, or essential but only how it appears to us. Instead it is a bizarre alternative to relativism in which the real, hidden, and essential do very much exist,

but communicate only by way of the unreal, apparent, and inessential. It would be as if mushrooms communicated with their own qualities, not directly or through rhizomal networks, but via radio waves. A real object is real and has a definite character, but its essence is first produced from the outside through causal interactions.[18]

The essential claim here is that, for Harman, the stable, dispositional properties of an object are in some sense emergent on the properties that arise when that object interacts with others.[19] This turning of the normal picture of emergence on its head is what allows his system to be fiercely anti-reductionist in the sense I have articulated above.[20] Harman's universe really is surprises all the way down.

When put together with his account of Heidegger, this yields Harman's fourfold ontology, where things split across two axes into real and sensual objects and real and sensual qualities. In works such as 2011's *The Quadruple Object*, Harman has begun cataloguing and developing theories of fundamental philosophical categories such as space, time, causality, metaphor, humour, beauty, charm, sleep, and so on in terms of relations between the objects' four poles. For example,

> The banal state of time and eidos is this: object and qualities seem compressed into a unit, and only in special cases do they appear in explicit strife: fission, as we have called it. The opposite holds for essence and space, where the real object is never counterposed with its sensual and real qualities except in the case of their fusion. For it is not at all the case that space is constantly with us in experience: rather, experience is a kind of hologram in which all near and distant objects touch us directly and spatial distance is merely inferred. And though it may sound surprising at first, it is also not the case that a real object has an articulated essence, because its essence is produced only once in a while. So much for the banal state of things.[21]

Without having to dig into the fourfold metaphysics, we can begin to appreciate how Harman uses objects' resistance to their own over- and undermining as an impetus to think of them as withdrawn reserves of their own potential interactions. Garcia, on the other hand,[22] sees the objects' resistance as motivating an understanding of them as brute differentiators between that which they contain (again, his technical term is comprehension) and that which contains them.

If Harman's fundamental bifurcation is between what is made present when an object interacts with another (sensual properties and objects) and what is not made present (their corresponding real properties and objects), Garcia's is between the things that compose an object and the things, such as relational structures, that an object helps compose (again, in Garcia's terminology, those things that *comprehend* the object, and those the object itself *comprehends*). And, as already noted, for Harman the real object is the thing that resists being exhausted by its interaction with other objects; for Garcia the real object is the thing that resists being exhausted by its constituents and the structures that the object helps constitute. There thus is an astonishing similarity between the starting points of the two systems, noted by Garcia in the introduction to *Form and Object*.

There are also a lot of differences, though. First, Garcia has no analogue to Harman's externalisation of Husserl and hence no distinction between Harmanian real properties and sensual objects. Second, Garcia adds to his initial differential model a sort of Spinozistic doubling of what we might call (Garcia does not use this terminology) modes of entities. Considered objectively, an entity ('object') is the differentiation in the sense I have described, between all of the objects that it contains and all of the objects containing it. Considered formally, the entity ('thing') is the mere differentiation between what Garcia calls 'matter' and 'world'. In virtue of his technical characterisation of these latter two concepts (a characterisation I will describe in Chapters 3 and 5), Garcian things are radically different from traditional metaphysical posits. Nonetheless, his things play the same role as what analytic philosophers call 'bare particulars', mere bearers of individuality which are all that is left when the differentiating properties are subtracted from an object. Entities considered as 'things' are paradoxical in the same way that bare particulars are; they secure an object's individuality yet are themselves completely indiscernible from one another. In both cases, the goal is to prevent the slide to Hegelian holism that threatens when relations are used to individuate objects.[23]

Garcia's other major innovation is an account of intensity (which I discuss in Chapter 8) to explain temporal aspects of entities. Just as Harman articulates regional ontologies (accounts of what distinguish important kinds of beings from one another) with his basic fourfold framework, in Book II of *Form and Object*

Garcia's basic differential model, plus intensity, allows him to develop novel and interesting theories of an astonishing number of kinds of entities, including events, time, life, animality, humanity, representation, art, rules, culture, history, economies, values, classes, genders, ages of life, and death. In most of these cases, Garcia articulates the kind in terms of an antagonistic struggle over time between various attempts to under- and overmine the object, the kind in question always refusing to be pinned down as it changes. It is a strange kind of post-Foucauldian upside-down Hegelianism, one where the dialectical tension often ends up being an engine of persistence rather than change. Remember that, for Garcia, we can develop a fully comprehensive over- and undermining theory of some kind only to the extent that we no longer need think of the kind as an object (in Garcia's terminology, the kind is tending towards 'compactness'). Garcia describes important kinds of entities as if the kind in question is itself an active agent resisting its own compactness.

No-Matter-What is Something, First Sense

For Garcia, anti-reductionism naturally lends itself to ontological liberality. The most natural way to deny being to some putative class of entities is to argue that those entities are nothing over and above the entities to which they reduce. Strictly speaking, there are no rocks, because rocks are really nothing over and above the subatomic particles composing rocks. And it is unclear how such assertions pan out if no sense can be made of the claim that the true propositions about rocks are reducible to our best theory of the behaviour of the rock's constituents and other things at that scale.

But a mere rejection of under- and overmining is not itself an ontology. Garcia's capsule credo expressing his rejection is 'no-matter-what is something', or its equivalent 'no-matter-what is not nothing'. In Chapter 4 we will be in a position to exhaustively explain what Garcia means by 'no-matter-what', which ends up being a central technical notion for him. For our purposes here, it is sufficient to note that in colloquial French, *n'importe quoi* simply means 'anything'. Here we thus need discern what Garcia means by claiming anything is something. He distinguishes two senses.

Everything that is – even if it is vacuous, false, nothing, or groundless – is *something*. The problem is understanding *in what sense* it is something. To think of an object as complex and elusive is precisely to discover how to grasp it.

In the second sense, the assertion that 'no-matter-what is something' marks the permeability of all the barriers by which one can claim to protect and limit the import of *that which is something*. In fact, one cannot prevent anything from being quite simply 'something', even if it is something illusory, a chimera of the human mind, or a mirage. (FO 23)

If for Quine, to be is to be the value of a bound variable,[24] for Garcia to be is to be the bearer of a property. This is the first sense of his affirmation that anything is something. Every thing is some kind of thing. But it is the second sense that concerns us here, Garcia's affirmation that there are no exceptions to the empire of things.

In this context, it is very important that reductionism is just one of the ways philosophers typically deny that some putative things are really things. In Chapter I of *Form and Object*, Garcia considers two other strategies: (1) anthropocentric claims that human entities, qualities, and their practices are so ontologically distinct from the non-human realm that humans should not be considered things, and (2) seemingly anti-anthropocentric claims that human practices and qualities are 'less than things': that is, epiphenomena of a deeper reality that might be constituted by objects or by what Garcia calls 'more than things'. The first is a paradigmatically *anti-reductionist* strategy for denying that no-matter-what is something. The second strategy is often reductionist (and hence not discussed by Garcia after he has bid farewell to reductionism), except when employed by process philosophers, which we shall discuss in Chapter 4.

In the opening discussion of Chapter I, Garcia counters the anthropocentrist by discussing 'six clear strategies that reduce the extension of possible things' (FO 23). These concern logical contradictions, linguistic inexpressibles, transcendental conditions on knowledge, cultural taboos, the sacred, and human moral and political agency. We will consider his comments about logical contradictions in our next chapter, since Garcia's affirmation of such is part of how he obliterates the Scylla and Charybdis of analysis and dialectics. In all of the other cases, Garcia makes the claim that in attempting to characterise the phenomena in question as beyond the realm of things, we only at best end up characterising the properties of the thing in question, and are presupposing that the thing is in fact an object after all. For example, in his discussion of objects that are prohibited by taboos, he writes:

> The prohibition, while preventing what is prohibited from being a thing, a practical, discursive, or thinkable object, distinguishes what is prohibited and makes it particularly important as a thing. Taboos exist in order to someday be lifted, for by prohibiting this or that from being objects, we in fact make them objects. The more they are prohibited, the better they are defined, delimited, and determined.
>
> Nothing forms an object better than a long-standing cultural status of concealment and prohibition. (*FO* 27)

As an example, consider menstruation, which was so taboo in the communities that produced the Old Testament book of Leviticus that merely touching a menstruating woman resulted in ritual uncleanliness.

> 19 When a woman has a discharge of blood that is her regular discharge from her body, she shall be in her impurity for seven days, and whoever touches her shall be unclean until the evening. 20 Everything upon which she lies during her impurity shall be unclean; everything also upon which she sits shall be unclean. 21 Whoever touches her bed shall wash his clothes, and bathe in water, and be unclean until the evening. 22 Whoever touches anything upon which she sits shall wash his clothes, and bathe in water, and be unclean until the evening; 23 whether it is the bed or anything upon which she sits, when he touches it he shall be unclean until the evening. 24 If any man lies with her, and her impurity falls on him, he shall be unclean seven days; and every bed on which he lies shall be unclean. 25 If a woman has a discharge of blood for many days, not at the time of her impurity, or if she has a discharge beyond the time of her impurity, all the days of the discharge she shall continue in uncleanness; as in the days of her impurity, she shall be unclean. 26 Every bed on which she lies during all the days of her discharge shall be treated as the bed of her impurity; and everything on which she sits shall be unclean, as in the uncleanness of her impurity. 27 Whoever touches these things shall be unclean, and shall wash his clothes, and bathe in water, and be unclean until the evening. 28 If she is cleansed of her discharge, she shall count seven days, and

after that she shall be clean. 29 On the eighth day she shall take two turtledoves or two pigeons and bring them to the priest to the entrance of the tent of meeting. 30 The priest shall offer one for a sin offering and the other for a burnt offering; and the priest shall make atonement on her behalf before the LORD for her unclean discharge.

As if all of this isn't enough, the authors of Chapter 20 Verse 18 up the ante. Now the punishment dictated for a man lying with and seeing a naked menstruating woman is banishment for both of them! The man who has seen what is supposed to be hidden now must himself be permanently hidden from society. Such proscriptions are common among ancient tribal peoples, surviving today among the Huaulu of Indonesia and Dogon Mali, where menstruating women are segregated from men in separate huts and in the forests and fields where they work.

When compared with cultures that do not have such taboos, Garcia's point becomes clear. Attempts to render menstruation invisible only serve to make it much more visible. In cultures with the taboo, it is immediately clear who is menstruating and who is not. Although he does not provide a citation, Garcia certainly starts with the example of taboos because the anthropological work of Claude Lévi-Strauss (along with Roman Jakobson's linguistic work) provided such an impetus for structuralist thinkers such as Jacques Lacan, Michel Foucault, Louis Althusser, Roland Barthes, Gilles Deleuze,[25] and Jacques Derrida. For these thinkers, the anthropological taboo became paradigmatic for the way in which a structure (such as language, the unconscious, society, the economy) in some manner constitutively presupposed a realm inexpressible or unknowable from within that structure, but which nonetheless functions as an essential condition of possibility for that structure.

In the context of the early stages of Garcia's project, the structuralist conceit that every structure presupposes a reality inexpressible relative to that structure is only of concern to the extent that it might entail an exception to the realm of things. For example, one might say that we must not consider God a thing, because to do so is to treat God as just another object within the universe that God created. Kantians make a similar claim about the transcendental subject, which is somehow responsible for imposing causal relata upon the various phenomena that it perceives. But it is a weird sort of imposition, for it cannot be a causal one, since causes are just relata between phenomena perceived by the subject. Indeed, Garcia's enemy here is precisely this kind of transcendental thinking. It is no accident that Deleuze begins 'How Do We Recognize Structuralism' with 'Structuralism cannot be separated from a new transcendental philosophy, in which the sites prevail over whatever occupies them.'[26] And this becomes clearest if we attend to the manner in which A. W. Moore differentiates empirical from transcendental idealism.

> Let *s* be a kind of sense-making. Then idealism with respect to *s* may for these purposes be defined as the view that certain essential features of whatever can be made sense of in accord with *s* depend on features of *s* itself. Empirical idealism, as I intend it, includes the rider that this dependence can itself be made sense of in accord with *s*. Transcendental idealism, as I intend it, includes the rider that it cannot.[27]

Again, consider causality. Idealists claim that causality only holds in virtue of the subject's imposition of causal relata upon experienced phenomena. To say that one billiard ball hitting another causes the other to go in the pocket is really to say something about how the human mind structures and organises its experiences of the balls. But what is this kind of structuring and organising? For the empirical idealist, the human mind's causality here is no different from the causality immanent in billiard ball phenomena. For the transcendental idealist, it must be some radically different kind of property. When contemporary Heideggerians critique 'onto-theology' or talk about 'ontological difference', they are affirming transcendental idealism in Moore's sense.

For Garcia's project, the relevant forms of problematic transcendental thinking are ones that express this difference (between some range of phenomena to be explained and that which is taken to ground or make possible that range) in terms of the transcendent realm not consisting of things. In all such cases, Garcia argues that the very manner in which the realm of things is differentiated from the realm of transcendental non-things paradoxically involves treating the putative non-thing as a thing. For example, with respect to the unknowable, Garcia writes,

> The surrounding walls of knowledge do not give me access to the castle of transcendence. But they do not prevent me from identifying

and locating what I do not know. 'What I do not know' is clearly something, neither all nor nothing nor any thing. (*FO* 29)

With respect to human autonomy he writes,

> Every moral system of distinction between things and what cannot be something is doubly condemned: first, by distinguishing what must not be something and by reifying it (the 'human person'); second, by denying the possibility of placing all things on an equal footing, which is the very condition of their comparison and of their relative importance. (*FO* 29)

It's the first point that is of import here. To distinguish a thing is, for Garcia, to distinguish it, or her or him, *as a thing*. Thus, it is impossible to delimit the class of non-things. The division always collapses because once they are delimited, they are things. As we shall see in Chapter 3, this is exactly the kind of argument that Graham Priest uses when he critiques attempts to block limit paradoxes. And we shall also see that much of what Garcia says only makes sense if one sees a version of this argument paradoxically applied to Garcia's own philosophy.

Readers sympathetic to Deleuze and the process philosophical tradition in philosophy, which includes Friedrich Schelling, Henri Bergson, A. N. Whitehead, Gilbert Simondon, and Wilfrid Sellars, will cavil at precisely this point, because, for process philosophers such as Deleuze (who explicitly argues as much in 'What is Structuralism?') the realm of processes does form a transcendental condition for the realm of individuated things in which we find ourselves. Of course, it is impossible to disconfirm such a rich tradition in a few short paragraphs, chapters, or even books. In Chapter 4, I discuss the process tradition in slightly more detail, presenting some of the main reasons why philosophers such as Harman and Garcia place their chips on the fundamentality of objects.

But first, we must consider another neither/nor, this one concerning philosophical methodology itself.

Notes

1. Because his theory of being entails that to be is to be determined, Garcia is not a Meinongian none-ist. Non-existent objects have

properties and so *are* for Garcia. The Meinongian grants some ontological (and much semantic) dignity to the non-existent while nonetheless equating existence and being. See Graham Priest's *Towards Non-Being* for the most complete recent articulation of none-ism. Likewise, Garcia is also more liberal than Meinong and other followers of Brentano in the sense that Garcia is not committed to the claim that something is an object only if it is the object of intentionality. See the discussion in Harman's 'Garcia's Jungle'.

2. See the discussion of undermining and overmining, some of which is presented below, in Harman's *The Quadruple Object* as well as the meditation on reductionism throughout his *Prince of Networks: Bruno Latour and Metaphysics*.

3. Harman, *The Quadruple Object*, p. 8.

4. Harman, *The Quadruple Object*, pp. 10–11.

5. Luc Ferry and Alain Renaut, *French Philosophy of the Sixties: An Essay on Antihumanism*, had a point when they claimed it was impossible to really understand the *soixante-huitard* philosophers unless you at least initially see them as instancing the formula '= (late Heidegger + some combination of Nietzsche, Freud, and Marx)'.

6. See my unpublished manuscript, 'Philosophy of Mind', for an overview.

7. This is one of the upshots of Wilson's *Wandering Significance*.

8. For an example that comes very close to this absurd limit, see Alexander Galloway's 'The Poverty of Philosophy: Realism and Post-Fordism'.

9. See Cat Jordie's *Stanford Encyclopedia of Philosophy* article on the unity of science.

10. In passing, we should note that Cartwright's *Nature Capacities and Their Measurements* and Dupré's *The Disorder of Things: Metaphysical Foundations of the Disunity of Science* are themselves important forerunners which need to be entered into dialogue with recent continental metaphysicians, as Cartwright and Dupré also defend realist metaphysical views that take seriously our explanatory limitations.

11. From Todd Wiscombe, David Ruy, and Todd Gannon's interview with Harman, 'The Object Turn: A Conversation'.

12. Harman, *Towards Speculative Realism*, p. 100.

13. In retrospect, Mark Ohm and I perhaps should have translated the French *différence* as 'differentiation' and 'differentiator' in these contexts. 'Difference' sounds much too much like set-theoretic subtraction. But what you get by set-theoretic subtraction is what

Garcia calls 'form'. What Garcia means by *différence* here is that which differentiates between what the object contains and what contains the object. I explain this in greater depth in Chapter 4.

14. For the fuller Whig history from which some of this is excerpted, see my and Mark Ohm's 'Actual Properties of Imaginative Things: Notes Towards an Object-Oriented Literary Theory'.

15. Dialectical and temporal progress sometimes diverge. Note that Harman's 'A Fresh Look at *Zuhandenheit*' was written in 1999, while Speculative Realism did not exist until the infamous 2007 Goldsmith symposium where Harman, Ray Brassier, Ian Hamilton Grant, and Quentin Meillassoux all critiqued philosophical anthropocentrism ('correlationism') in their disparate ways.

16. Far, far too many commentators (paradigmatically Robert Brandom in *Tales of the Mighty Dead*) try to foist an even more radical Cartesianism on Heidegger by claiming that, for Heidegger, understanding cannot be pre-linguistic. This is a non-starter though. It is uncharitable both since the view itself is so implausible and because it only works as Heidegger exegesis via misunderstanding the German word *Rede*. See Mark Okrent's 'On Layer Cakes' for a definitive rebuttal on both counts.

17. This is the primary locus of Harman's fundamental disagreement with the kind of capacity metaphysics picture of object-oriented ontology presented canonically by Levi Bryant in *The Democracy of Objects* and developed in a slightly different key in my and Mark Silcox's 'The Emergence of Emergence'. All of this work should be seen as a development of the views articulated by Nancy Cartwright in *Nature's Capacities and Their Measurement*. Adjudicating the issue of whether capacity metaphysics approaches really can honour the extreme anti-reductionism of members of the Stanford School and object-oriented ontologists will require a careful comparison of Harman's account of real properties with Cartwright's account of capacities.

18. Harman, *The Quadruple Object*, pp. 106–7.

19. In conversation, Charles Pence has helpfully characterised Harman's view of the connection between real and sensual qualities as Alexander Bird's view of causal relations (see, for example, John W. Carroll's *Notre Dame Philosophical Reviews* piece on Bird's *Nature's Metaphysics: Laws and Properties*) combined with what many would take to be an upside-down grounding relation (see Rick Bliss and Kelly Trogdon's *Stanford Encyclopedia of Philosophy* article on metaphysical grounding). This probably isn't *quite* right

(among other things, reversing the grounding relation ends up changing Bird's view of laws in exactly the way Harman would take them to be in need of being amended), but I think it is very helpful for connecting Harman's thinking with emerging traditions in analytic philosophy, as is the work of the Stanford School mentioned earlier.

20. Another way to think about the reversal of the emergence/grounding relation in Harman's thought is that it is an expression of his conviction that reality is radically non-linguaform, for the real qualities we discover loosely capture aspects of reality that we can picture with our conceptual/linguistic resources. These concerns map closely on to analytic debates about whether actualist theories of possibility generally suffer the problems of 'book realism', which takes the actual world to be an actualisation of the book that correctly describes it. For Lewisians such as John Divers (in *Possible Worlds*) the implausibility of this is a dispositive reason to not take there to be a metaphysical difference between the actual world and possible ones. But one might take the very dilemma between modal realists and actualists to be a reason to develop a theory of modality not involving possible worlds.

21. Harman, *The Quadruple Object*, p. 130.

22. For Garcia's own take on his divergences from Harman, see his 'Crossing Ways of Thinking: On Graham Harman's System and My Own', as well as Harman's response 'Tristan Garcia and the Thing-in-itself'.

23. Harman's major criticism of Garcia in 'Tristan Garcia and the Thing-in-itself' concerns whether entities qua things can stop this slide. I discuss this criticism in Chapter 9.

24. The phrase comes from Quine's influential essay 'On What There Is'.

25. If we use the definition of structuralism given in Deleuze's 1967 'How Do We Recognize Structuralism?', then it is clear both that Deleuze and Derrida were paradigm structuralists and (perhaps) that post-structuralism never was. I was taught in college that the paradigm 'post-structuralist' thought (attributed to Derrida) is that each structure constitutively presupposes something radically at variance with it. But in 1967 Deleuze argues that this has been a key part of structuralism all along. I don't mean to downplay Derrida's importance by writing this. Prior to his own fame, he was a prominent student in some of Lacan's seminars and my sense is that Derrida the student profoundly influenced Lacan the teacher. Incidentally, Deleuze's essay is also wonderful for seeing

how a process metaphysics can come out of structuralism; the non-structure presupposed by structures becomes for Deleuze the virtual realm of intensive differences.

26. Deleuze, 'How Do We Recognize Structuralism?', p. 174.
27. Moore, *The Evolution of Modern Metaphysics*, p. 142.

2

Neither Analytic Nor Dialectic I: Horizon

The speculative moment in recent continental philosophy is largely motivated by a dilemma faced by phenomenologists. Phenomenology attempts to articulate the structures that must be presupposed for people to have experiences of objects. But then, the speculative thinker poses a question: are these structures themselves properties of objects? If the answer is yes, then phenomenology is already part of metaphysics, albeit the small part concerned with elucidating our own cognitive navels. That is, if human beings are objects in the world, and phenomenology is in the business of describing how humans experience the world, then metaphysics must be possible. Of course many phenomenologists will reply[1] that phenomenology is transcendental in the sense that the conditions articulated for access to objects are not themselves properties of an object. The transcendental subject is not itself an object. The speculative return to metaphysics happens when one rejects this distinction as well as its accompanying anthropocentrism. Once classic phenomenology is reinterpreted as a metaphysics of the subject, which itself is an object among other objects in the world, then classic phenomenology can be mined in a guerrilla fashion to help us understand non-human objects.

The return to metaphysics in analytic philosophy follows quite a different pattern. If continental philosophers found the royal road to philosophy to lie through the characterisation of the human subject, early analytic philosophers found it in characterisation of human language. Given the primacy of language to human subjects, these projects are not nearly as distinct from one another as is commonly supposed. And just as the speculative moment in continental philosophy opens up a vast trove of phenomenological resources for analytic metaphysicians, the death of 'analysis' in analytic philosophy is highly instructive for continental metaphysicians. Indeed, Garcia's discussion of events and time in Book II of *Form and Object* (discussed in Chapter 8 below) is itself a fantastic piece of analytic philosophy, building on earlier analytic thinkers' work.

Being reasonably clear about how 'analysis' failed in analytic philosophy has a twofold payoff for understanding Garcia's system. First, speculative realists should take heart in the way the failure of analysis supports the return to metaphysics. As I will show, the death of analysis was occasioned by the realisation that information about the world could not be easily shaved off from information about word meaning. This is a linguistic version of the speculative realist's criticism of attempts to shave off metaphysical content from phenomenological content. Early analytic philosophy was a form of linguistic neo-Kantianism in exactly a parallel manner that early phenomenology was a form of cognitive neo-Kantianism. Second, Garcia's brief comments on analysis might lead a reader unfamiliar with analytic philosophy to think that he is eschewing the whole tradition. But mainstream contemporary analytic philosophy is on Garcia's side here.

Another confusion we must forestall with respect to Garcia involves his distancing himself from 'dialectical' thinking, the rejection of which formed one of the major birth pains of the analytic tradition. Clarity here is doubly important since Speculative Realism's revolt against Kantian strains in contemporary philosophy has commonalities with German idealists such as Schelling, Hegel, and Schopenhauer. When Schelling writes 'I am nature'[2] he is rejecting the distinction between transcendental and empirical subject in precisely the manner that speculative realists reject phenomenology's transcendental pretensions. For we now see Kantian speculation about the human mind as metaphysics, not what we do instead of metaphysics. And, though I will not develop this thought here, Hegel's deconstruction of the Kantian distinction between the noumenal realm of things in themselves and the phenomenal realm of human experience[3] also finds echoes in Garcia.[4] Below, I will show the main sense in which Garcia is a dialectical thinker and the sense in which he is not. Like Hegel, he is interested in tension and contradiction, but unlike Hegel[5] he holds that these tensions are often *not* productive of change. In fact, Garcia turns this on its head. Part of what it is to be an object is to resist sublimation into the structures that contain the object in question.

With respect to philosophical methodology, 'analysis' is the semantic version of undermining, where word meanings are understood in roughly the same way, as composed of simpler meanings, the grasping of which is necessary and sufficient for grasping the semantically complex word. 'Dialectics' for Garcia tends to correspond to understanding concepts in terms of their relations to their place in the argumentative structures in which they occur. This is the conceptual version of Harman's overmining, for example the historical role that the concepts of chairs play (as opposed to the historical role of the chairs themselves).

> Every analytic reduces the possibility of being something to some logical, rational, or pragmatic conditions. Every dialectic reduces the possibility of being something to its mediation by another thing. Instead, we demonstrate our commitment to that solitary something in each thing that can never be reduced to anything else. This irreducibility is the 'chance' of each thing, and the ground for the dismissal of both analytic and dialectical ways of thinking. We reject ways of thinking that reduce things exclusively to natural, social, or historical things. (FO 8)

It might seem natural to leave it at that and begin our explanation of the manner in which the technical components of Garcia's system avoid undermining and overmining. However, the price of doing that would be to potentially miss the manner in which the pure ontology of things/objects in *Form and Object*'s Book I ties to the various regional ontologies of Book II. Pure ontology investigates what is in common to *all* things, which for Garcia includes electrons, tables, melodies, numbers, ghosts, oceans, wistfulness, and ideas. Regional ontologies articulate what is distinctive about different kinds of things. In Garcia's case, he must articulate the specific ways that a kind of object, such as humanity, constitutes itself by resisting its own undermining and overmining.

Garcia's denigration of reductive explanations is meant to apply to his own metaphysical explanations, which assume a paradoxical character in virtue of this. The paradoxical nature of Book I's pure ontology becomes a kind of motif, which I refer to as the dialectics of persistence, that then gets reiterated when Garcia examines the kinds of objects discussed in Book II. We cannot really understand this unless we are maximally clear about the way Garcia departs from traditional dialectical thinking. In addition, Garcia's division of entities into two modes (object and thing) in his pure ontology can only really be motivated by examining tensions in dialectical thinking, which we consider here and in the next chapter.

Analysis

So-called 'analytic philosophy' gets its name from many of its earliest practitioners, who held the curious conviction that the proper task of philosophy is the analysis of meaning. In the revolutionary period of the movement, a ferment best exemplified by A. J. Ayer's *Language, Truth, and Logic*, the notion of 'analysis' tended to borrow uncritically from Kant's characterisation of analytic judgements. In *The Critique of Pure Reason*, a proposition is analytic if (1) denying it leads to a contradiction, and (2) the meaning of the predicate is contained in the meaning of the subject. Part of the development of formal logic by analytic philosophers was an attempt to make sense of the first criterion. Kant's containment metaphor, as applied to the task of analysing word meanings, was widely adopted until Quine's 'Two Dogmas of Empiricism' convinced most analytic philosophers that it was misleading at best.

To get a feel for the hegemonic rule of the containment metaphor during the wild days of analytic philosophy, one need only glance at G. E. Moore's characterisation of definitions where he argues that 'good' is actually not definable.

> Let us, then, consider this position. My point is that 'good' is a simple notion, just as 'yellow' is a simple notion; that, just as you cannot, by any manner of means, explain to anyone who does not already know it, what yellow is, so you cannot explain what good is. Definitions of the kind that I was asking for, definitions which describe the real nature of the object or notion denoted by a word, and which do not merely tell us what the word is used to mean, are only possible when the object or notion in question is something complex. You can give a definition of a horse, because a horse has many different properties and qualities, all of which you can enumerate. But when you have enumerated them all, when you have reduced a horse to his simplest terms, you can no longer define those terms. They are simply something which you think of or perceive, and to anyone who cannot think of or perceive them, you can never, by any definition, make their nature known. It may perhaps be objected to this that we are able to describe to others, objects which they have never seen or thought of. We can, for instance, make a man understand what a chimaera is, although he has never

heard of one or seen one. You can tell him that it is an animal with a lioness's head and body, with a goat's head growing from the middle of its back, and with a snake in place of its tail. But here the object which you are describing is a complex object; it is entirely composed of parts, with which we are all perfectly familiar – a snake, a goat, a lioness; and we know, too, the manner in which those parts are to be put together, because we know what is meant by the middle of a lioness's back, and where her tail is wont to grow.[6]

Just as objects have parts, so do the definitions that seek to characterise them; the parts of the definitions correspond to the parts of the things in question. We should note that Moore does not mean 'material part' by part, since the yellowness of the lion's fur would count as a basic part of the lion for him. It should be clear that this sense of analysis is a canonical example of undermining, applied by early analytic philosophers to word meanings.

Understanding Garcia's system requires appreciating the sad fate of 'analysis' so construed, the reasons why the overwhelming majority of so-called 'analytic philosophers' no longer believe that the proper task of philosophy is the analysis of meanings. It is not difficult to construct a Whig history of this rejection if we focus on the fate of Frank Ramsey's and Rudolph Carnap's[7] brilliant method of recasting implicit definitions as explicit ones. For an immediate problem with the containment metaphor for analyticity is that many definitions don't even seem to have a subject–predicate form, so the idea of truths by definition as being those where the meaning of the predicate is contained in the meaning of the subject ends up determining that many true definitions are not true by definition.

To illustrate this, we can consider one of the standard ways that addition is recursively defined over the natural numbers.

i. $\forall x(x + o = x)$
ii. $\forall x \forall y(x + s(y) = s(x + y))$

The first claim says that any number plus zero equals that number and the second says that any number plus the successor of another number equals the successor of the two numbers. If we add enough axioms characterising the successor function, which takes a number as an argument and delivers that next number in the natural number line, then this gives us a mechanical procedure to calculate sums. For example, if we wanted to determine what three plus two is we would run ssso (since three is the successor of the successor of the successor of zero) and sso (two) through our axioms.

1. ssso + sso = s(ssso + so)   by ii
2. s(ssso + so) = s(s(ssso + o))   by ii
3. s(s(ssso + o)) = s(s(ssso))   by i

In this manner, as long as successor means what we think it does, the definitions allow the determination of any two arbitrary sums.

However, note that the axioms are not of the subject–predicate form. We just seem to have a couple of sentences involving addition that mathematicians take to be central, but nothing like an explicit definition. Even worse, each sentence includes the very thing being defined! If we don't already know what '+' means how does '$\forall x \forall y (x + s(y) = s(x + y))$' give us useful information? In introductory logic courses circularity is usually taught as fallacious. If my child asks for a definition of 'jejune' it would be perfectly unhelpful to say that it is what is in common to all jejune things, and this is precisely because such a definition (though providing necessary and sufficient conditions) would not help someone who doesn't already know the meaning of the term come to grasp it.

Fortunately, Ramsey and Carnap developed an ingenious technique to turn implicit definitions such as occur in mathematics into something more pleasing to philosophers laboring under Kant's characterisation of analyticity. First we can conjoin our axioms together into one sentence.[8]

$$\forall x \forall y ((x + o = x) \wedge (x + s(y) = s(x + y)))$$

This just says that, for any two numbers, adding zero to the first one is equal to the first one, and adding the first one and the successor of the second one is equal to the successor of adding the two numbers together.

Then, we existentially quantify out with respect to each of the non-logical terms in the axiom. For simplicity, we will follow modern usage and treat '=' as a logical relation (in Peano Arithmetic proper, axioms guaranteeing reflexivity, symmetry, transitivity, and closure are added for identity).

$$\exists M_1 \exists M_2 \forall x \forall y[(x\ M_1\ o = x) \wedge (x\ M_1\ M_2(y) = M_2(x\ M_1\ y))]$$

This just says that there exist two functions M_1 and M_2[9] such that for any two numbers the M_1 function takes the first one and zero to the first one, and M_1 takes the first one and M_2 applied to the second one and yields M_2 applied to what M_1 delivers when applied to the two numbers.

Then, we can transform this into an explicit definition of addition by just saying that a plus b equals by definition the output of M_1. We can say that plus is the property such that

$$a + b = c \ _{def} \exists M_1 \exists M_2 \forall x \forall y[(x\ M_1\ o = x) \wedge (x\ M_1\ M_2(y) = M_2(x\ M_1\ y)) \wedge c = (a\ M_1\ b)]$$

The right hand side of the definition is the Ramsey sentence for plus. To be fair, this isn't quite a simple subject–predicate judgement of the form Kant considered. But it does seem to give us hope for legitimating the containment metaphor. The concept of plus contains all of the concepts necessary in articulating plus's Ramsey sentence, which exposes the logical relations between all of the predicates necessary for understanding that word. And note how '+' does not occur on the right-hand side of the definition, which considerably mitigates the concern about the intrinsic circularity of implicit definitions.

This property of Ramsification became the most important one for philosophers of mind trying to analyse the meaning of words such as 'pain', 'pleasure', 'belief', and 'desire'.[10] The problem was that any full account of some mental concept involves reference to other mental concepts. For example, people in pain typically desire not to be so. Philosophers of mind who hoped that analysis could help solve the mind–body problem in favour of the body rightly saw this as a problem. If every definition of a mental concept made reference to other mental concepts, then one hasn't explained the mental in terms of the non-mental. Luckily then, full Ramsification of ordinary psychological talk would solve this problem. There would be one Ramsey sentence not containing any psychological predicates for the entire theory and each mental term could be defined in terms of the variable existentially quantified out for that term, analogous to the manner in which we have defined addition in terms of M_1 above.

This being said, the question immediately arises about *how much* information needs to be packed into a Ramsey sentence. Note that our definition of '+' actually completely fails unless M_2 really is the successor function. Let's say 's' were the identity function, the function that takes an object to itself. Then our Ramsey sentence would define '+ o' not '+' (in mod 1 arithmetic the functions are the same).[11] And what would our definition say if 'o' didn't exist in the first place? Much more needs to be added to our Ramsey sentence, in particular both to secure that 'o' exists and that 's' has its intended meaning. And standard Peano axiomatisations prevent variant arithmetics that make true our definition but also make true claims that are clearly false of the natural numbers (in particular, one needs an existence axiom for 'o' and three axioms ensuring that 's' is an injective function and that zero is not the successor of anything). But such axioms themselves are not in anything like subject–predicate form and they also display a kind of circularity. Fortunately, in the case of mathematics one can just extend the Ramsey sentence to incorporate all of these new axioms.

To get a better idea of how this works, and to see its ultimate limitations, let us consider what is revealed when we partially Ramsify the most recent version of George Dickie's institutional theory of art. The theory itself offers up a set of explicit definitions that exhibit the kind of circularity that we might have once found disturbing about implicit ones:

> An artist is a person who participates with understanding in the making of a work of art.[12]
> A work of art is an artifact of a kind created to be presented to an artworld public.[13]
> A public is a set of persons the members of which are prepared in some degree to understand an object which is presented to them.[14]
> The artworld is the totality of all artworld systems.[15]
> An artworld system is a framework for the presentation of a work of art by an artist to an artworld public.[16]

If we want to take the second such sentence as the definition for 'work of art', we are immediately confronted by the kind of circularity decried in introductory logic classes. We can only understand the claim that 'A work of art is an artifact of a kind to be presented to an artworld public' if we know what an artworld public is. But when we push through the definitions we are led to the definition of 'artworld system' which mentions 'work of art' again.

Ramsification to the rescue? Let's see. The process begins by replacing all of the art-centric predicates with variables.

1. An X_1 is a person who participates with understanding in the making of an X_2.
2. An X_2 is an artifact of a kind created to be presented to an X_3 public.
3. A public is a set of persons the members of which are prepared in some degree to understand an object which is presented to them.
4. The X_3 is the totality of all X_3 systems.
5. An X_3 system is a framework for the presentation of an X_2 by an X_1 to an X_3 public.

Now the logical conjunction of these sentences is the institutional theory with variables replacing the art-relevant terms. Let us call this T(1,2,3,4,5). This Ramsification then allows us to easily express the institutional theory as an explicit definition of 'work of art' in the following manner:

T(1,2,3,4,5).
y is a work of art $=_{def} \exists X_1 \exists X_2 \exists X_3 [T(1,2,3,4,5) \wedge X_2(y)]$

And, as with our Ramsey sentence for addition that did not include axioms for the successor function, we can see that this fails to provide necessary and sufficient conditions. Let X_1 be an academic, X_2 be academic publications, and X_3 be the research community. Academic publications are not artworks, but the schema provided by the five definitions yields a Ramsey sentence that defines academic publications just as much as it does works of art.

The overriding issue for analysis then concerns exactly how much information needs to be added to a definition such that (1) understanding the definition is sufficient for understanding the word and (2) the definition only contains information relevant for understanding the word. In analytic philosophy, the thesis of the inextricability of meaning from belief (hereafter *the inextricability thesis*)[17] is the denial of the claim that there is any fact of the matter about the proper division of information merely relevant to a word's meaning from associated meaning about the world that might involve the denotation of the word in question. One problem is that centrality of information relevant to ability to use a word correctly is highly context-sensitive, depending upon the target audience and the level of expertise the linguistic community demands of members of that audience. A dictionary for primary school children and a dictionary for engineers will have radically different definitions of the same terms. From expectations of lexical mastery for primary school children one would say that the information in the engineers' dictionary was not information about the meanings of the words, but added world information. Which dictionary is correct in this regard? The inextricability thesis entails that this very question makes no sense.

A few hundred years of lexicography have disabused us of the myth that there could be a dictionary from a God's-eye view that included all and only information relevant to word meaning such that we could determine whether two speakers who disagree substantially agreed on the meaning of the central terms (and hence disagreed about the way the world is) or were merely using the terms in different ways.

If we were very liberal about adding information that might seem to do with the world and not merely with the meaning of 'work of art', we could end up with a definition that is not easily falsifiable in the way the institutional theory of art is. But, as Jaegwon Kim argues in his influential critique of Ramsification in the philosophy of mind, this carries a very high price, as

> we had better make sure that the underlying theory is true. If our T is to yield our psychological concepts all at once, it is going to be a long conjunction of myriad psychological generalizations, and even a single false component will render the whole conjunction false. So we must face this question: What is going to be included in our T, and how certain can we be that T is true?[18]

But, given this requirement, we cannot just add all of the beliefs that various people have about what makes something a work of art; there is *a lot* of substantive disagreement about what counts as a work of art! Consider Kim again with respect to the philosophy of mind.

> These reflections lead to the following thought: On the Ramsey-Lewis method of defining psychological concepts, every dispute about underlying theory T is going to turn out to be a dispute about psychological concepts. This creates a seemingly paradoxical situation: If two psychologists

should disagree about some psychological generalization that is part of theory *T*, which we could expect to be a very common occurrence, this would mean that they are using different sets of psychological concepts. But this would seem to imply that they could not really disagree, since the possibility of disagreement presupposes the sharing of the same concepts. How could I accept and you reject a given proposition unless we shared the concepts in terms of which the proposition is formulated?[19]

This, in essence, is the problem that beset classical analytic philosophy, and much contemporary analytic philosophy of mind and language can only be seen as attempts to come up with theories of meanings and concepts that answer Kim's final question.[20] But almost nobody would still accept the view that the royal road to philosophy lay in writing dictionaries.

Part of the problem is that philosophy is not a *descriptive* enterprise concerning what people actually *do* believe, but rather a *normative* one concerning what people *ought to* believe. Since all conceptual resources are not equal, philosophers need in part to try to characterise the concepts that one *should* deploy if one wants to be capable of having the beliefs that are conducive to wisdom. Strangely, at the very beginning of the wild years, G. E. Moore exhibited a then uncommon awareness of this very issue.

What, then, is good? How is good to be defined? Now, it may be thought that this is a verbal question. A definition does indeed often mean the expressing of one word's meaning in other words. But this is not the sort of definition I am asking for. Such a definition can never be of ultimate importance to any study except lexicography. If I wanted that kind of definition I should have to consider in the first place how people generally used the word 'good'; but my business is not with its proper usage, as established by custom. I should, indeed, be foolish if I tried to use it for something which it did not usually denote: if, for instance, I were to announce that, whenever I used the word 'good', I must be understood to be thinking of that object which is usually denoted by the word 'table'. I shall, therefore, use the word in the sense in which I think it is ordinarily used; but at the same time I am not anxious to discuss whether I am right in thinking it is so used. My business is solely with that object or idea, which I hold, rightly or wrongly, that the word is generally used to stand for. What I want to discover is the nature of that object or idea, and about this I am extremely anxious to arrive at an agreement.[21]

But when this insight is married to the inextricability thesis, the end result is the not very surprising claim that philosophers (along with physicists, librarians, and tug boat captains) would like to have true beliefs about the kinds of things (such as goodness, in Moore's case) that interest them. If the inextricability thesis were false, then the task of philosophy would plausibly be to delineate what everyone should believe about the meaning of philosophically interesting words. But if there is no fact of the matter principally differentiating word meaning from related information about the world, then any attempt to analyse word meanings will bleed over into defences that one should view the world in some substantive way. The death of analysis, like that of transcendental philosophy, is the rebirth of metaphysics.

This is not to eschew all explanation of objects (even words and their meanings) in terms of parts. When Garcia himself critiques overmining, he sometimes does so in terms of the necessity of undermining! Consider this section from the very end of Book I.

> By looking at an organism part by part, I cannot obtain the meaning of the parts from the whole. There would only be a possible synthesis, and never an analysis. I could count from one to a very large number, but I could not return to a smaller number from this number. Soon, the whole world would appear to me as a *big compact thing*, a being comprehending each thing absolutely, in such a way that I could never pick out from this world things that compose this world, and from these things I have little by little returned to this world. (*FO* 103)

Analysis is a vital part of understanding the multiplicity of the world. As with undermining generally, Garcia's concern about its limits should not be taken as denial of its successes.

At the risk of repeating myself, let me again state that part of this success is the moral that analytic philosophers have drawn from the failure of analysis. For many analytic philosophers, analysis was what one did instead of metaphysics. But the way that analysis failed suggests that metaphysics is inevitable. For once we give up on the idea that there is a principled distinction between dictionary information relevant to word meanings and encyclopedic information about the world, what sense are we to make of previous attempts to analyse words such as 'knowledge'? One could consign epistemology to the flames, since its earliest analytic incarnations rested on bogus views of language. This would be mistaken though, as the overwhelming amount of the theory of knowledge just now becomes seen as part of metaphysics. Someone who develops a theory of justification to make sense of knowledge as a kind of justified, true belief is simply developing a theory of something in the world, knowledge. We were doing metaphysics all along. Our concept of knowledge, and the dictionary definitions we might give of knowledge, might have to be revised substantially because knowledge doesn't have the properties we thought it did. All of our attempts to develop a theory of it might ultimately be frustrated. But they are attempts to characterise something in the world, not attempts to characterise facets of our views about knowledge that are true in virtue of meaning.

Dialectics

The chapters in Book II of *Form and Object* consider a history of how our theory of some kind of thing (life, humanity, classes, gender, death, and so on) changes over time as we rocket back and forth in attempting to understand the kind in question using methods of natural science and understanding the role of the kind in human culture. In some sense, Garcia is presenting several Hegelian *tours de force*, as dialectics often involves characterising the subtle ways a concept shifts in light of historical and argumentative pressure. But the weird thing about Garcia's dialectics is that they often never resolve. There is no end of the story where we have a natural scientific story that explains the kind in question such that it plays the role it does in broader culture. Instead, we see that the very tensions become constitutive of the kind in question. Thus Garcia in a sense preserves dialectic, albeit in a radically altered form.

There are two ways that Hegelian dialectic tends to get presented in the secondary literature. The traditional manner[22] presents dialectical logic as always involving a thesis, which falls apart upon critical scrutiny; an antithesis, which is simply the denial of the thesis and which also falls apart under critical scrutiny; and synthesis, which somehow gets what was right about the thesis and antithesis without falling apart (at least until the synthesis serves as a thesis for a further bit of dialectic).

To see how this works, let our thesis be scientific determinism, the idea that a completed science in some sense contains the resources to predict the future with 100 per cent accuracy. Some people have argued that the world described by the determinist[23] is self-refuting in the sense that there is no place in a deterministic world for human beings who could discover and use the very sciences that seem to suggest determinism. Doing science requires creatively thinking of different hypotheses and how to test them, and rationally assessing the result. Is there any place in the deterministic universe seemingly described by classical physics for such creativity and rationality? If not, then we have the weird result that the existence of science shows that we are not just robots determined to follow the laws described by that science. But the *mere rejection* of determinism would yield the view that some events occur for no reason whatsoever. And this completely fails to address what was problematic about scientific determinism, for it seems to entail that we do things for no reason whatsoever. A robot with a random number generator in its head dictating certain actions is still a robot.

The synthesis would in some sense get what is right about determinism and indeterminism without falling apart (at least for the same reasons). With respect to human freedom, note that most worthwhile freedoms presuppose a radical narrowing of possibilities. For me to have the freedom to decide whether to learn a given song on the guitar, I have to have already taken a lot of guitar lessons. If my parents had just let me do everything I'd wanted to, I'd be much less free today. Or consider libertarian approaches to healthcare. If most of us had to approach every aspect of our healthcare in the same manner that we approach purchasing cars, we would have no time for anything else (not to mention the lack of freedom that untreated illness causes). The 'freedom to choose' is often vastly less free, in part because the lack of certain freedoms is precisely what gives us the time and abilities to exercise a higher freedom of making rational choices about things that are important to us.

While many of Hegel's arguments can easily be put in the structure of thesis/antithesis/synthesis, this picture of dialectic actually describes the earlier German idealist, Fichte, as well as some of Marx's appropriations of Hegel. Recent English-language scholarship[24] presents a different picture. Here, the three phases are (1) abstract (finite understanding), (2) dialectical (negative reasoning), and (3) speculative (positive reasoning). For Hegel, the mental facility of the understanding is the part of us that applies categories to the world. For a variety of reasons this faculty is forced to affirm the laws of excluded middle (P or it is not the case that P) and non-contradiction (it is not the case that (P and it is not the case that P)). This forces us into an either/or kind of thinking. For example, we characterise 'freedom' in such a way, and then any act must be 'free' or 'not-free' according to that characterisation. Then the dialectical phase is where we find the problems inherent in the either/or conceptualisation itself. This leads to scepticism and despair. But the speculative phase of positive reason allows us to overcome our previous rigid dichotomies and see the world closer to the way an infinite intellect might.

For Hegel, abstract thinking is both a feature and a bug. Since we are forced to understand the world and communicate this understanding with our finite intellects, we constantly have to oversimplify things. But this kind of either/or oversimplification gets us into trouble. As for the second stage, 'dialectic', much contemporary continental philosophy can only be considered as permanently stuck there, endlessly attempting to undermine dichotomies. Indeed, the word 'deconstruction' has come to mean precisely this for most people who use the term. The 'speculative turn in recent continental philosophy' can thus be seen as an attempt to move past purely negative critique.

For German idealists, the move to the third step, speculation, was not particularly mysterious. The undermining of dichotomies revealed contradictions in how we see the world. But contradictions are themselves calls to change the theory that gave rise to them. The further speculative tendency is to see these processes of thought as incarnate in reality itself, characterising historical and natural processes thus in terms of contradictions arising and being resolved. Consider Friedrich Schelling's description of time.

> Whoever takes time only as it presents itself feels a conflict of two principles in it; one strives toward development, and one holds back inhibiting [*hemmend*] and striving against development. If this other principle were to provide no resistance, then there would be no time, because development would occur in an uninterrupted flash rather than successively; yet if the other principle were not constantly overcome by the first, there would be absolute rest, death, standstill and hence there would again be no time. But if we consider both of these principles to be equally active in one and the same essence, we will have contradiction straight away.[25]

And this isn't just with respect to the past and future, but everything existing: 'Thus, the principles we perceive in time are authentic inner principles of all life, and contradiction is not only possible but in fact necessary.'[26] And as we have noted the way that contradictions spur changes in our set of beliefs, so are contradictions in nature spurs to historical and natural processes.

> Although men – in both living and knowing – seem to shy away from nothing so much as contradiction, they still must confront it, because life itself is in contradiction. Without contradiction there would be no life, no movement, no progress; a deadly slumber of all forces. Only contradiction drives us – indeed, forces us – to action. Contradiction is in fact the venom of all life, and all vital motion is nothing but the attempt to overcome this poisoning.[27]

The job of the speculative thinker on this account is to engage in the process of dialectic in order to describe the dialectical nature of reality.

But Garcia's speculative move is not a mere recapitulation of dialectics after a seventy-five year or so interregnum. For Garcia does *not* think that tensions and contradictions revealed by the second stage of dialectics must be resolved into new consistent theories.[28]

> Lastly, we refuse to dialectically arrange contradictions. For a dialectician, our theory may appear to go nowhere, to sink into relativism, to make everything and anything possible, to prove to be inconsistent and, worst of all, flat, since it does not hierarchise things formally. (FO 8)

But, unlike the standard-issue deconstructionism,[29] Garcia doesn't stop there, because he *does* accept that the unresolved contradictions tell us something important about the nature of reality itself. Unresolved contradictions in our thinking about the world are no barrier to metaphysics if those unresolved contradictions represent the way the world is.

Indeed, in Garcia's initial discussion of the typical strategies by which philosophers attempt to explain phenomena as if those phenomena are not objects, Garcia explicitly considers contradictory objects. In this context he makes much the same kind of arguments that Graham Priest does in *Towards Non-Being* to the conclusion that contradictory objects must have some dignified ontological status, since we talk about them and distinguish them from one another.

> A contradiction must have a determination *a minima* in order to remain the contradiction that it is. If what is white and non-white could be absolutely no-matter-what, it could be exclusively white, and therefore not be contradictory and not be no-matter-what. (*FO* 26)

Admittedly, not very much hangs on this bare admission. We will have to examine the sense in which contradictory objects play a role in Garcia's metaphysics. We begin in the next chapter by articulating the sense in which the world is contradictory for Garcia, as this forms (as I will show) a territory separated by some of the major fault lines in contemporary metaphysics.

More generally though, if conceptual tension is a motor of change for the German idealists, it is a principle of persistence for Garcia. Things are what they are (both synchronically and dia-chronically) because they *resist* being the kinds of things that we can tell unified, consistent stories about. This move informs nearly every aspect of Garcia's system, from the differential model of objects/things in Book I to the tragic conception of existence and philosophy itself worked out Book II.

Notes

1. The best contemporary discussion of these issues is to be found from the various authors in Steven Crowell and Jeff Malpas's *Transcendental Heidegger*. The intelligibility of Husserl's claim that the phenomenal subject is transcendental is also presented as a key hinge in Okrent's *Heidegger's Pragmatism* and Moore's *The Evolution of Modern Metaphysics*. It seems clear to me that from very early in his career Heidegger wanted to break with the view, but it is not at all clear to me that he ever succeeded.
2. See Iain Hamilton Grant's *Philosophies of Nature after Schelling*.
3. For Hegel's send-up of Kant's transcendental dialectic (which forms the main argument for the distinction between phenomena and noumena in the *First Critique*), see the discussion in Priest's *Beyond the Limits of Thought*. For a reading of Hegel as more straightforwardly undermining the distinction see the discussion in Braver's *A Thing of This World: A History of Continental Anti-Realism*.

4. Though not in Harman! Harman preserves the distinction between noumena and phenomena but, in the boldest of speculative moves, views it as holding between any two objects.

5. In *Beyond the Limits of Thought* Priest interprets Hegel's view of infinity as affirming true contradictions.

6. Moore, *Principia Ethica*, pp. 7–8.

7. See Stathis Psillos's 'Ramsey's *Ramsey*-sentences*' for an account of the history of the concept arising out of the interplay between Ramsey, Carl Hempel, and Carnap. For a longer description of how Ramsey sentences do and don't work, see my *Philosophy of Mind*.

8. I'm not here considering full Peano arithmetic with either a first-order induction axiom scheme or second-order induction axiom. Ramsifying this requires the second-order axiomatic form of induction. The fact that second-order logic does not have a decidable consequence relation ends up in a profound way also reining in what one might take to be philosophically accomplished by Ramsification in particular and analysis in general. See the discussion of artificial intelligence and limitation results in Silcox's and my *Philosophy Through Video Games*.

9. For simplicity's sake I've left '+' and 's' as functional signs instead of using predicates corresponding to the characteristic functions corresponding to them. See the discussion of Ramsey sentence functionalism in my *Philosophy of Mind* for a more standard presentation.

10. For a full account of this, see my *Philosophy of Mind*.

11. See Roy Cook's and my 'What Negation is Not: Intuitionism and "0 = 1"' and my 'Tonking a Theory of Content: An Inferentialist Rejoinder' for discussion of some surprising philosophical consequences of mod 1 arithmetic, which you get by removing the Peano axiom that states that zero is not the successor of anything and adding the axiom that zero equals one.

12. Dickie, 'The Institutional Theory of Art', p. 98.

13. Dickie, 'The Institutional Theory of Art', p. 99.

14. Dickie, 'The Institutional Theory of Art', p. 100.

15. Dickie, 'The Institutional Theory of Art', p. 100.

16. Dickie, 'The Institutional Theory of Art', p. 101.

17. As far as I know, this way of putting it is due to Dummett, in his influential 'The Significance of Quine's Indeterminacy Thesis'. It's very weird that Dummett shows so little awareness that his interpretation of Quine undermines his own 'molecularism' about meaning. See my dissertation, 'Slouching Towards Vienna: Michael Dummett and the Epistemology of Language'.

18. Kim, *Philosophy of Mind*, pp. 108–9.
19. Kim, *Philosophy of Mind*, p. 109.
20. For anyone worried about how all this might play out with respect to philosophical methodology, a very good place to start is Tamar Szabo Gendler and John Hawthorne's edited anthology, *Conceivability and Possibility*.
21. Moore, *Principia Ethica*, p. 6.
22. For example, Lloyd Spencer and Andrzej Krauze's *Introducing Hegel*, p. 14.
23. I *think* Schelling was the first person to make this kind of argument, though it clearly builds on the way that Descartes's actual argument for dualism involved the claim that language showed that humans could not be machines. See Iain Hamilton Grant's *Philosophies of Nature After Schelling*. John McDowell's critique of 'bald naturalism' in *Mind and World* is an updated version of Schelling's argument, albeit McDowell is much clearer than Schelling about how the real tension concerns the place of normativity in a naturalistic world.
24. For a brief account, see Robert Stern's *Hegel and the Phenomenology of Spirit*, p. 15. For the cutting-edge discussion of this question, see Brady Bowman's *Hegel and the Metaphysics of Absolute Negativity*.
25. Schelling, 'Ages of the World', p. 123.
26. Schelling, 'Ages of the World', p. 124.
27. Schelling, 'Ages of the World', p. 124.
28. I'm not claiming that Hegel thinks they are. Perhaps at the very end of the dialectic (if there is such a thing for Hegel), when matter has fully become self-conscious spirit, then spirit is aware of its own contradictory nature.
29. My colleague Deborah Goldgaber argues (pers. comm.) that Jacques Derrida is not a deconstructionist in this sense. She is working through an interpretation of Derrida as a speculative thinker both in the sense above and in the sense in which Harman reads Heidegger.

3

Neither Analytic Nor Dialectic II: The World of Object-Oriented Ontology

In Chapter 1, we saw how Graham Harman and Tristan Garcia's object-oriented ontology is centrally motivated by the conceit that one can offer a speculative metaphysics of objects in terms of their radical resistance, an important instance of which is their ability to elude our attempts to reduce them to their constituents or the structures in which they are placed. But the astute reader will have noticed a rather substantial problem. All of the object-oriented explanations actually *do* involve specifying objects' constituents and the structures in which they are placed! Harman's fourfold represents the internal structure of any object (undermining) and the manner in which objects paradigmatically relate to one another (overmining). Both the objective and formal modes of Garcia's own differential model are relational structures (overmining) in which all entities find themselves, and intensity operates as a basic property the possession of which (undermining) allows entities to temporalise themselves. To the extent that object-oriented ontologists really are offering speculative systems of metaphysics, they seem to be trying to do what they themselves take to be impossible.

Is this a feature or a bug? To find the answer we must pose the problem in a more general manner. Metaphysics tries to give us explanations of what reality must be like such that what we know about it is true. But suppose for argument that part of what we know about reality is the impossibility of providing an explanation of what reality must be like such that what we know about it is true. Then the metaphysician would have to provide an account of what reality is like such that metaphysics is impossible. Is this the position that object-oriented ontologists find themselves in? If so, is it even a remotely sensible project?

Of course the issue is too general and large to answer here. But I think I can present a few things that are relevant to addressing it.

First, the paradox in question should not be thought of as something just affecting Harman and Garcia. Rather, I will show here that it is an instantiation of what Graham Priest calls inclosure paradoxes, paradoxes that arguably arise whenever philosophers think deeply enough about totality. I take it to be a virtue of Harman and Garcia's views that the issue is set in such bold relief for them. Likewise, we will see that other aspects of their systems are actually best understood as being in response to inclosure paradoxes applied to the limits of explanation. To the extent that paradoxes at this limit reflect something about our post-modern predicament,[1] Harman and Garcia have something to teach us.

The OOO Paradox

The easiest way to see how this paradox is an instance of Graham Priest's inclosure schema is to first understand the sense in which all such paradoxes instantiate the form of Russell's Paradox.[2] Russell's Paradox can be understood simply as follows. Intuitively, most collections of objects do not contain themselves. A carton of eggs is not an egg. But some collections do contain themselves; the set of all sets definable in less than twelve words is definable in less than twelve words, and hence a member of itself. But most of the sets that typically concern us are not self-membered. So consider the set of all sets that do not contain themselves, which we can call R. Now assume (for *reductio*) that R contains itself. But that means that it satisfies its own definition of being a set that does not contain itself. So our supposition that it contains itself leads to a contradiction. From this we conclude that it does not contain itself (discharging the assumption that it does contain itself).[3] But then R is a member of the set of all sets that do not contain themselves, which is R. So now we have that it both does and doesn't contain itself. Contradiction!

What should one say about this kind of thing? Priest shows that there are exactly four kinds of responses. This follows from his great discovery that an astonishing number of traditional paradoxes fit the following schema:

Inclosure Schema:
(1) $\Omega = \{y \mid \varphi(y)\}$ exists and $\psi(\Omega)$ Existence
(2) if $x \subseteq \Omega$ and $\psi(x)$ (a) $\delta(x) \notin x$ Transcendence
                                 (b) $\delta(x) \in \Omega$ Closure

At first glance, this is a formidable piece of symbolism. Rather than attempting to gloss over it here, I will first explain it with respect to Russell's Paradox below and then show the paradox for object-oriented ontology to be an instance of it. This application will be clear without too much exercise of patience even to readers for whom logical notation is rough going. For now note that in *Beyond the Limits of Thought* Priest gives values for φ, ψ, and δ to derive the paradoxes of Russell, Burali-Forti, Mirimanoff, Kant (according to Priest's reconstructed 'Fifth Antinomy'), König, Berry, Richard, Berkeley, Weyl, and Montague, as well as the traditional liar paradox involving a sentence that expresses its own falsehood. In addition, as noted above, he is able to present a guerrilla retelling of the history of philosophy (including Plato, Aristotle, Cusanus, Aquinas, Anselm, Leibniz, Berkeley, Kant, Hegel, Cantor, Russell, Frege, Quine, Davidson, Derrida, Wittgenstein, Heidegger, and Nāgārjuna) in terms of the schema.

For Priest, Russell's Paradox has pride of place, in part because it is 'the heart of Cantor's Paradox' and 'undoubtedly the simplest of all the set-theoretic paradoxes'.[4] We will explain the connection with Cantor below, but Priest's key insight is that the 'Russell set', the set of all sets that are not members of themselves, is arrived at by applying Cantor's own diagonalisation function to the identity function of the set of all pure sets.[5] A pure set is one such that neither it, nor any of its elements (nor their elements, nor their elements, and so on) contain ur-elements, which are elements that are not themselves sets. A pure set either might not bottom out, being at the top of an infinite sequence of sets that have other sets as members (this is permissible in non-well-founded set theories) or (as in more standard approaches) bottoms out always with instances of the empty set, the set that has no members (and there is only one such set because sets are distinct only if one has a member that the other lacks).

Priest's discussion is largely informal, but his inferences are not hard to present in natural deduction systems. Doing so is helpful for convincing analytically minded readers that what I am going to call the OOO Paradox (the one arising from the fact that explanations of what objects are like such that they resist under- and overmining themselves are instances of under- and overmining) is not an epiphenomenon of continental confusion, but rather actually (even according to the analytic naysayer) a real thing. For readers unfamiliar with this kind of notation, be assured that I will summarise everything in natural language.

We can begin our formal excursus by defining Cantorian diagonalisation in the usual manner. Where f_A is a one-place function defined over the set A, $\text{diag}(f_A)$ equals the set of x in A that are such that x is not a member of the object delivered when f_A is applied to x (the object denoted by $f_A(x)$). Thus:

$$\text{diag}(f_A) = \{x \in A \mid x \notin f_A(x)\}$$

This is the key function that Cantor constructed to show that the cardinality (the number of things in the set) of any set is less than the cardinality of the set of all of that set's subsets. Cantor proved that if we start with a function from a set to its own powerset (the set of all subsets of the initial set), the set delivered by diag will of necessity not be among the members delivered by the initial function from the set to its powerset. Any proof that establishes this with respect to some set and its powerset is now called a proof by diagonalisation. Since the set delivered by diag is not among the members delivered by the initial function, it follows there is no function from a set to its powerset that uniquely connects each member of that set with its powerset (that is, there is no one to one, onto, function). But if we let id (for identity) be the function that takes every object to itself (a function into, but not onto, the set's powerset), we define the diagonal set of the identity function applied to the set A as:

$$\text{diag}(\text{id}_A) = \{x \in A \mid x \notin \text{id}_A(x)\}$$

But since by definition $\text{id}_A(x) = x$, we can replace $\text{id}_A(x)$ with x in the above, giving us:

$$\text{diag}(\text{id}_A) = \{x \in A \mid x \notin x\}$$

Now assume that A is V, the collection of all pure sets. Since V contains everything, the set of x in V is the same as the set of all x.

$$\text{diag}(\text{id}_V) = \{x \in V \mid x \notin x\} = \{x \mid x \notin x\}$$

This is the Russell set, the set of all sets that are not members of themselves, R from our informal discussion above.

And now we can consider Priest's inclosure schema for Russell's Paradox. We should note that part of what makes Russell's Paradox the simplest such one is that it is in the family of paradoxes (including the Burali-Forti and Mirimanoff paradoxes, and Kant's Fifth Antinomy) where the ψ in Priest's schema can be a trivial property such as being self-identical. Thus we don't need to represent it. Also, since $\Omega = \{y \mid y \in V\}$ is equal to V, we can simplify the inclosure schema thus:

Priest's Inclosure Schema for Russell's Paradox:
(1)   V exists[6]   Existence
(2)   if $x \subseteq V$ (a) diag(id$_x$) $\notin x$ Transcendence
                      (b) diag(id$_x$) $\in$ V   Closure

The contradiction is arrived at by the characteristic self-application of (a) Transcendence and (b) Closure to V itself, which yields the contradiction (a) diag(id$_V$) $\notin$ V and (b) diag(id$_V$) $\in$ V. Since (2) is a universally quantified claim about all x, all we are doing here is instantiating (2) with x. Consider:

(2)   if $V \subseteq V$ (a) diag(id$_V$) $\notin$ V   Transcendence
                      (b) diag(id$_V$) $\in$ V   Closure

Since by the definition of 'subset'[7] (x is a subset of y if, and only if, all members of x are members of y) every set is a subset of itself, and Transcendence and Closure apply to all subsets of V, they apply to V itself, yielding the contradiction expressed by lines (a) and (b) above. The Russell, diag(id$_V$), set is an element of V and is not an element of V.

From the nature of the contradiction we can see why Priest uses the words 'Transcendence' and 'Closure'. Once applied to V, the Transcendence lemma shows that the diagonalising function yields a value *external* to the postulated totality (the set of all sets), and thus a thing which is not itself a set. On the other hand, the Closure lemma shows that the same function yields a value *inside* the postulated totality, a set. So the value of the function when applied to the set of all sets would contradictorily be both a set and not a set.

Clearly the self-application of the schema to the totality V yields a contradiction. The interesting work then is always demonstrating Transcendence and Closure with respect to all of the subsets of the totality in question. In the case of Russell's Paradox, Closure follows immediately. Since, by hypothesis, V is the set of all pure sets, any pure set is an element of it by definition. Transcendence is a bit trickier, but, in the case of Russell's Paradox, formalisable in a Fitch-style system without too much sweat,[8] as is shown in the Appendix of this chapter.

A typical response to such paradoxes is to refuse to assert the Existence of the totality in question. Kant's original response to his mathematical antinomies (discussed in Chapters 5 and 6 in *Beyond the Limits of Thought*) is the model of how to attempt such a thing, and for Priest, ZF set theory, which carefully builds up sets from below and prohibits talking about the entire universe of sets, is a modern-day version of Kant's gambit. But there are other possibilities. ZF set theory contains open sentences such as $x \notin x$, or $x = x$, which seem (to someone who hasn't already accepted standard set theory crafted in response to the paradoxes) to characterise sets from the outside. The first is true of all sets that are not members of themselves (the Russell set). The second is true (by the standard logical account of identity) of everything. Unfortunately, talking about the collection of such objects as if it is a set in set theory yields a contradiction via Russell's Paradox. ZF set theory carefully builds up the universe of sets (the universe of sets not being itself a set in ZF set theory) such that (as far as we can tell) no such sets can be constructed satisfying paradox-inducing formulae. In Von Neumann's set theory, sentences such as $x \notin x$, or $x = x$ express proper classes,[9] which are like sets but prohibited from being members of anything. Thus Closure is blocked, since Closure states that the Russell class $\mathrm{diag}(\mathrm{id}_V)$ (the class of all sets that are not members of themselves) is a member of V. And the proof to Transcendence can be blocked by adopting weaker logics, such as the De Morgan logic developed by Hartry Field in *Saving Truth From Paradox*.

Priest himself critiques such solutions and argues that inclosure paradoxes are sound arguments involving true contradictions. For Priest, for example, the Russell set really is both a member of the universe of sets (Closure) and *not* a member of the universe of sets (Transcendence). This also standardly involves adopting a logic weaker than full classical. In paraconsistent logics it is not the case that any proposition follows from a contradiction.[10]

To the extent that our paradox is an instance of the inclosure schema, it will be the case that solutions will instantiate one of Priest's four types: (1) denial of Existence, (2) denial of Transcendence, (3) denial of Closure, or (4) acceptance of true contradictions. And our paradox is arguably such an instance. Without in any way specifying its extension (do fictional or possible entities count?) let 'T' denote the totality of all that is. Then, where x is some subset of all that is, let $e(x)$ denote the set of objects we are ontologically committed to by the metaphysical explanation of the objects in x. Characterised this way, we can easily generate what Joshua Heller and I have elsewhere[11] (with respect to our formulation of Kaplan's Paradox) called a quasi-Priestian inclosure schema for object-oriented ontology that clearly demonstrates a contradiction.

Quasi-Priestian Inclosure Schema for the OOO Paradox:
(1) T is   Being
(2) if $x \subseteq T$ (a) $\neg\,(e(x) \subseteq x)$ Transcendence'
                           (b) $e(x) \subseteq T$ Closure'

The Being claim merely states that everything that is, is. I don't use Priest's 'Existence' because one might, like Garcia as well as Priest in his later work such as *One*, want to hold the Meinongian view that non-existent objects *in some sense* have being and are part of the totality we talk about when we make universal claims. It is clearly analogous to Priest's 'V exists', which claims that the set of all sets exists. Transcendence' states that for every subset of the Totality, an explanation of the objects in that subset will be not ontologically committed to a set of objects in that subset. The schema is simply Priest's Transcendence with subsethood replacing set membership. In both cases an entity is asserted to be outside some other collection. And it is precisely Garcia's claim about what happens when we take undermining and/or overmining explanations to be complete. For Garcia and Harman, objects only exist to the extent that they *resist* their dissolution into the parts and structures that we use to explain them. A complete undermining explanation is just ontologically committed to the relevant parts of the object and a complete overmining explanation is just committed to the structure in which the object occurs.

And Closure' holds for the same reason that it does with respect to Russell's Paradox. Since T is the totality of everything that is, the set of objects to which the explanation of x commits its adherents is a subset of T. And, finally, in the same manner as Russell's Paradox, the contradiction is apparent when we self-referentially instantiate Transcendence' and Closure' on T itself, which (since T is a subset of itself) entails that the entities to which our explanation of T commits us are not a subset of T (Transcendence': $\neg(e(T) \subseteq T)$) and that the entities to which our explanation of T commits us are a subset of T (Closure': $e(T) \subseteq T$).

Seeing the argument as an inclosure paradox allows us to be clear about the four possible kinds of solutions. One can, analogously to ZF set theory, refuse to grant being to T. Markus Gabriel is the most prominent contemporary philosopher connected with Speculative Realism to defend a realist ontology that denies the existence of a world in the sense of a totality.[12] It is a position starkly at odds with the conclusions of most people initially enthusiastic about the speculative realist critique of correlationism. The initial hope was that affirming the primacy of speculative metaphysics over epistemology was an affirmation of our ability to develop maximally general accounts of reality, considered in its general maximality. Until Gabriel's work is brought into conversation with Harman's and Garcia's (as well as the anti-metaphysical strains in Badiou),[13] it's not at all clear how we can do speculative metaphysics if we must deny, or prescind from even mentioning, the being of T.[14]

Or one can try something analogous to Von Neumann set theory, giving some ontological status to entities such as T and e(T) but disallowing us from taking them to be subsets of anything. To say that e(T) is a subset of T, as Closure' states, is equivalent to stating that e(T) is an element of the set of T's subsets. So if e(T) is a proper class, and thus cannot be an element of anything, then Closure' is blocked. And, perhaps not surprisingly, we do find that what distinguishes Tristan Garcia's concept of 'world', the entity that contains ('comprehends' is Garcia's technical notion that models both predication and set-theoretic membership for him) everything, is that the world cannot itself be contained.

Weirdly though, Garcia is committed to the world not containing itself *not* because Russell's Paradox shows that commitment to the being of the world would give rise to a contradiction, but rather because a central proposition of Garcia's differential model of objects/things entails that an object/thing cannot be a member of itself. This is because, for Garcia, an object/thing is that which differentiates that which comprehends it from that which it comprehends. But if an object contained itself, it would not be differentiated from either. Whenever Garcia uses a cognate of 'compact' he means to be referencing this (for him) impossibility. We shall see in Chapter 5 how compactness forms one of the primary antagonists in the story he is telling.

Given that nothing comprehends itself for Garcia, the world as that which comprehends everything else is really that which comprehends everything that does not comprehend itself. But this is exactly homologous to the Russell set, the set that contains everything that is not a member of itself! But the argument for Transcendence (see the Appendix at the end of this chapter) shows that the Russell set itself is a member of itself. And Closure shows that the set of all sets is self-membered. Similarly, by the identical argument, Garcia's world would then be a member of itself. But this is metaphysically prohibited by Garcia's differential model of objects/things and his commitment to everything being a thing.

Should Garcia reject Closure' with respect to the OOO Paradox? To do so would be to argue that the totality of entities posited in explaining the world are themselves class-like enough to be incapable of being elements of other sets or classes. I must confess that this is something I have absolutely no intuitions about. More significantly, as I will show below, in every other respect Garcia actually agrees with the reasons Priest gives against denying Existence, Transcendence, and Closure. Thus, though Garcia *metaphysically* opposes self-membered sets, of all the new continental metaphysicians he is closest to endorsing Priest with respect to the OOO Paradox.[15]

The final possible response would be the denial of Transcendence'. One could do this by resisting the claim that overmining and undermining explanations are eliminative in the sense that Garcia takes them to be. However, the burden of proof of such an argument is arguably very high in this case, since what is ultimately involved is the explanation of the Totality of beings, the point in the inclosure paradox where Transcendence' is applied to the totality itself. But, at least in continental philosophy, it is an old saw that one cannot explain the totality of things in terms of things in that totality. Whenever a continental philosopher uses the phrase 'onto-theology' this is what she is critiquing. Although the thought is usually traced back to Heidegger's account of the ontological difference between being and beings,[16] an earlier version of it occurs in Hume's critique of the a posteriori arguments for the existence of God in his *Dialogues Concerning Natural Religion*. Assume that the natural theologian is correct to conclude that God exists because everything that exists is in need of an explanation in terms of a designer. But what about God? If God is part of everything that exists, the natural theologian's argument would entail the existence of a superGod who designs God and everything else. But then we'd need a supersuperGod, a supersupersuperGod, and so on, up until infinity. Hume assumes everything that exists cannot be explained in terms of the very entities that are part of everything.

Assuming that Hume and Heidegger are correct about ontotheology, the denier of Transcendence' has two choices here. The first involves differentiating the transcendental from the empirical in a way that affirms that the ultimate explanation of the transcendental preconditions of the totality of things does not involve positing things at all. For example, one could say that we are constrained, prior to any experience, to experience events as causally interrelated. The hope would be that one could affirm this as a prior constraint on our experience of all things without having to ontotheologically posit some new transcendent thing in virtue of which the constraint holds. This is why A. W. Moore, in his recent *The Evolution of Modern Metaphysics*, differentiates empirical from transcendental idealism in the following manner:

> For my purposes, the crucial distinction between the two kinds of idealism with which Kant himself is concerned – the distinction that I wish to generalize – turns on the following question. Is the dependence of the world of our experience on our experience of it of a piece with, or does it utterly transcend, what we can know about that same world through experience?[17]

Recall our discussion in Chapter 1 of the manner in which Garcia sharply criticises a variety of such approaches, which proliferated during the heyday of French (post-)structuralist studies of knowledge, culture, language, religion, and morality/politics. Garcia utilises the same kind of limit argument that German idealists used against Kantians, that Meillassoux uses against the correlationist,[18] and that Graham Priest uses against his opponents. I return to this argument below, as Garcia's use of it is part of the reason that his view is closer to Priest's than that of contemporary neo-Kantians.

But there is a more general problem that all transcendental approaches face. It is impossible to articulate transcendental preconditions without using empirical language. For example, Kant uses causal language with respect to how causality itself is instituted by the transcendental subject.[19] But then how are we to make sense of this language? If we take it at face value, then, as German idealists argued, the very distinction between empirical and transcendental has broken down and we are back to where we started. And according to Okrent's *Heidegger's Pragmatism*, this is actually the key insight that motivated the late Heidegger to affirm the 'facticity' or ultimate contingency of totality. If interpreters such as Mark Okrent and Lee Braver[20] are correct, then Heidegger's account of *Ereignis* or 'the event of appropriation' is actually nothing over and above an affirmation of this radical contingency. We ultimately cannot explain why we are given the universe in which we find ourselves. Here Transcendence' is blocked at the price of lapsing into quietism.

Unfortunately, philosophers are not very good at being quiet, and end up saying all sorts of things about that which they maintain we cannot say anything. The simple act of articulating that which one should be quiet about violates the prohibition of speaking out about that subject. Derridean, though not Badiouan,[21] talk about the 'the problem of the event'[22] can best be seen as an attempt to say more by engaging in something homologous to traditional negative theology. Derrida's late work, such as *Rogues*, is replete with statements about what an event is not. An event not only cannot be predicted but could not be understood prior to its occurrence. In his important 'Autoimmunity' interview he piles up these eight negations: 'unappropriability, unforeseeability, absolute surprise, incomprehension, risk of misunderstanding, unanticipatable novelty, pure singularity, [and] absence of horizon'.[23] The hope of accumulating such negations is always somehow to grant us access to the transcendent without violating the strictures that differentiate the transcendental from the empirical. But the worry is that it only succeeds here to the extent that it fails. To the extent that empirical understanding is really being avoided, is the negative theologian lapsing into nonsense? If something a priori cannot be subsumed under any possible rules by which we are able to positively describe things, how can we even say that it possibly exists? This is why Adrian Johnston seeks to consign this kind of thinking to the wastebasket:

Like the Romantics and Pietists before them, numerous post-idealists in the nineteenth and twentieth centuries end up promoting a facile mysticism whose basic underlying logic is difficult to distinguish from that of negative theology. The unchanging skeletal template is this: There is a given 'x;' This 'x' cannot be rationally and discursively captured at the level of any categories, concepts, predicates, properties, etc. Yet, nevertheless, the only true task of authentic thought is to circle endlessly around this sacred void of ineffability, repeating *ad infinitum* (and *ad nauseum* [*sic*]) the gesture of grasping at the purportedly ungraspable. The names of this empty 'x' vary while the pattern stays constant: Will, Life, Power, Temporality, Being, Other, Flesh, Difference, Trauma, and so on (up to even certain pseudo-Lacanian versions of the Real). Not only is this boringly predictable negative theological cookie cutter an all-too-easily grasped conceptual scheme of its own – even if one were totally to concede the truth of one or more of these ineffabilities as they are held up by their numerous enthusiastic advocates, there is so much more of greater interest and urgency for thinking to do than to remain absorbed in the sedentary meditative exercise of doing nothing but fixedly staring into a dark abyss.[24]

I'm not endorsing this, just noting it as a genuine issue.[25] I hope that situating Johnston's concern in terms of our OOO Paradox and attempts to avoid Transcendence' ultimately suggests responses for those of us prone to use the vocabulary Johnston is mocking. In this regard it is very interesting that in footnote 98 of the first chapter of *The Politics of Logic*, Paul Livingston reconstructs Derrida's reading of Karl Schmidt in *Rogues* (one of the key texts for Derrida on the event) in terms of an inclosure paradox! Likewise, Chapter 14 of Priest's *Beyond the Limits of Thought* presents Derrida's thoughts about *différance* in terms of an inclosure paradox. This lends itself to a rereading of Derrida as a key instance of the kind of paradoxico-metaphysics that I attribute to Garcia below.[26] For Garcia there is a sense in which metaphysics is both necessary and impossible. We cannot help but to treat the totalities of most interest to us as if they constitute the world, but in doing so we think of such totalities as both closed and transcendent, leading to contradiction. And for the paradoxico-metaphysician the world itself is the inconsistent totality that generates these contradictions when we interact with it. If our metaphysics is contradictory, that is because it accurately reflects reality.

Metaphysics as Art?

Before beginning to describe Garcia's own particular variety of paradoxico-metaphysics, I want to consider another promising strategy besides that of Markus Gabriel's consistent pluralities or Garcia's inconsistent totality. Above, we saw that the traditional attempts to block Transcendence' with respect to metaphysical explanation all seem themselves to face something much like the very inclosure paradox of which Transcendence' is a part. The transcendentalist and the quietist both end up doing that which they are not supposed to be able to do by their own doctrines (treating the transcendental subject as an empirical one, speaking the supposedly unutterable), and it is not clear that what Johnston characterises as negative theology succeeds at actually saying anything.

Harman's work provides a fundamentally different way to block Transcendence', one that has commonalities with some interpretations of Heidegger, Deleuze, and Derrida.[27] An interesting thing about Harman's fourfold is that it allows his philosophy to be reflexively applied to itself in two ways, depending upon whether the metaphysician's task is to be understood in terms of the relation between Harmanian sensual objects and real qualities, or in terms of the relation between sensual qualities and real objects. Remember that the sensual qualities are those properties manifest when objects interact with one another, the phenomenal object the object manifest when objects interact, the real qualities the essential properties that are posited to explain interaction (and for Harman the essential properties are in some sense emergent), and the real object the infinite reserve never exhausted by its interactions.

At first glance one would think that metaphysics is to be understood in terms of what Harman calls 'theory', with the metaphysician confronted by sensual objects and trying to discern the real qualities underlying these objects. On this view, Harman's own fourfold is the result of Harman the metaphysician discerning and deliminating the (in some sense second-order) real qualities of being a real object, of being a real quality, of being a sensual quality, of being a sensual object, as well as all of the real relational properties between the bearers of these properties.[28]

The fact that Harman himself baptises the link between sensual objects and real qualities 'theory' might seem to license this meta-metaphysical view. His model is Husserl's eidetic reduction, subtracting the changing, accidental features of our experience to get at the essential qualities beneath.

> By stripping away this surface noise through Husserl's method of eidetic variation, what we attain is not the same featureless unity for every sensual object – a 'bare particular,' in the terms of analytic philosophy. Instead, we approach what Husserl calls the *eidos* of an object.[29]

The eidetic properties play a role in securing the identity of the object and in explaining the behaviour of the object that we see.

> The sensual object has a vague and unified effect on us, not usually articulated into its various eidetic features. It is always fused in advance with its own eidos. Only theoretical labor can dissemble or reverse-engineer the bond between them. The word *theory* can serve as our term for the fission that splits a unified sensual object from the real qualities it needs in order to be what it is. We will have to decide later whether animals, plants, and airplanes are also capable of theory in some primitive sense. But for now, we can already see that theory is a kind of fission between a sensual object and its multitude of real traits.[30]

The way Harman describes eidetic reduction strongly suggests that he would consider the scientific attempt to map and measure various of nature's capacities (when understood as consistent with what we noted in Chapter 1 about the manner in which real qualities are in some sense emergent) as an instance of 'theory'. But if this is right, and if it were the case that metaphysics were also theoretical, Harman would straightforwardly face the OOO Paradox, as his own explanation would be another variety of undermining.

But if we turn to Harman's characterisation of the relation between the sensual qualities and real objects, another tantalising possibility arises. The metaphysical name for this relation is 'space' for Harman, but when he is talking more epistemically, he uses the term 'allure', which for him denotes the various ways that real objects manifest themselves in spite of the fact that they are inextricably withdrawn from the sensual properties that arise when they interact with other objects.

There are times when these sensual qualities are placed into orbit around the ghostly withdrawn melon (allure), but this occurs on a purely *ad hoc* basis, and the melon could hardly care less even if it were a deeply emotional creature.[31]

Unlike with theory, Harman *does* come close to explicitly self-reflexively characterising his own endeavour in terms of allure, stating that,

allure is a special and intermittent experience in which the intimate bond between a thing's unity and its plurality of notes somehow partially disintegrates. This is an important point that will require further development. But clearly it is just the sort of thing we are looking for: the entire method of this book hinges on drawing up a geographic atlas of the bonds and joints between the four poles of being, mapping their union and dissolution.[32]

As stated, this is consistent with the geographic atlas itself being a work of theory. But when we look at Harman's instances of how allure works, we see that in each case he describes an aesthetic operation that is non-theoretical yet nonetheless has the epistemic function of giving us a pre-theoretical understanding of what reality is like (or rather, as close as one can get, given his withdrawn model of objects).

As seen with the cypress-flame of Ortega and even the wolf-system of Black, what happens in metaphor is that we somehow become attuned to the inner ingenuousness of things. The truly executant flame and wolf can never be perceived by any other object. But neither does metaphor leave us stranded at the level of perceptible qualities. Somehow, it manages to put the very sincerity of a thing at issue, by somehow *interfering with the usual relation between a thing and its qualities* – and this is precisely what charm means. Indeed, it seems likely that all forms of beauty and fascination have this sort of structure.[33]

Harman shows that our aesthetic appreciation of humour, beauty, cuteness, and other hypnotising experiences such as tragic and horrific art all involve this kind of bringing to presence the ability of things and their normal qualities to be divorced. The most straightforward case he describes is beauty:

But a similar cutting of the bond between an agent and its traits occurs in beauty, in which a thing or creature is gifted with qualities of such overwhelming force that we do not pass directly through the sensual material into the unified thing, but seem to see the beautiful entity lying beneath all its marvelous qualities, commanding them like puppets.[34]

For Harman, an event is funny if it is appropriate to take a demeaning kind of pleasure in the incongruity revealed between a withdrawn object and its sensual qualities, and an event is tragic if solicitous sadness is the appropriate response to the same. Thus does Harman accommodate Bergson's theory of humour as the intrusion of the mechanical on the non-mechanical and (though he never mentions this) Mark Twain's insight that humour is when someone else breaks their leg and tragedy when I stub my toe. For Harman, our ability to have enchanting aesthetic experiences is the closest we get to withdrawn real objects, precisely because these are fundamental experiences of the withdrawal in action. His theories of metaphor and horror[35] present the function of art in part as the production of such experiences.

This is somewhat speculative with respect to Harman, but all of it strongly suggests a distinct strategy for blocking Transcendence' (remember that the apostrophe merely denotes that we are talking about subsets instead of elements as in Priest's original inclosure schema). If metaphysical explanation were properly characterised as a species of allure, rather than theory, then there would be no reason to think that explanation of a Totality must proceed in terms of entities outside of that Totality. One of the things creative artists do is make sense of things in new ways. Part of how someone writing a narrative history gets their new perspective across is by arranging things already at hand in novel ways.

Metaphysics then would be a bit Janus-faced, using language in common to over- and undermining explanations but to a fundamentally different purpose. Independent of the question of whether this is in general a good bit of meta-metaphysics, sustaining it with respect to Harman means carefully considering whether it makes sense to see his descriptions of the fourfold as really analogous to what is going on when writers in other genres use words to put into play the operations of cuteness, horror, beauty, humour, and tragedy. Is philosophical wisdom really analogous to what is delivered to someone who responds properly to aesthetically valuable experiences?

I think that it is for Harman. In a recent interview marking the second release of *Quentin Meillassoux: Philosophy in the Making*, Harman sharply differentiates philosophy from natural science in the following way:

> Science is supposed to provide *knowledge*, of course, replacing vague proper names with lists of properties truly possessed by things. One fails as a scientist if one cannot replace a name such as 'Pluto' with increasingly accurate properties of what we now call the dwarf planet Pluto. But this has never been the case in the arts. We do not understand a painting by Picasso by discovering an ever-lengthening list of true facts about it. The goal of art is not to create paraphrase-able imagery, but to create something to which no paraphrase ever does justice. The same goes for history. Here, factual research in the archives is only one part of the work. To understand Napoleon or Suleiman the Magnificent requires going beyond the verifiable facts and understanding an object that lies somewhat beyond knowledge. The same holds for philosophy. Socrates gives us no *knowledge* about virtue, friendship, or justice. Philosophy is not a proto-science from which the sciences are spin-offs. The reverse is actually the case: the pre-Socratics are certainly scientists, but in my view not quite philosophers. They speculate about the ultimate physical root to which everything can be reduced – this is a scientific aspiration, and not a philosophical one, as shown by Socrates' jail cell remarks distancing himself from Empedocles' naturalism.[36]

Clearly, Harman's view is that the philosopher is more akin to the artist than the natural scientist. If I am right that, on his own view, the function of metaphysical explanation is to generate a kind of allure, then Harman is not only consistent in his own beliefs, but consistent with respect to the threat of the OOO Paradox.[37] If art constitutes a kind of non-ontotheological explanation, and metaphysics is art, then metaphysics might avoid both Transcendence' and making invidious distinctions between the empirical and transcendental, or what can and cannot be said.

Paradoxico-Metaphysics

At first blush it looks clear that Garcia's account of 'world' as being such that it is not included in any other object (adopted for metaphysical, not logical reasons) commits him to rejecting

Closure'. Remember that Closure' claims that for any explanation of some set of entities x, the collection of entities that explain x (which we denoted as $e(x)$) are a subset of the totality T. But if the class of entities that explain T, $e(T)$, cannot be an element of any class, then it cannot be an element of T's powerset, and hence $e(T)$ cannot be a subset of T. Since Garcia already in effect takes T (the world) to be a proper class, this would seem to be an easy way out for him.

Priest shows both that Kant's rejection of Closure is the key to Kant's attempt to solve his third and fourth antinomies concerning causation and grounding, and how this attempted solution constitutively involves the distinction between the unknowable noumenal realm of things as they are in themselves and the phenomenal realm of things as they appear to us.[38] This is because Kant wants to maintain that noumenal causation and God exist, so to block his antinomies he cannot block the analogue of Priest's Existence.

It is no accident, then, that Garcia comes so close to reviving a distinction between an unknowable noumenal realm and a knowable phenomenal one precisely when he is discussing world.[39] Many passages in *Form and Object* read as if 'big thing' and 'universe' is a phenomenal (accessible to human perception and explanation) correlate to the noumenal (in some sense radically transcendent) 'world'.[40] For example:

> One of the strongest human tendencies is the desire to represent the world; every human being vaguely knows or senses that when the world appears to them in the form of *something*, it is because this something is not truly the world. But it is precisely this consciousness of the world that contributes to the desire to represent and to try to understand the world. I want to capture the world, but I only obtain a very big thing. But I always see glistening in the things their inverse, their negative, and their world.
>
> Thus, human beings produce more and more comprehensive *big things*: cosmological theories, arguments about the formation of matter, history, sociology, evolution, religious representations, metaphysics, and so on. (FO 84–5)

For Garcia, while 'the world' is predicated of things when we say that things are in the world, we cannot predicate anything of the world because by his model of predication this would be to say that the world is comprehended by something else (and, again, here 'comprehension' is Garcia's technical notion that is supposed to include set-theoretic containment and predication). But at the same time we can't help finding ourselves doing just this. To the casual reader, the easiest gloss on this would be Kantian, with the world a ghostly, noumenal thing in itself, which we wrongly approximate via our representations of big things, which are not worlds precisely because they can be comprehended by other things.

But this really cannot be right. First, it is impossible to reconcile Garcia's opening salvo against 'philosophies of access' with a fundamental division of reality into an unknowable world as it is in itself and the phenomenal universe of significance to human beings, with Garcia (in the role of a philosopher of access) just describing the phenomenal universe. Second, as we showed in Chapter 1, Garcia himself uses varieties of the anti-transcendental limit arguments to great effect at the very beginning of his book, critiquing accounts of knowledge, culture, language, religion, and morality/politics that we associate with the French (post)-structuralist neo-Kantian conceit that some kind of entity cannot be a thing because it plays a transcendental role with respect to the domain of things.

Priest is a little more explicit than Garcia about the premises involved in his version of the limit argument: (1) the Principle of Uniformed Solution, which states that similar paradoxes should have similar solutions, and (2) the Domain Principle, which in its simplest formulation is Cantor's view that 'For every potential infinity there is a corresponding actual infinity'. Here we need only focus on the latter.

When Priest actually uses the Domain Principle, he intends something stronger than Cantor's principle, stating for example that

for any claim of the form 'all sets are so and so' to have determinate sense there must be a determinate totality over which the quantifier ranges. It would clearly be wrong to suppose that this totality is a set satisfying the axioms of Zermelo-Fraenkel set theory, or of some other theory of sets; but that there *is* a well defined totality seems to me to be undeniable. Moreover, it is clearly a totality that we can think of as a single thing, since we can legitimately refer to it as *that totality*: the totality of sets.[41]

Although Priest presents this in terms of set-theoretic paradoxes, he applies the principle to other ones. We can thus get at its general essence by presenting it thus:

Priest's Domain Principle:
For any claim of the form 'all *x*s are so and so' to have determinate sense, there must be a determinate totality over which the quantifier ranges. We refer to this totality and so must include it to the group of objects over which we might quantify.[42]

If this is correct, then one cannot claim that the set of all sets does not exist. The fact that Priest makes claims supposedly true of all sets shows that he is committed to the totality of sets existing. He also argues that the standard Von Neumann method of blocking Closure in terms of proper classes actually also ends up blocking Existence when the paradox is run on the totality of sets and classes, a totality over which the free variables of VN set theory range.[43]

Priest's argument for the Domain Principle extends Cantor's own argument to argue that sentences with free variables will have completely different senses depending upon the totality over which those variables are taken to range.

For example, consider the claim 'Let z be a root of the equation $ax^2 + bx + c = 0$. Then z has at least one value.' This is true if z may be complex; false if z must be real.[44]

Thus, for a sentence to have a determinate sense there must be some totality over which the referring expressions are taken to range.

As Priest is aware, in most if not all of the cases where he actually brings the Domain Principle into play, he is making an inference associated with the German idealist critique of Kant. A. W. Moore christens this bit of reasoning 'the limit argument' and characterises it thus:

First Premise: The Limit-Drawing Principle: We cannot properly draw a limit to what we can make sense of unless we can make sense of the limit.
Second Premise: The Division Principle: We cannot make sense of any limit unless we can make sense of what lies on both sides of it.

Conclusion: We cannot properly draw a limit to what we can make sense of.[45]

Priest articulates the 'not drawing a limit' in terms of not excluding entities from the domain of discourse, thus the name Domain Principle. Over and over again, throughout the entirety of *Beyond the Limits of Thought*, Priest shows that opponents of Existence, Transcendence, and Closure end up violating the very limits they have to articulate to block the parts of the paradox they try to oppose. Garcia's use of this same argumentative strategy (as recounted in Chapter 1 above) against some of the same opponents places him firmly in Priest's camp. It is not at all clear why it should work against Garcia's (post-)structuralist opponents and not against Garcia himself on world. This is not actually a criticism of Garcia, however, as I think it is clear that he is aware of this.

For, as we have noted, Garcia (like Priest and Paul Livingston) believes that there are true contradictions. Not only does he reject the typical analytic philosopher's horror of contradiction, for example when he argues that contradictory entities such as non-square squares are distinct from non-triangular triangles, but he also distances himself from dialectical attempts to see true contradictions as things that exist but are consistently resolved either in historical movement or via conceptual revolutions.

> Lastly, we refuse to dialectically arrange contradictions. For a dialectician, our theory may appear to go nowhere, to sink into relativism, to make everything and anything possible, to prove to be inconsistent and, worst of all, flat, since it does not hierarchise things formally. (FO 8)

And some of the most interesting chapters in Book II of *Form and Object*, those involving humanity, arts and rules, gender, adolescence, and death, do characterise the kind in question as intrinsically contradictory, where our best undermining and best overmining theories of them perpetually contradict one another, and these contradictions are a constituent part of how the kind resists its reduction either way. For example, in his discussion of death Garcia argues that facts relevant to one's own self justify stoicism in the face of death and facts relevant to one's place in a social structure refute stoicism. For Garcia, the conflicting norms in no way cancel each other out. They rather characterise an irre-solvably inconsistent normative reality.

The perceptive reader will have noted that Garcia includes 'metaphysics' in the discussion of world that I quoted earlier. He continues in an increasingly paradoxical vein:

> In other words, the fact that the world is not something makes the local progress in the knowledge of objects possible, while ultimately precluding it. Since the world is not something, a faint colour of failure always stains all human, artistic, scientific, religious, and metaphysical pictures of the world, including the one in this book. (*FO* 85)

The Coda to the book actually consists in a set of moving reflections on this very failure, yet paradoxically articulated in terms of the very system he has just developed.

When we put all of these considerations together, Garcia fits much better into the class of thinkers that Paul Livingston calls 'paradoxico-critics', a class including Deleuze and Derrida, members of which Livingston presents as accepting the truth of certain limit contradictions. Garcia is unique in doing this with respect to the contradiction as applied to the possibility of meta-physical explanation itself. As such, he is a systematic, speculative metaphysician who provides a model of what reality is like such that systematic, speculative metaphysics is impossible. In articu-lating the failure, he is committed to Closure' failing for world. World cannot be comprehended/contained by any object, which for Garcia is to affirm that nothing true can be predicated of world. Yet, like the physicist who takes her model of the cosmos to be a model of totality, Garcia must predicate things of world just to explain how things cannot be predicated of world!

This is slightly different from Priest's dialetheism with respect to Russell-type paradoxes. Priest defends the view that the paradoxi-cal sets both are and are not members of themselves. The analogue for Garcia would be to defend the view that the world both does and does not comprehend itself. But Garcia's view is that that the world is both incapable of being comprehended at all and yet nonetheless is comprehended. The analogous set-theoretic view would be that paradoxical sets are both proper classes (incapable of being members of other sets/classes) and not proper classes. I do not know whether this difference from Priest is one that makes a difference with respect to set theory. With respect to Garcia's metaphysical system, the important issue hinges on his meta-physical prohibition of self-comprehension (self-membership in set theory), which would undermine his basic differential model of being that we have begun to sketch.

There is a nice self-referentiality here as well. Just as metaphysics as constitutively tied to allure is, for Harman, itself a part of the metaphysical explanation, the true contradiction that characterises Garcia's enterprise is reflected in the things themselves, according to his own system. His absolute bifurcation of objects as differentiators between that which is in them and that which they are in leads to the regional ontologies in Book II of *Form and Object*, where our best overmining and best undermining theories of things contradict one another and there is no reason to think that the contradictions will be resolved. Just as Garcia explains objects as the very things that frustrate their own explanations, his metaphysical explanation of the world is as a sort of limit case of an object that frustrates metaphysical explanation, limiting because the tension between undermining and overmining in the case of the world comes from the fact that the world cannot be overmined, since we cannot predicate anything of it. But in making this very affirmation, we do predicate something of it.

Appendix: Proof of Transcendence

Priest's inclosure schema for Russell's Paradox was given above as:

(1) V exists   Existence
(2) if $x \subseteq V$ (a) $\text{diag}(\text{id}_x) \notin x$ Transcendence
                           (b) $\text{diag}(\text{id}_x) \in V$ Closure

As noted, the contradiction is arrived at by characteristic self-application of (a) Transcendence and (b) Closure to V itself, yielding the contradiction (a) $\text{diag}(\text{id}_V) \notin V$ and (b) $\text{diag}(\text{id}_V) \in V$. This is licensed because any set is a subset of itself, and Transcendence and Closure apply to all subsets of V.

As noted above, in the case of Russell's Paradox, Closure follows immediately. Since V is the set of all pure sets, *any* pure set, including itself, is an element of it by definition. Establishing transcendence requires making one assumption explicit:

1 $\forall z(z = \{y \in z \mid y \in y\} \cup \{y \in z \mid y \notin y\})$ FACT

This says that any set is the union of two of its subsets: (1) the one composed of elements of that set that are members of themselves, and (2) the one composed of elements of that set that are not members of themselves. Since, by the law of bivalence,[46] a set either is a member of itself or is not, this exhausts the possibilities and so hence the union of the two subsets is always equal to the superset z. We continue (note that the proof is described in natural language immediately following the deduction):

2. | $x \subseteq V$ — assumption for $\forall$ introduction
3. || $\text{diag}(\text{id}_x) \in x$ — assumption for $\neg$ introduction
4. || $x = \{y \in x \mid y \in y\} \cup \{y \in x \mid y \notin y\}$ — 1 $\forall$ elimination
5. || $\text{diag}(\text{id}_x) \in \{y \in x \mid y \in y\} \cup \{y \in x \mid y \notin y\}$ — 3,4 = elimination
6. ||| $\text{diag}(\text{id}_x) \in \{y \in x \mid y \in y\}$ — assumption for $\cup$ elimination[47]
7. ||| $\text{diag}(\text{id}_x) \in \text{diag}(\text{id}_x)$ — 6 definition $\in$
8. ||| $\text{diag}(\text{id}_x) \in \{y \in x \mid y \notin y\}$ — 7 definition of $\text{diag}(\text{id}_x)$
9. ||| $\text{diag}(\text{id}_x) \notin \text{diag}(\text{id}_x)$ — 8 definition $\in$
10. ||| $\bot$ — 7, 9 $\neg$ elimination
11. ||| $\text{diag}(\text{id}_x) \in \{y \in x \mid y \notin y\}$ — assumption for $\cup$ elimination
12. ||| $\text{diag}(\text{id}_x) \notin \text{diag}(\text{id}_x)$ — 11 definition $\in$
13. ||| $\text{diag}(\text{id}_x) \in \text{diag}(\text{id}_x)$ — 11 definition $\text{diag}(\text{id}_x)$
14. ||| $\bot$ — 12, 13 $\neg$ elimination[48]
15. || $\bot$ — 5, 6–10, 11–14 $\cup$ elimination
16. | $\text{diag}(\text{id}_x) \notin x$ — 3–15 $\neg$ introduction
17. $\forall x(x \subseteq V \rightarrow \text{diag}(\text{id}_x) \notin x)$ — 2–16 $\forall$ introduction

We (2) start with an arbitrary x which is a subset of V, and (3) assume for *reductio* that the diagonalisation on the identity function applied to that x is itself a member of x. Then, (4) note that the x in question will be equal to the union set of two subsets, one consisting of members of x that are members of themselves and one consisting of members that aren't. Since we have assumed that the diagonalisation set is a member of x, it follows that (5) it is a member of this union. But then if we reduce to absurdity the assumption that it is in either of the two united sets $(6–10, 11–14)^{49}$ we will have reduced to absurdity the assumption that it is a member of x (15), and hence $(16, 17)$ proved that for any subset x of V the diagonalisation of the identity function on x is not a member of x. The two subproofs $(6–10, 11–14)$ both straightforwardly hinge on the definition of diagonalisation and set membership.

Notes

1. In light of this, it would be worthwhile to re-examine Lyotard's original discussion of Gödel's incompleteness theorems in *The Postmodern Condition*. Paul Livingston motivates what he calls paradoxico-criticism in *The Politics of Logic* via meditation on both Gödel's theorems and Russell's Paradox. I use the term 'paradoxico-metaphysics' for Garcia's position because of the strong homologies between Garcia's view and Livingston's account of social critique.

2. Harman mentions Priest's dialetheism in the penultimate essay of *Bells and Whistles*, 'A New Look at Identity and Sufficient Reason'. This is an important essay for understanding the key difference between Harman and Meillassoux. Timothy Morton also discusses Russell's Paradox and dialetheism in *Realist Magic: Objects, Ontology, Causality*. A detailed examination of how Morton's position intersects with the argument of this book is both ultimately necessary and desirable; like myself, Morton is motivated in many ways by his reading of Harman.

3. Just to be maximally clear to any non-proof theorists, from the meaning of R we have that if R is true then it is not the case that R is true. But such a claim is logically equivalent to the claim that R is not true. So the falsity of R rests only on the conditional.

4. Priest, *Beyond the Limits of Thought*, p. 129.

5. Seeing this connection with Cantor's argument is pretty insightful. The way Russell's Paradox is almost always presented misses it because it proceeds by noting that if the set of all sets exists then the Russell set would also exist as a subset of it. Priest (*Beyond the Limits of Thought*, p. 130) shows that this more standard manner of presentation is also an instance of the inclosure schema.

6. This does *not* say that V exists as a set in the sense that we typically mean set in standard set theories. It just says that V exists. As will be clear from the discussion, one of the main virtues of Priest's schema is that we can understand standard set theories in terms of how they characteristically respond to the inclosure schemas.

7. Again, we mean to be talking about the pre-theoretic notion of subset that is common to variant set theories. That V isn't a set by most of these theories is irrelevant. See previous note.

8. The advantages of doing this are multiple. In addition to the epistemic gain, actually producing a gap-free proof in a proper (normalisable) natural deduction or sequent calculus system both gives one deeper insight and suggests more clearly the range of possible reactions. For a clear demonstration of this, see, for example, Neil Tennant's magnificent 'A New Unified Account of Truth and Paradox', which trades on the strange proof-theoretic properties of proofs to paradox, properties that would never have been revealed if Tennant left things to mathematical English.

9. To be fair, the defender of Zermelo–Fraenkel set theory (ZFC with the standard addition of the axiom of choice) can also say that such sentences express proper classes, but classes such that ZFC cannot, on pain of contradiction, quantify over. It should be clear in what follows how this view also runs afoul of Priest's Domain Principle.

10. This is *very* hard. Suppose that you derive a contradiction P and it is not the case that P. From P it follows that P or Q is true. But then from P or Q and it is not the case that P, it follows that Q is true. The paraconsistent logician has to articulate where this argument goes wrong. In 'The Bearable Inconsistency of Being', Joshua Heller and I suggest an interpretation of Badiou where classical logic is correct yet there are still true contradictions, which are guideposts for when not to employ classical logic. The hope is to marry a paraconsistent pragmatics with a classical semantics.

11. In our 2014 'Meillassoux's Dilemma'. As far as I can tell, one can, with a bit of artificiality, gerrymander a properly Priestian inclosure schema from a quasi-Priestian one. Since A is a subset of B only if A is an element of the powerset of B, one can run the paradox in question with respect to the powerset of the totality in question. This strikes me as unnatural and unnecessary, as it might raise other issues.

12. See Markus Gabriel's *Fields of Sense: A New Realist Ontology* and *Why the World Does Not Exist*.

13. In *The Politics of Logic*, Paul Livingston presents Badiou as the paradigm thinker of consistent pluralities. See Joshua Heller's and my somewhat laboured attempt to save Badiou from the criticisms that follow from this in our 'The Bearable Inconsistency of Being: Badiou Beyond the Limits of Thought'. On further reflection, I think it might be the case that Gabriel can be read as a properly

speculative Badiou. On this map of the conceptual terrain, Gabriel would be to Livingston's constructivist thinkers as my paradoxico-metaphysicians (Priest and Garcia) are to Livingston's paradoxico-critics. Harman might be seen as straddling Livingston's conceptual map, as he agrees with Gabriel that the world does not exist, but is nonetheless a relentless critic of any kind of constructivist strands.

14. Most analytic metaphysicians try to get by through not thinking about totality, but just exploring their little bits of dialectical space. But the issue inevitably crops up. Kaplan's Paradox can pretty easily be presented as an inclosure paradox with respect to the totality of possible worlds. In Joshua Heller's and my 'Meillassoux's Dilemma' we do just this in our demonstration that Badiou and Meillassoux came very close to independently discovering Kaplan's Paradox. Likewise, the pressing issue of 'extraordinary modal contexts' just is the issue of how to make sense about modal claims about collections of possible worlds, including the totality of possible worlds. See Josh Parsons's 'Against Advanced Modalizing'. One can, of course, say that our e function makes no sense because there is no reason to think that a set of entities could ground everything. But one can't *just* say this. One of the main virtues of Markus Gabriel, and Meillassoux and late Heidegger in a very different register (with respect to their affirmations of absolute contingency), is that they develop metaphysical systems (though, to be fair, neither Gabriel nor Heidegger would endorse this use of the term 'metaphysical') that license saying this.

15. In 'Meillassoux's Dilemma' Joshua Heller and I argue that Meillassoux's critique of correlationism commits him to a Priestian take on Kaplan's Paradox, a take that actually undermines the argument for contingency presented in the latter part of Meillassoux's *After Finitude*.

16. The best account of what this amounts to, both as a general issue and with respect to Heidegger's thinking, is Mark Okrent's *Heidegger's Pragmatism*.

17. Moore, *The Evolution of Modern Metaphysics*, p. 142.

18. This is one of the key claims that distinguishes my and Joshua Heller's reading of Meillassoux in 'Meillassoux's Dilemma'.

19. See Desmond Hogan's 'Noumenal Affection' for a wonderful over-view and discussion of related issues. For some reason, contemporary Kant scholars take it to be a principle of interpretive goodness that one can clear Kant of the charge. But it's not at all clear to me (nor to A. W. Moore, from his discussion) that the resulting Kant

can do the philosophical work Kant wanted to do with respect to Hume's challenges to alethic and deontic modality. So the worry is that we get a consistent Kant at the price of his philosophical irrelevance. Getting rid of the inconsistent Kant who gave rise to German idealism would be an incalculable philosophical loss.

20. Okrent's *Heidegger's Pragmatism* and Braver's *Groundless Grounds: A Study of Wittgenstein and Heidegger and* present the two clearest accounts of Heidegger's purported *Kehre* in terms of his view that the transcendental manner in which our understanding of beings is grounded is itself without grounds.

21. For Badiou the problem of the event is the problem of radical novelty. In part because of his distance from Heidegger (something arguably not shared by any of the other great post-structuralists), one can explicate the problem for him in a way that differentiates it from issues of transcendental grounds. There is thus actually significant overlap between Badiou's problem space and that of the object-oriented ontologist. See Badiou's *Being and Event* and the rich discussion of Badiou in Livingston's *The Philosophy of Logic*.

22. I have to thank my colleague François Raffoul, who is writing a book on the (Derridean) problem of the event, for hours of illuminating discussion on this topic. I should also cite Daniel Smith, whose unpublished 'An Event Worthy of the Name: A Name Worthy of the Event' has also been extraordinarily helpful.

23. Derrida, 'Autoimmunity: Real and Symbolic Suicides', p. 91.

24. Johnston, 'Points of Forced Freedom: Eleven (More) Theses on Materialism', p. 93.

25. For the Harmanian, Johnston is here committing a Meno's Paradox-type fallacy, where the only two possible epistemic states are Knowledge with a big K and the kind of circling around an ineffable void that he so ably mocks. Harman's doctrine of the primacy of aesthetics is in part motivated by trying to understand Socratic *philosophia* as different from either of these (and distinct from Heideggerian practical comportment as well).

26. Conversations with Deborah Goldgaber have been extremely helpful here.

27. For examples of the relevant interpretation of all three, see the discussion in Moore's *The Evolution of Modern Metaphysics*. Conversations with Gregory Schufreider have been very helpful here, and I particularly look forward to his book on Mondrian that develops these themes in a different direction (for hints, see Schufreider's 'Sticking Heidegger with a Stela: Lacoue-Labarthe, Art

and Politics'). Schufreider's interventions are particularly interesting in this context for two reasons: (1) they do not rest on reading the early Heidegger as a failed transcendental thinker as standardly do analytic accounts of 'the turn', and (2) Schufreider takes very seriously the idea that the philosophical instantiation of what I'm calling aesthetic forms of sense making might require different modes of writing. Whether Harman substantially disagrees or just instances an aesthetic sensibility at odds with many readers of Heidegger is, I think, both interesting and possibly underdetermined. For an (albeit in the end highly critical) interpretation of Derrida, see Harman's own discussion in Chapter 9 of *Guerrilla Metaphysics*.

28. One might think this is inadmissible because Harman would be saying that the property of being a sensual quality is itself a real quality. I don't find such an issue compelling. First, it is really the same issue Frege faced with the notorious 'The concept horse is not a concept' problem, and it is not clear to many commentators (for example, see the discussion in Moore's *The Evolution of Modern Metaphysics*) that this is really a problem. But more interestingly, the view that whenever a relation between two objects is instantiated, then a distinct object also exists actually does metaphysical work for Harman. A given sensual quality for Harman is also a fourfold object in its own right. This gives rise to a regress, but in the contexts in question clearly not a disqualifying one.

29. Harman, *The Quadruple Object*, p. 27.

30. Harman, *The Quadruple Object*, p. 104. I should note that Harman does at one point (*ibid.*, p. 28) say that 'allure' (which I go on to describe below) is used when we gain epistemic access to real qualities. I take it that this is the case for the reasons given in two notes previously. Real qualities are themselves objects with a fourfold structure. We approach them qua real objects via allure.

31. Harman, *The Quadruple Object*, p. 106.

32. Harman, *Guerrilla Metaphysics*, p. 143.

33. Harman, *Guerrilla Metaphysics*, p. 141.

34. Harman, *Guerrilla Metaphysics*, p. 142.

35. Clearly, much more needs to be said above. The most important text I haven't discussed above is Harman's account of Lovecraft in his recent *Weird Realism: Lovecraft and Philosophy*.

36. Harman, 'An Interview with Graham Harman'.

37. A fuller account would not only closely examine Harman's recent Lovecraft exegesis, but also think this whole issue through with respect to the manner in which, in *The Evolution of Modern*

Metaphysics, A. W. Moore commends 'creative' approaches to metaphysics such as (according to Moore) Nietzsche's, Carnap's, Bergson's, and Deleuze's. I find Moore's discussion hampered by the fact that he is not explicit about the content of the affirmation that metaphysics is intrinsically creative. He means much more than the claim that it takes creativity to do it well, but isn't explicit enough about what this comes to. Given the very high quality of every other aspect of Moore's discussion, connecting what he is saying about creative metaphysics with Harman's thinking would have non-trivial applications concerning what we are to learn from Nietzsche, Carnap, Bergson, and Deleuze.

38. Priest, *Beyond the Limits of Thought*, pp. 96–8.
39. A fuller treatment would compare this with the way in which Kant took metaphysics to be both impossible and unavoidable.
40. My student James Harris has argued (pers. comm.) that Garcia's doctrines about the thing's solitude should be seen as a variant of Schopenhauer's account of the noumena as undifferentiated. Exploring the similarities and differences here would be rewarding for a number of reasons, not only (though also) as a challenge to my interpretation of Garcia in post- as opposed to neo-Kantian terms. On the other hand , Schopenhauer's relationship to Hume and Kant might be argued to be importantly similar to Harman's with respect to Heidegger and Husserl, for Schopenhauer the speculative move being realising that since he is a thing in the world, so is will. For all of the other ways in which Schopenhauer was Kantian, his speculative move contains at least the seeds of a radical *anti*-Kantian response to Humean worries about necessity.
41. Priest, *Beyond the Limits of Thought*, p. 281.
42. Put this clearly, the principle is suspiciously similar to Frege's Comprehension Axiom, which entails that the set of all sets exists. See also Priest's 2005 discussion of the Characterisation Principle (in *Towards Non-Being*) which holds that for any property there is some possible object that this property is true of. I should also note that the Domain Principle is consistent with the contextual determination of quantifier range. I can truly say that everyone is here without meaning to say that everyone in the universe is here.
43. Priest, *Beyond the Limits of Thought*, p. 164.
44. Priest, *Beyond the Limits of Thought*, p. 125.
45. Moore, *The Evolution of Modern Metaphysics*, p. 135. As Moore notes, the best the transcendental idealist can do in response to this is to bifurcate sense, affirming the first premise with respect to

a thin sense which is used to characterise both the empirical and the transcendental, and rejecting the second principle with respect to the thick sense used in her characterisation of the empirical. Moore rejects transcendental idealism because he does not find such approaches ultimately satisfactory.

46. One need not use bivalence if one is already talking about the Russell set, so intuitionism doesn't block the proof.

47. There's no reason to cavil at my treating union as a logical notion. We could easily lengthen the proof by turning the claims into disjunctions and then using disjunction elimination.

48. Treating inferences of this form as negation elimination instead of absurdity introduction is required for (1) having normalisable systems, and (2) taking minimal logic to be defined entirely in terms of introduction and elimination rules, with intuitionist logic arrived at by adding the absurdity rule (from absurdity anything), and classical logic arrived at by adding one of the classical negation rules such as double negation elimination.

49. Incidentally, lines 11–14 show why merely prohibiting sets that include themselves will not block Russell's Paradox. Assuming that the Russell set is the universal set only makes the proof shorter, because lines 6–10 are not then needed.

4

No-Matter-What

The most difficult issue that Mark Ohm and I faced as translators of *Forme et Objet* concerned Garcia's repeated use of the phrase *n'importe quoi*, which we render as 'no-matter-what'. The final section of Chapter 1 above was entirely concerned with what is meant by one sense of Garcia's claim that no-matter-what is something. But the phrase occurs in many other contexts, for a total of 189 times throughout the text. It is not only used to express Garcia's ontological liberalism but also his account of how matter composes things (I will discuss this latter use in Chapter 6 below). And Garcia's *n'importe quoi* denotes a real, and very strange, entity.

This chapter has three purposes: first, to justify the coinage of an idiomatic English phrase; second, to show how all of the odd and seemingly contradictory things that Garcia says about no-matter-what actually describe an interesting, consistent entity; and third, to provide Garcia's argument that no-matter-what exists. Some of the discussion requires formal languages; given that Garcia countenances contradictory entities, it's very important to establish that no-matter-what is not one of them. And Garcia's argument for the existence of no-matter-what is interesting in its own right, as it is also a novel (as far as I have been able to ascertain from studying the history of set theory) argument for the existence of the empty set.

Translation

In most of this book, I've just used Ohm's and my English versions of Garcia's technical terms, but the translational issues were so difficult with respect to *n'importe quoi* that much of the discussion below of necessity must discuss the French locution.

Interestingly, the most important concept in Book I of *Form and Object* also denotes something *without importance*, *n'importe quoi* ('anything'). This is why, in an ordinary, exclamative sense, the expression *c'est n'importe quoi!* may translate as 'it doesn't matter!' and so on. In this sense, *n'importe quoi* is close to 'nothing'. But when I say '*it* doesn't matter', I clearly characterise *something* as having the property in question. In other words, *n'importe quoi* is not *absolutely* nothing since not mattering is at least something, however many other forms of disapprobation we might bring to bear on it. Like Heidegger's infamous discussion of *das Nichts* ('the Nothing'), Garcia's usage both deviates from colloquial French and cleverly combines the quantificational sense of the phrase ('for all x') and something more denotational and name-like.

A historically attuned reader will recall Rudolf Carnap's excoriation of Heidegger in his 1932 'Überwindung der Metaphysik durch Logische Analyse der Sprache' for committing just this same supposed sin. According to Carnap, Heidegger treated *Nichts* as if it were a name with a specific denotation, rather than a quantificational expression meaning 'it is not the case that there exists an x such that'. And this is actually a felicitous comparison, given what we have said above about the connections between Graham Priest and the object-oriented continental ferment. In *Beyond the Limits of Thought*, Priest demonstrates not only that Carnap was wrong about Heidegger but why it was interesting that he was wrong. One can, in fact, use the logic that Carnap helped create and popularise to make perfect sense of Heidegger's argument as giving voice to the very kind of inclosure paradox we considered above.

Something similar can be achieved with respect to *n'importe quoi*. This will not only forestall potential uncharitable Carnaps among us, but will also bring to the forefront central properties of no-matter-what. Again, as with Heidegger, Garcia's usage of the term departs substantially from the colloquial. While one might argue about how important the issue of *Nichts* really is to making sense of either the substantive disagreements between Heidegger and Carnap or to Heidegger's *œuvre* considered in itself,[1] no-matter-what is a fundamental part of Garcia's systematic metaphysics.

In *Forme et objet*, the phrase *n'importe quoi* occurs with no preceding article: (1) as a simple predicate after some conjugation of *être* (for example, 'Que rien ne soit n'importe quoi . . . ');[2] (2) as a subject noun phrase (for example, *N'importe quoi peut être quelque chose* . . .);[3] (3) as a direct object (*Prenez – ou ne prenez pas – n'importe quoi* . . .);[4] (4) as an adjectival quantifier (for example, *tout tabou est donc différent des autres de telle sorte qu'un tabou n'est jamais n'importe quel tabou* . . .);[5] and (5) after a preposition (*Pour accéder à n'importe quoi* . . .).[6] Some of the above uses occur in quotation marks (for example, « *n'importe quoi* » *n'est rien d'autre que l'expression du refus d'accorder quelque importance que ce soit à ce qu'est ceci, à ce qu'est cela, à ce que peut être tout ce qui peut être*).[7] The phrase occurs with a preceding definite article (*le*): (1) as a subject (for example, *Le « n'importe quoi » n'a pas d'intérêt* . . .);[8] (2) after a preposition (for example, *Si une contradiction est une porte d'accès au n'importe quoi* . . .);[9] (3) after a partitive (for example, *C'est le monde plat du n'importe quoi*);[10] and (4) as a demonstrative (for example, *Et c'est ce n'importe quoi qui nous intéresse ici*).[11] Some such uses occur in quotation marks (for example, *Le refus physique ou métaphysique du « n'importe quoi »*).[12]

Garcia's philosophical prose is in fact generally so clear that were it not for the fact that the phrase represents a central metaphysical category, there would have been no special difficulty for Ohm and me. We could have just used cognates of 'anything' in many places, for determiners affix 'the concept of', and then fiddle further with the syntax of the English sentences to secure quantificational (that is, 'for all x') readings when needed. But doing this would have actually radically confused Garcia's metaphysics, which, like Heidegger's, actually demands that the reader give phrases with quantificational interpretations simultaneous name-like[13] interpretations.

Another solution would have been to stay closer to the French syntax and mark the phrase as philosophical by rendering it 'Anything' with a capital 'A', in the sense that it used to be standard to translate Heideggerian *Sein* with capital B 'Being' in English. But translating *n'importe quoi* in this way would also lead to much confusion, for the literal combinatorial meaning of the three words actually does work for Garcia as well. For it is central to no-matter-what that it be *absolutely undetermined*, not any kind of 'what' that can be determined via predicate or property.

94   Garcian Meditations

Nothing is No-Matter-What

In addition to the odd way that *n'importe quoi* is both quantificational and name-like, a first-time reader is likely to think that Garcia is simply saying incoherent things about no-matter-what. Here I will present just a few instances that *seem* contradictory, all from Book I, Part I, Chapter I, though Garcia repeats these claims throughout Book I.

On the one hand, Garcia claims that something can never be no-matter-what, that nothing can be no-matter-what. For example:

> Something is never no-matter-what. I could not find something in the world which would be no-matter-what. (*FO* 21)
> That nothing is no-matter-what means that there does not exist any object, event, god, or idea that would be 'no-matter-what'. (*FO* 30)

In seeming contradiction to these assertions, we are simultaneously told both that no-matter-what can be something and that no-matter-what is something.

> Nonetheless, no-matter-what is not nothing. On the contrary, no-matter-what – that is to say, 'equally this *or* that *or* any other thing' – is something. (*FO* 23)

But then Garcia is saying both that no-matter-what is something and that nothing is no-matter-what. Moreover:

> From this we can claim that it is incompatible to be something and to be no-matter-what. Everything which is not no-matter-what is something. (*FO* 27)

Again, how can it be incompatible to be something and to be no-matter-what while at the same time it is the case that no-matter-what is something?

The answer to this question requires attending to one essential facet in Garcia's theory of being, most clearly presented in Part III of Book I. Remember that Garcia's notion of 'comprehension' is not intrinsically epistemic nor tied to human or animal capacities. For Garcia, any object that includes another *in any way* can be said to comprehend that other object. With this proviso, we have the following:

The subject is always the part, and the predicate is the whole, the set. When I say that x is y, I mean that x belongs to y, that x is a part of y, that x composes y, and that x takes part in y's matter. x is y – that is, that x is comprehended by y. Since x is y, y comprehends x, y is external to x, and y is 'outside' x.

The first major consequence of interpreting 'being' as the inverse of comprehending derives from the product of an 'anti-symmetric' relation. It may seem that being is the sign of a symmetric identity relation: if a is b, then b is a. No! Being is anti-symmetry *par excellence*. If a is b, then b cannot be a. Being means nothing other than this one-sidedness [*ce sens unique*]. (FO 109)[14]

Garcia presents us with an easy way to read off the direction of the comprehension relation from natural language. Whatever the subject of a sentence refers to is always comprehended by whatever the predicate refers to. And not only the problem sentences involving no-matter-what conform to this pattern:

When I say that 'the wall is white', I am aware that I am claiming something about the wall. But in fact, I am primarily expressing my judgement about whiteness. I am saying that the wall is comprehended in whiteness, is among white things. I am not expressing a quality of the wall, being white. If that were the case, the wall would comprehend, among other qualities, the fact of being white, as if this quality were hung to the coat rack of the thing. No, rather, I am expressing a quality of whiteness. This whiteness can comprehend the wall. The wall can count within the set of what is white. In the sentence 'the wall is white', the *thing* is not primarily the wall, but whiteness. Otherwise, I ought to say that whiteness is the wall – that is, that the wall comprehends the whiteness in the things which compose this wall. Likewise, I often say 'I am a person', I think that I am expressing one of my determinations, namely, personhood. No, I am expressing one determination of the set of humanity which is able to contain and comprehend me. If I want to assert the fact that humanity counts among the things that compose me, I ought to say that a person is me – some personhood is in me. (FO 109)

It is very important to realise that this is Garcia's considered opinion.

In the introduction to *Form and Object* he writes things that might lead one to think that abstract properties are part of the constitution of an object, and hence comprehended by those objects in Garcia's technical sense. Consider again our piece of slate, which

> possesses certain qualities of cohesion and of solidity that allow one to dissociate it from its environment, handle it, transport it, and consider it quite simply as 'something'. What is it composed of? It contains quartz, clay-like minerals, mica, some traces of feldspar. And all these components themselves have a certain atomic structure. But in a wider sense, they also enter into the constitution of the rock as 'thing': its rectangular form, the irregularities of its surface, the porphyroblasts coated with pyrite, its sombre colour, its delicate texture, its weight, its fragility, and all the primary or secondary qualities by which we can recognise the black slate.
>
> We say that this is *all that is in this thing*, all paths of being that lead to the constitution of this black slate in my hand. (*FO* 12)

But Garcia's considered view is that the qualities of the object are *not* part of what constitutes the object. Rather, the object is part of what constitutes these qualities, which comprehend the object.

Showing how the anti-symmetry of being renders the seemingly contradictory claims about no-matter-what consistent sheds bright light both on Garcia's account of being and what he is affirming in his claims earlier in the book with respect to no-matter-what. This is particularly important to be clear about because, as I will show in Chapters 6 and 10, anti-symmetry is one of the key formal properties that for Garcia allows objects to resist dissolution into the Hegelian whole. The way this works with respect to the problem passages concerning no-matter-what ends up being a model for how it works for everything.

First, consider the claim that nothing is no-matter-what. The most important meaning of this for Garcia is if we take 'nothing' in the quantificational sense and no-matter-what as name-like. Then we are saying all things are such that they do not enter into the no-matter-what, or equivalently that all things are such that the no-matter-what does not comprehend them. No-matter-what comprehends nothing.

So the no-matter-what is contained in other things (in 'some-thing') but itself contains nothing, the exact inverse of Garcia's world which is a container of every thing but which is itself not contained.

Given that being is being comprehended, and that this is anti-symmetric, if nothing is no-matter-what, then (for Garcia) no-matter-what is not nothing. This entails the other sense of Garcia's claim that no-matter-what is something. Something comprehends no-matter-what. This is quantificational; there exists at least one thing that comprehends no-matter-what.

Now let us recover our pre-Carnapian innocence and think of the quantificational phrase 'something' as name-like. To make this maximally clear, we will tread a small distance towards Heideggerian usage and talk of 'the something'. Then, to say that no-matter-what is something is to say that no-matter-what enters into the something and that the something comprehends no-matter-what.

Now let us consider the claim that no-matter-what is something with 'no-matter-what' understood quantificationally. Then, to say that no-matter-what is something is to say that anything is something. As Garcia sometimes puts it, 'anything can be something', which is exactly the sense of the phrase we explicated in the final section of Chapter 1. Like Meinong, or perhaps more so, when Garcia says 'anything' he really means *anything*.[15] For Garcia, any thing, whether existent or not, possible or not, imaginary or not, consistent or not, presentable to human consciousness or not, and so on, is a thing.

We have seen that for Garcia to be is to be comprehended, and when we put this together with his understanding of the claim that anything can be something we get the further claim that to be is to be determined. So when Garcia says that no-matter-what is something in the second sense, the sense where no-matter-what has a name-like interpretation and something is understood quantificationally, he is simultaneously claiming that it possesses properties and attributing being to it.

No-Matter-What is Something, Second Sense

In the final section of Chapter 1 above, we considered Book I, Part I, Chapter I, Sections 15–21 of *Form and Object*: Garcia's discussion of six distinct strategies that preclude no-matter-what from being something: logical, linguistic, epistemic, cultural, religious, moral/political. In each case, Garcia opposes the claim that some category picks out non-things by noting that within that category determinations are made. In other words, each strategy denies that something has what Garcia calls a 'minimum-of-whatness' (*FO* 26), that is, a minimum determination. Unlike no-matter-what, these things are not *absolutely* indeterminate.[16]

For example, to the logician who denies that there are true contradictions, Garcia deftly points out that we can differentiate contradictory entities; the squared circle is necessarily circular while the non-white white is not. As we showed in Chapter 1, this is how he defends the claim that anything is something. Garcia argues that to attribute a determination is to talk about a thing. To be is to be determined. It is in this sense, then, that no-matter-what (anything) can be something.

But then once one holds that to be is to be determined, Garcia's argument that no-matter-what has being follows naturally. All one must do is consider an entity that lacks all determination, and note that lacking all determination is itself a determination. And for Garcia, the no-matter-what names precisely this determination of lacking all determination. Consider a representative passage:

> What do we mean by claiming that a clementine is something, that a segment, pip, orange colour, weight, unity, its falling, two, three, the word 'clementine', or its idea are something, just as me, you, an animal, or the earth are something? We have assumed that a clementine is not *another thing*, that it is only *something*. More precisely, we have assumed that a clementine is not no-matter-what. A clementine is *this* clementine. But this clementine is not *that* clementine. Therefore, it is a matter of something, it is a matter of no-matter-what. The word 'clementine' is neither the word 'Australia' nor an animal nor the end of a storm. When this clementine is something, it is not that clementine or something else. No-matter-what, we have said, is this *or* that *or* its opposite *or* something else. No-matter-what is something, anything.
>
> A clementine is not this *or* that *or* its opposite *or* anything else. It *matters* that a clementine be something, that is, that it can be this or that, but that it absolutely cannot be this or that or anything else. If a clementine is no-matter-what, then it is not a matter of a clementine. (*FO* 52)

For a clementine to be something it must be determined in some way, but no-matter-what's only determination is that it lacks all determination.

This is clearly a *prima facie* paradoxical notion, but we can see why Garcia must embrace it. Garcia's anti-reductionism pushes him to the bold Meinongian claim that anything (no-matter-what) is something. While critiquing specific forms of reductionism inconsistent with this claim, he argues that all that is necessary for being something is possessing some determination. But then what about the concept of just being anything? For this concept to be maximally inclusive it must lack any determination whatsoever. But 'lacking any determination whatsoever' is itself a determination. So it would seem to both lack and possess determinations.

One might say that this no-matter-what is itself thus a contradictory entity, but Garcia's model of being provides a way out of the paradox. Let us step back and consider all of the things that lack all determinations. By describing the collection thus, we provide a determination, so everything in this 'collection' is both determined and not determined. So, on the assumption that this is a contradiction we should reject,[17] we now know that nothing is in this collection. But now we have a 'thing' such that nothing is (in) this thing! Moreover, this thing is something, as it has a determination, being the collection of all things that have no determination.

In the next section I provide a formal derivation in standard logic of this. Before doing so I want to note that what I hope to have done here is provide a rational reconstruction of the reasons that led Garcia to characterise the no-matter-what as being something while at the same time affirming that nothing is no-matter-what. Along the way we have come to appreciate how important it is that comprehension is an anti-symmetric relation. When we discuss Garcia's model of entities qua things as differentiators between matter and world, we will see that our understanding of no-matter-what as being the metaphysical floor, not comprehending anything while being comprehended itself, renders it in some ways a limit concept for matter. At that point our labours here will pay rich dividends.

Formal Derivation

As far as I can tell, Garcia actually presents a novel paradox, and (again, as far as I can tell) a novel solution. Not *entirely* novel, as the no-matter-what has commonalities with the empty set that forms the basis of standard set-theoretic universes in mathematics. But somewhat novel because standard set theories either simply assert the existence of an empty set via axiom, or prove it using a restricted comprehension axiom with respect to a claim that some object is not identical to itself. In both cases, the axiom of extensionality, which holds that two sets are identical if they have the same members, is later employed to show that there is only one empty set.

The no-matter-what is distinct from the empty set in several ways. First, it is not clear that the normal derivation would work for Garcia, since in his account of beauty he allows that things can be more or less themselves. Making sense of this formally might require differentiating metaphysical identity from the reflexive, symmetric, and transitive relation so many of us know and love in mathematics. Likewise, Garcia's anti-reductionist differential model of objects is arguably inconsistent with the axiom of extensionality, so it is not clear that one could go on to strictly establish that there is exactly one no-matter-what. The axiom of extensionality asserts that two sets are identical if they have the same members. But if objects really are the differentiators between the things they comprehend and that which comprehends them, then two objects might comprehend the same objects but be comprehended by different objects. From this perspective, set-theoretic membership is perhaps just that special case of comprehension where extensionality holds.[18] As noted in note 13, and discussed in Chapter 6 below, Garcia's model of counting (in common with the Geach-Kraut view of individuation) arguably precludes providing either ordinality or cardinality to the no-matter-what, again in contrast to the empty set's role as the starting point for both measures.

With these provisos in mind, here is a formal proof of the existence of no-matter-what. The Garcian claims are (1) the unrestricted (second-order!) Comprehension Axiom which would be one way of articulating the claim that to be is to be determined, (2) line 13 ($\forall x(x \notin a)$), which would be one formal way of expressing the claim that nothing is no-matter-what, and (3) the conclusion, line 15 ($\exists y \forall x(x \notin y)$) which would be one way of expressing the claim that no-matter-what is something. Here are the rules that might be found controversial.

Second-Order Comprehension:
   Where y is the only free variable in $\Phi[y]$, $\exists x \forall y(y \in x \leftrightarrow \Phi[y])$.[19]
Second-Order Existential Introduction ($\exists^2$ introduction):
   Where b is a term of type 0, $\Phi[b] \vdash \exists P(P(b))$

Second-Order Existential Elimination ($\exists^2$ elimination):
> Where b is a term of type o, $\exists P(P(b))$ |- R when it can be shown that there is some Q that doesn't occur in P, nor in any assumptions upon which $\exists P(P(b))$ rests, such that $Q(b)$ |- R.

We start by considering the determination of having no determinations, which we express as $\forall P\neg Px$, meaning for all determinations, x does not have that determination. Then the beginning of the proof is an instance of Second-Order Comprehension applied to the determination of having no determinations.

1. $\exists x\forall y(y \in x \leftrightarrow \forall P\neg P(y))$	by Comprehension
2. $\mid \forall y(y \in a \leftrightarrow \forall P\neg P(y))$	assumption for $\exists$ elimination ('a' is arbitrary)
3. $\mid\mid [b]$	assumption of arbitrary name 'b' for $\forall$ introduction
4. $\mid\mid b \in a \leftrightarrow \forall P\neg P(b)$	2 $\forall$ elimination
5. $\mid\mid\mid b \in a$	assumption for $\neg$ introduction
6. $\mid\mid\mid \forall P\neg P(b)$	4,5 $\leftrightarrow$ elimination
7. $\mid\mid\mid \exists P(P(b))$	6 $\exists^2$ introduction
8. $\mid\mid\mid\mid Q(b)$	assumption for $\exists^2$ elimination ('Q' is arbitrary)
9. $\mid\mid\mid\mid \neg Q(b)$	6 $\forall^2$ elimination
10. $\mid\mid\mid\mid \bot$	8,9 $\neg$ elimination
11. $\mid\mid\mid \bot$	7, 8–10 $\exists^2$ elimination
12. $\mid\mid b \notin a$	5–11 $\neg$ introduction
13. $\mid \forall x(x \notin a)$	3–12 $\forall$ introduction
14. $\mid \exists y\forall x(x \notin y)$	13 $\exists$ introduction
15. $\exists y\forall x(x \notin y)$	1, 2–14 $\exists$ elimination

Comments: (1) From a logical perspective, two things are interesting here. First, the use of second-order resources (the quantification over properties P in $\forall P\neg Px$), which is not the norm in set theory. I do not know if this presents any special problems. Note that, as far as I can tell, one could do the above with Comprehension restricted to subsets of other existing sets, but one would still need the second-order version. Second, I have not proved that there is exactly one no-matter-what. This would require an axiom of extensionality, which in this context would fit neither with (a) Garcia's central intensionalist contention that an object is not determined by that which is comprehended by the object, but rather that the object is the differentiator between that which it comprehends and that which comprehends it, nor (b) Garcia's semi-Geach-Kraut-type theory of how counting is relativised to a sortal property, considered in Chapter 6 below.

(2) Even given this, tension with Garcia's framework might be argued to arise from two sources: (a) in this context Garcia might have good reason to restrict the Comprehension Axiom, since an unrestricted axiom would entail the existence of sets that are members of themselves, and (b) the conclusion could be parsed in natural language as saying that something is such that nothing is it, which might be parsed as something is no-matter-what, which Garcia denies. I take the first to be part of a collection of important questions concerning what a Garcian philosophy of mathematics would look like. In any case, as long as some object exists, the proof should work with second-order comprehension axiom restricted in the usual manner (only applying to subsets of already existing sets). The second seems less important to me. The conclusion is not in English, and in English should literally be read as 'There exists a y such that, for all x, x is not a member of y'. There seems nothing amiss about someone who accepts Garcia's metaphysics to read this in English as 'no-matter-what is something', with no-matter-what getting a name-like reading, that is, that which has no members is something. Consider that '$\exists y(Happy(y))$' can be read as that which is happy is something.

Notes

1. For the former, cf. Michael Friedman's *A Parting of the Ways: Carnap, Cassirer, and Heidegger* and Peter Gordon's *Continental Divide: Heidegger, Cassirer, Davos*. For the latter, see Harman's *Tool-Being*.
2. Garcia, *Forme et objet*, p. 30.
3. Garcia, *Forme et objet*, p. 61.
4. Garcia, *Forme et objet*, p. 29.
5. Garcia, *Forme et objet*, p. 36.
6. Garcia, *Forme et objet*, p. 30.
7. Garcia, *Forme et objet*, p. 30.
8. Garcia, *Forme et objet*, p. 30.
9. Garcia, *Forme et objet*, p. 36.
10. Garcia, *Forme et objet*, p. 41.

11. Garcia, *Forme et objet*, p. 39.
12. Garcia, *Forme et objet*, p. 50.
13. I say 'name-like' for two reasons: (1) Carnap's quibble actually concerned *das Nichts* which is a determiner-noun noun phrase, but still name-like because the determiner normally functions to pick out one entity; and (2) much more important, even though Garcia uses the phrase *le n'importe quoi*, it would be a category error in Garcia's view to say there was *one n'importe quoi*. While differentiating his position from Quine and Leibniz, Garcia explicitly states in an introductory footnote that *oneness* or *identity* is not a requirement of *n'importe quoi*; being and unity do not come together for Garcia. Moreover, as I develop this theme in Chapter 6, we will see that Garcia's view of counting has much in common with the Geach-Kraut view of indiscernibility, where identity only makes sense relative to a sortal predicate (or more metaphysically, a property of the right sort). But, as we note above, there is neither predicate nor property to do such work with *n'importe quoi*.
14. In the French passage, Garcia actually uses the word 'transitive' in the grammatical sense. But this would be unclear to an English reader as it is absolutely clear that he means 'symmetric' in the mathematical sense. Given this, his 'non' should be 'anti-'. Mathematically, the four words are the same in both languages. Again though, this also means that being is intransitive in the sense that it takes no direct object, it is unidirectional. Remember that the other crucial aspect of Garcia's theory of being is the denial of compactness, entities being (in) themselves. In other words, the relation between something and itself is anti-reflexive. This yields another seeming contradiction of a Fregean 'the concept horse is not a concept' type, that is, 'no-matter-what, through the milieu of something, is not no-matter-what. Something is in fact that which "detaches" no-matter-what from no-matter-what; no-matter-what is a thing, and a thing is that which is not no-matter-what' (*FO* 52).
15. However, it should be noted that Garcia distances himself from Meinong and various neo-Meinongian currents. See Garcia's 'Après Meinong. Un autre théorie de l'objet'.
16. As with the example of a clementine that follows, Garcia makes this point rather brilliantly elsewhere, when one tries to remove all determinations from something (in the example, a tree). See Garcia's 'Crossing Ways of Thinking: On Graham Harman's System and My Own'.
17. Since Garcia is committed to inconsistent objects (given that they

possess determinations), this is a way open to him, albeit one he does not take. In fact, one of Garcia's most profound discussions (located in Book I, Part I, Chapter V) concerns the manner in which the dialetheist must face the fact that mere inconsistency is not sufficient grounds for rejection. This is one of many places that there are fruitful grounds for dialogue between Priest and Garcia. In Chapter 6 below, I contrast Garcia's model of anti-symmetric resistance with Priest's recent defence of dialetheic gluons in accounting for the unity of objects.

18. I hope that we will reach a point of analytic-continental cross-cultural conversation where formal ontologists will regularly work on figures like Garcia. Anyone attempting to come up with an axiomatic theory of Garcian comprehension could do worse than start by combining insights from Nelson Goodman's 'A Genuinely Intensional Set Theory' with mereological approaches that take the constitution relation to be irreflexive, anti-symmetric, and transitive.

19. Note that one can obtain a similar proof using Graham Priest's stronger 'Characterisation Principle', some form of which Garcia is committed to. Instead of forming a set of things characterised by a given property, the Characterisation Principle allows us to name one of the things so characterised: where y is the only free variable in $\emptyset[y]$, then for some term t, $\emptyset[t/y]$. Then what you get corresponds to lines 6–11 of the proof I go on to represent. As is already abundantly clear, there are a variety of open issues between Priest and Garcia, not least of which concern dialogue between Priest's appeal to possible worlds to save the characterisation principle from slingshot-type arguments (for example, let the predicate be 'y = y and A', let the unused name be 'fred', then you get 'fred = fred and A', which entails that A is true for any A) and Garcia's critique of possible worlds in Book I, Part II, Chapter III of *Form and Object*. And of course an unrestricted Comprehension Axiom is problematic in that it yields Russell's Paradox.

5

Neither Substance Nor Process II: Two Modes

Garcia's anti-reductionism leads him to hold that objects are not exhausted by their constituents and relations to other objects. Chapters 2 and 3 were largely concerned with teasing out the paradoxical meta-metaphysical effects facing any philosopher who shares this view. Here we begin the transition to Garcia's system proper, showing how his differential view of objects leads him to reject both substance and process metaphysics. A concern raised by Graham Harman about the extent to which Garcia avoids problems with process ontology will place us in a position to begin a more rigorous explication of his characterisation of entities as differentiating objects/things.

I should note here that Garcia's scattered comments about substance versus 'vectoral' (process) ontologies are sometimes cryptic, yet one of his main motivations is avoiding problems that characteristically beset each tradition:

> Substantiality tends to compact being in the final stage of its process, overdetermining self-saturated things or things in themselves. The pure eventuality of the vectors of being tends to dissolve and disseminate being, and transforms things into effects, illusions, or secondary realities. Our concept of a thing fits neither the first nor the second model. The first produces a thing which is too much a thing, which is 'compact', while the second generates a thing which is not enough of a thing, which is only a construction or ephemeral projection. Our aim is the following: to conceive of a model that is neither too strong nor too weak, and to represent things that are really in the world without being in themselves. (FO 11)

It's almost as if he assumes that the reader is already dissatisfied with both traditions and searching for an alternative.

How does one refrain from turning these objects into substances, making them compact, as if they existed in themselves? Conversely, how does one not dissolve them into pure eventiality, potentiality, or becoming? Quite simply how does one retain *things* – neither too closed on themselves nor, too transient? (*FO* 7)

In order to get reasonably clear about Garcia's motivation we must get reasonably clear about the traditions of substance and process ontology. In addition, we must show how their traditional problems fit into Garcia's anti-reductionism and critique of compactness. Given the richness of both metaphysical schools, 'reasonable clearness' will have to be stretched somewhat, albeit not to the breaking point.

Substance: The Classical View

In order to best understand what classical substance was supposed to do, it will be helpful to revisit the denizens of Plato's cave, continuing the quick history of metaphysics we began in the Introduction. In dialogues such as *Phaedo*, the *Republic*, *Theaetetus*, and *Timaeus*, Plato seems to be motivating his own views as a solution to the threats of scepticism and relativism, though it is difficult to tell, since he presents the views as belonging to his character, Socrates. Plato's enemies, Greek sophists such as Protagoras, appealed to the constant changeableness of the world we perceive, as well as the fact that different people believe such different things, in an attempt to undermine the very concept of an objective reality about which we can attain genuine knowledge.

Plato's theory of forms responds to the sceptical challenge by bifurcating reality into a changeable realm of things that perceptually appear to us (the interior wall of his mythic cave) and a realm of forms consisting of entities that are unchangeable and unperceivable yet nonetheless intelligible (the sun outside). Plato holds that we are able to make sense of the change we perceive because we have an intellectual grasp of the unchanging forms that are instantiated by the object before and after the change. So, for example, if I perceive a whiteboard being coloured red, this makes sense to me because I have a grasp of the form of whiteness and the form of redness. For Plato then, true knowledge is the knowledge of the changeless abstract entities that are instantiated or copied by the changeable realm of perception. The form of red exists eternally and unchangeable, and it is instantiated at various places and times in the history of the changeable world of appearances.

To the extent that Alfred North Whitehead was correct when he wrote 'The safest general characterisation of the European philosophical tradition is that it consists of a series of footnotes to Plato',[1] this is because European philosophers have generally taken Plato to ask the right questions while simultaneously giving the wrong answers. Both substance and process ontology can be seen as different answers to the problem of what reality must be like given that we perceive a world that is constantly changing. For Aristotle, substances are similar to forms in that their changelessness plays a role in explaining how we can have knowledge of the changing world of appearances. But, unlike Plato's forms, Aristotelian substances do not exist in a separate realm. For Aristotle there is no outside the cave, but substances are used to block the idea that this leads to idealism or scepticism. Once substances are posited, the objects on the cave's wall are no longer mere projections from the sunlit realm of forms but rather properties of objects that exist in their own right.

Aristotle's primary substances are characterised as

(1) Being objects of predication but not being themselves predicable of anything else (at least, not in the way entities in the other categories are . . .).
(2) Being able to receive contraries. (4 a10) A substance can go from being hot to being cold, or from being red to being blue, but the instance of blue in an object cannot similarly take on and lose a wide range of attributes.
(3) [Such that] if substance did not exist it would be impossible for things in any of the other categories to exist. There could be no instances of properties if there were no substances to possess them.[2]

Substances are not eternal for Aristotle. Secondary substances (not to be confused with what some philosophers call 'secondary properties') denote the essential properties a primary substance has. And if changes end up causing the thing in question to no longer possess one of its secondary substances, then the thing in question has ceased existing. If Fido (primary substance) stopped being a dog (Fido's secondary substance), then Fido would stop existing, replaced by whatever matter is left after Fido's destruction. Nonetheless, primary substances are enduring precisely because

they remain the same as their *non-essential* properties change
(they only cease to exist when their essential properties cease to be
instantiated).

Garcia surveys the broad tradition of substance ontology and
finds that the core concept is of something existing in itself.

> Aristotelian substance, 'what is neither claimed of a subject nor in a
> subject', the primary meaning of being, substratum of qualities, quan-
> tities, and other categories; Thomist substance, an essence which exists
> in itself; Cartesian substance, this thing 'which exists in such a way
> that it only requires itself to exist'; simple, monadic Leibnizian sub-
> stance, 'which enters into composites: simple, that is, without parts';
> Kantian substance, this 'substratum which remains while everything
> else changes'. The ancient, medieval, and classical ways of thinking
> about substance implicitly show us what is distinct about our time:
> an absence of substantiality in our conception of things and of the
> world. The various lines drawn from one thesis to another represent
> the outline of substance, the key-term of what we have lost (and there-
> fore, negatively, of what we have gained): existence in itself; simples
> in composites; ground of all things; mode of being of what is in the
> things without anything being in it, without anything being affirmed
> of it; self-sufficiency; permanence; existential necessity; and so on.
> The signs of what we grew estranged from – the idea of substance –
> together and separately mark the concept of a thing in itself, which is
> distinguished from things insofar as these things can be in them and
> by them, without this thing in itself ever being by another thing and in
> another thing except itself. (*FO* 41–2)

Garcia's rejection of substance ontology is then based on his rejection of the idea that anything is in-itself.

With respect to substance ontologies, note that when Garcia
writes that something is 'in' something, he often means to denote
predication. So, in his way of speaking, a substance's properties would be in that substance. Thus, when Garcia writes that
a substance is 'in itself' he means to denote that the substance is
in a sense predicated of itself. By definition it is not predicated of
anything else, but rather is the ultimate bearer of the properties we
pick out with predicates. While we consider an object to be a substance bearing properties, it is nonetheless the case on this picture
that the substance in a sense *is* the object. Garcia tries to argue
that this in-itself status causes the substance to bifurcate into two

objects: the 'it' which is the bearer of properties, and the 'itself' which is the substance which is the bearer of itself.

> In one sense, there is necessarily substance insofar as modes are in it as in another thing. In another sense, there is necessarily substance insofar as it is in itself. Every substance is understood perniciously in two senses: the *itself* and the *it*. We will see later that this concerns a 'formal' sense (the 'itself') and an 'objective' sense (the 'it'). Substantiality confounds these two senses.
>
> No substance can ever be in itself in the same way as that which is in it is in it – since that which is in it is not in itself, and therefore is in it *as in another thing.* On the one side, there exists a substance that one is in as in another thing ('it'). On the other side, there exists a substance that one is not in as in another thing ('itself'). Substance is thus itself *and* substance is it.
>
> Substance is what makes a thing more than a thing. Substance is always what makes a thing *two* things.
>
> The idea of substance assumes that a thing may not be double or split. But by trying to constitute a thing as *one*, it always produces *two* things: one *it*-thing and one *itself*-thing. The problem is then how to explain that the two are the same. But the gap between the two can never be entirely bridged. (*FO* 42)

I don't think that this is a very good argument.

To see where it goes wrong, let us differentiate the property of being the substance that something is from all of the other properties a substance might possess. Call the first type Sproperties and the second type just properties. Then, Garcia's argument is the following.

1. Let us call the substance which is the bearer of an object's properties 'it'.[3]
2. Let us call the substance which is the bearer of its Sproperty (the property of being the substance it is) 'itself'.
3. Assume for *reductio* that 'it' and 'itself' denote the same thing.
4. The properties of 'it' inhere in another thing (the substance that is distinct from those properties).
5. So 'it' has properties that inhere in another thing (something other than these properties).
6. The Sproperty of 'itself' does not inhere in another thing (it inheres in itself).

7. So 'itself' has a property that does not inhere in another thing.
8. But (on the assumption that 'it' is the same as 'itself'), since 5 and 7 contradict one another, 'it' must be distinct from 'itself'. So we have two things instead of one thing.

The problem is that 5 and 7 would only contradict one another if 5 stated that 'it' *only* had properties that inhere in another thing. And Garcia gives us no reason to suppose this. And if 'it' and 'itself' denoted the same object then it would be true that 'it' also had one property that does not inhere in another thing, its Sproperty.

Luckily, his text doesn't depend on this argument's validity, as the rejection of substance ontologies and the very idea of anything being in itself actually follows straightforwardly from Garcia's differential model of entities. If objects are that which differentiates what they contain from what contains them, then an object that contained itself would be differentiated from itself. Or, put another way, the object could not be because it would have nothing to differentiate itself from. This is the sense in which 'compactness' is a tendency towards dissolution for Garcia, and the real reason why the 'itself' in the previous argument is prohibited.

This prohibition of objects being in themselves ends up constituting a central plank in Garcia's theory of being. As noted above, Garcia uses 'comprehension' as a term to apply to that which is common to what is picked out by more precise notions such as set-theoretic membership, predication, and various forms of containment. Given this terminology, the prohibition of objects being in themselves becomes the claim that comprehension is anti-symmetric and irreflexive. No object comprehends itself. In light of this, let us consider again a previously quoted passage.

When I say that x is y, I mean that x belongs to y, that x is a part of y, that x composes y, and that x takes part in y's matter. x is y – that is, x is comprehended by y. Since x is y, y comprehends x, y is external to x, and y is 'outside' x.

The first major consequence of interpreting 'being' as the inverse of comprehending derives from the product of an 'anti-symmetric' relation. It may seem that being is the sign of a symmetric identity relation: if a is b, then b is a. No! Being is anti-symmetry par excellence. If a is b, then b cannot be a. Being means nothing other than this unidirectionality [*ce sens unique*].

If I am comprehended in something, then what I am in cannot be in me. If I am x, then x is not me. (FO 109–10)

It is important to remember that all of this follows from Garcia's anti-reductionist understanding of an object as that which differentiates what it comprehends from what comprehends it. An object cannot comprehend itself and be distinct from all of the things it comprehends.

Garcia's discussion of Ouroboros, the snake eating its own tail, vividly illustrates this point.

> Our snake representing the ideal return of eternal subsistence materialises both the hope and failure of a complete self-adequation to itself, apart from the world. If the Ouroboros could make what is in it correspond to what it is in, then it would become a solitary container and content. What is in the snake is its tail, the bottom-half of its body. What the snake is in is the top-half of its body, its mouth. Its body is divided in two, eaten and eating. It devours, as form, something, as object, which is only itself. (FO 73)

In Garcia's terminology, the Ouroboros is a symbol of the tendency towards 'compactness', which is perhaps the major antagonist in Garcia's text. For him, substance ontologies represent objects as achieving an impossible and undesirable ideal. Nothing is compact, yet the tendency towards compactness is manifest in the philosopher of mind's desire to see human cognition as transparent to itself, the mystic and introvert's desire to withdraw from the world, the human desire for an absolute freedom not made by the actual contingencies and limitations upon which freedom acts, the onto-theological (and for Garcia unavoidable) thought of the world as an object in the world, and the reductionist identification of an object either with that which composes it or with its place in the structures in which it occurs.

The univocity of comprehension for Garcia is metaphysically important. It really is the case that the desire to achieve perfect self-understanding for him has the same end as the desire to become an Aristotelian substance. Consider how he moves back and forth between the human subject and rocks in this passage.

> I do not comprehend myself, society does not comprehend itself, nature does not comprehend itself: each thing is exiled from what it

comprehends, and situates what the thing is outside what the thing comprehends.

The self is not something. The self is a process through which being and comprehension are mutually excluded, a process whereby what is a thing is not confounded with what a thing is.

Therefore, there is no self-consciousness. There is only conscious-ness of the world. The self is the shadow of a doubt of everything that casts some light. The self is what prevents every relation of self to self, and allows a relation to the world, to something other than itself. The self is only closed to itself as a thing is in the world. What is in itself goes outside the world, or, more precisely, is defined as 'compact', that is, as only being possible on the condition of its failure.

The rock's self is the process that precludes the rock being composed of itself, and that makes the rock be in something other than itself: a desert, the Earth, a topological model, a cognitive space, a postcard.

The rock's self has nothing different from the human self, myself, yourself, a cat's self, or an adjective's self. Our self does not make us singular, but binds us to our common condition as things.

The impossibility of being myself is equivalent to the impossibility of a rat being a rat itself, a drop of rain a drop of rain itself, the entire solar system the entire solar system itself – in other words, the impos-sibility of being a *compact* thing. (FO 62–3)

We shall have occasion to touch on more instances of the agonistic struggle between the forces of compactness and reality's pushback as we discuss the regional ontologies from Book II of *Form and Object*. Here I should just reiterate that I do not think that Garcia has offered a very good argument against substance ontology. The brief argument against things existing in themselves is only compelling if one *already* accepts Garcia's differential model of objects. But, if Garcia's negative claims about substance are sup-posed to be motivating that differential model, then we have a perfect circle. However, as I noted earlier, a natural way to read the text is rather that Garcia assumes that his reader knows that substance ontology is problematic and it is a virtue of his theory that it is not committed to substances. In this book I must leave open the question of the extent to which traditional problems with substance (such as those discussed in Howard Robinson's *Stanford Encyclopedia of Philosophy* article) can be reconfigured so as to apply to Garcia's model of being. Here it is enough to note that the univocity of 'comprehension' raises the stakes considerably, since abstract issues about the being and nature of substance can now be seen to ramify into nearly every area of justifiable human interest.

Process

As Harman argues in 'Tristan Garcia and the Thing-in-Itself', Garcia's rejection of things in themselves puts him in many ways close to the process ontology tradition of Whitehead and Bruno Latour (and arguably Heraclitus, Friedrich Nietzsche, Henri Bergson, Gilbert Simondon, Gilles Deleuze, as well as contemporary structural realists in analytic philosophy such as James Ladyman, Don Ross, and Steven French). The official remit of process ontology is to conceive of change as more fundamental than static being. Garcia characterises the tradition in this manner:

> One thus conceives of trajectories of being, identified with events, facts, powers, intensities, or intentionality. These vectors of being are primary. They carry, support, and displace being, but without ever obtaining an end point or objective consistency. In such a representation, what is in the world is not identity but difference, trajectory, becoming, a continuous projection of being which never leads to a compact being, closed upon itself. There is no in-itself. Being is never like the flight of a boomerang. Nothing is self-contained or sealed. The ontological plane is open and extends through flows, forces, and becomings. (*FO* 9–10)

The process perspective centrally involves rejecting the central Platonic conceit that was preserved by Aristotle, the idea that change must be explained in terms of metaphysically prior unchanging things, be they Platonic forms or Aristotelian substances. For process ontologists then, objects that persist over time are in some strong sense not fundamental. Garcia describes it thus:

> To account for the apparent existence of things, of identifiable and re-identifiable stable entities, this model views the possibility of determining figures at the intersection of different trajectories. These figures are sealed, like the sides of a triangle made of plumes of transient smoke emitted from three aeroplanes scanning the sky. An observer may have the impression of perceiving a triangle in the sky, a determined figure inscribed in the conjunction of three different events or trajectories. In this essentially contemporary vectorial model (found in certain Nahua

philosophies of Mexico, Nietzsche, Bergson, and evolutionary theory),
things are considered as secondary effects, constructions, or illusions
at the intersection of several events or vectors of being. (*FO* 10)

Garcia notes that this is a natural route for someone who rejects
substance to take. Remember that for substance ontologists there
is a sense in which the object itself *is* the substance that bears the
object's properties. If one accepts that the only model of objects
is in terms of persisting substances, then getting rid of substances
will involve getting rid of objects.

The manner in which process philosophers take change to be
prior to sameness over time always involves also thinking of ordinary objects as in some manner radically dependent upon more
basic relational structures. Harman writes,

> Whitehead and Latour pursue a de-humanized cosmos in which all
> relations between all entities are on equal footing. The human per-
> ception of a tree is no different in kind from a bird's or raindrop's
> collision with a tree, even if the human case turns out to be more
> intricate and fascinating. All entities are on the same plane in relation
> to each other, or as Whitehead puts it, in 'prehending' each other. We
> should salute this aspect of the emerging Whitehead/Latour relational
> ontology, and also salute its refusal to valorize one particular type of
> entity such as the natural, the simple, or the eternal. In principle these
> philosophies allow us to place supposed 'aggregates' such as machines
> and international banks on the same level as plants, animals, and
> atoms. What object-oriented philosophy rejects in this philosophical
> current is its tendency to treat entities as purely relational or agential.
> For Whitehead, entities turn out to be nothing more than their rela-
> tions; for Latour, they turn out to be nothing more than the sum total
> of their effects on other entities. As a result, there are no enduring
> things for these two philosophers, but only perishing instantaneous
> 'actual occasions' (Whitehead) or actors that exist in one time and one
> place only (Latour).[4]

The thought, which Garcia hopes to be able to reject, is that what
is really there is a total system that is always changing and we only
see self-identical objects by abstracting away from components of
the total system.

Process philosophy paradoxically leads to objects both multiplying faster than *Star Trek* tribbles and at the same time

disappearing into a unity, the relational system containing all of the other seeming objects.[5] The denial of real existence to objects persisting over time ends up multiplying the number of objects in the world by the number of possible divisions of time. But, unless one wants to think of these as just very short-lived substances, the identity of these objects also must be understood as holding in virtue of the relational processes in which they are parts. But then since these processes will contain other objects, the identity of an object is dependent upon other objects. To see how this follows, note that any two objects x and y are related in *some* way (for physical objects, just consider spatio-temporal relatedness), so for any object x, a change in any other object y will change the set of relations that, for the process philosopher, constitute x. But then, for the process philosopher, the only entity that behaves at all like an object in the ordinary sense of that term that Aristotle tried to capture with his doctrine of substance is the total world itself. Process philosophy almost always tends towards this form of holism. In the next chapter we will see that there are two ways to make this argument more precise: (1) via what is known as Bradley's Regress, and (2) more directly, via what can be called[6] the Putnam/Parmenides argument.

Harman argues that Garcia's non-substance ontology of objects as the differentiators between what they contain and what contains them is a relational ontology in the manner of process thinkers.

Although Garcia initially seems to agree on this point, by making the object the difference between that which is in it and that in which it is, rather than avoiding both undermining and overmining (as I aim to do) he seems to perform both reductive operations simultaneously. For if a tree is the difference between its physical components and its current contextual position, then it will be hyper-sensitively dependent on both of these. To remove one needle from the pine tree will obviously change the 'difference' between the tree's parts and its environment, and the same holds true if another nearby tree is knocked down. The only way to prevent such ontological hypersensitivity is to accept a tree-in-itself midway between the two extremes that is not overly sensitive to all changes in those extremes. But by excluding the thing-in-itself from the outset, Garcia ends up with a blatantly relational ontology, since objects will now inevitably shift whenever their inner or outer relations shift. I have argued against relational ontology for other reasons, but Garcia might have been expected to reject it due to his initial commitment to flatness. Despite his apparent celebration of an ontology more inflationary than Meinong's, Garcia excludes an entire class of entities from his world: objects-in-themselves not exhausted by their current relations. Instead of saying that the tree per se and the tree at T are equally real, he denies the tree per se altogether, thereby showing as much hostility to non-relational objects as either Whitehead or Latour.[7]

This leads to the two problems characteristic of process ontology.

First, one must always worry about whether the process ontologist can make good on her promise to overturn the Aristotelian order of explanation. Again, *pace* Plato and Aristotle, the process ontologist takes change as fundamental and to explain any stability we happen to perceive as somehow emerging out of change. But it is still very much an open question how successful they are. Garcia writes, 'The pure eventuality of the vectors of being tends to dissolve and disseminate being, and transforms things into effects, illusions, or secondary realities' (*FO* 11). For example, thinkers such as Simondon, Deleuze, and Manuel DeLanda articulate the idea in terms of a strict dualism between a subterranean, pre-individual realm of entities such as processes, flows, and virtualities, and the realm of objects that exist over time. Simondon's model for how the latter emerges out of the former is based on how crystals form out of suspensions.[8] Unfortunately, however, individual crystallisation always requires a 'seed' to start forming out of the non-individuated sludge. But such seeds are themselves ordinary objects that exist over time! So at least for Simondon, Plato and Aristotle have not been inverted, as substance over time has not been explained in terms of non-substantive processes. Instead, we have just replaced Plato's dualism with another, a dualism that Harman refers to as 'a two-storied house of virtual and actual',[9] with elements of the actual question-beggingly used to explain how the virtual becomes actual.

This problem is related to the second problem already suggested above, the disappearance of the actual. Process philosophers always risk the subsumption of discrete entities into the whole that they partly compose. For, as I have already noted, one way to avoid the question-begging explanations of actualisation is to affirm that all that *really* exists is the whole in which the actual objects are parts. Harman is again worth quoting at length on this tendency.

Holism is an idea once but no longer liberating. It is certainly true that objects determine one another by responding to each other, smashing into one another, and drawing each other into marriages, clubs, networks and other unions. But it is equally true that they do not thereby vaporize into a systematic totality. The nails and bolts in a table do contribute to the table as a total unified entity, but do not cease for that reason to be bolts and nails. Rather, their continued participation in the table is renegotiated at each moment, and can easily be broken off due to the actions of workmen or vandals, or simply by internal structural flaws that cause the bolts and nails to collapse. The insights of holism should not be abused in order to slander the true independence of the entities that orbit freely through the cosmos, not dissolved into a single-world system as Heidegger would have it, but ensconced in monstrous hybrid relationships even while retaining their integrity.[10]

While I think that Garcia escapes these criticisms, they are very important because they set in bold relief exactly why Garcia defends some of the strangest aspects of his system. In the Introduction to his book, Garcia writes,

> Unlike the 'flat ontologies' proposed thus far, we do not restrict ourselves to a plane of individuated and non-hierarchised entities, having recourse to the concepts of 'interaction' or 'emergence' in order to explain the appearance of totalities and organisational structures. We combine our *formal* ontology of equality with an *objective* ontology of inequality. (*FO* 6)

As we will discuss in the next chapter, for Garcia, entities have two modes: entity-qua-thing and entity-qua-object. In the above quote, Garcia is claiming that his division into formal and objective modes allows him not to need to give an account of the emergence of individuals out of relational structures in the manner of process philosophers. The entity considered in the formal mode, as a thing, is in many ways like an Aristotelian substance insofar as it is not individuated by its relation to other things. But the entity considered in the objective mode, as an object, *is* relationally individuated in the manner pointed out by Harman. Following Harman's insight, I will be able to show that Garcia's objects share non-trivial properties in common with Latour's actants.

For now, note that Garcia clearly claims a certain primacy for the formal mode insofar as he does explicitly reject the claim that relations to other objects could be prior to objects.

> It is a great logical mistake to make the existence of this something depend on its relation to something. Insofar as nothing is in itself, it is impossible to relate to something without this something existing outside itself. More precisely, it is impossible to be in relation to something that always arises from this relation. If I try to relate to something that only exists through this relation, it would be impossible for me to relate to it. I cannot relate to my relation to things, unless I relate to this relation as if it were *something*. This is possible, to the extent that the relation derives both from me and from *something other* than me. (FO 80)

Yet he does not want these somethings to be traditional substances. Somehow they must themselves still be mere differentiators between that which they contain and that which contains them.

As we quoted earlier from the book's Introduction, it is clear that Garcia wants his substantial cake after having already eaten it.

> How does one divide a persistent thing or something becoming into different objects? How does one refrain from turning these objects into substances, making them compact, as if they existed in themselves? Conversely, how does one not dissolve them into pure eventiality, potentiality, or becoming? Quite simply, how does one retain *things* – neither too closed on themselves, nor too transient? (FO 7)

When wedded to his anti-reductionism, this statement does nothing more than give voice to Garcia's desire to see entities as that which differentiate comprehended from comprehending while somehow still blocking the slide to the conclusion that the only real object is the totality of relations itself. In the next chapter we turn to this audacious effort.

The Putnam/Parmenides Argument

Prior to presenting Garcia's own model, I need to be a little more rigorous with respect to the claim that process philosophies lead inevitably to metaphysical holism,[11] the Parmenidean view that in some sense the only unified object is totality. In seeing exactly where the threat of holism arises, we are able to see exactly how Garcia attempts to block this threat.

The central planks of process ontology that yield holism are the views that differences, that is relations, are somehow prior to objects and that to the extent that objects really exist, they are somehow constituted by such relations. And as soon as we try to be reasonably rigorous about what proclaiming the primacy of difference might amount to, we see that putative objects become mere interchangeable placeholders in the relational structure that is supposed to ground them. The only thing that is not interchangeable with every other thing is the relational structure itself.

To demonstrate this, let us first consider Max Black's universe[12] consisting entirely of two completely indiscernible spheres. One cannot differentiate them by saying that the first sphere is on the left and the other on the right, since one isn't in the universe to move them about. Each sphere has the exact same intrinsic and relational properties as the other sphere. One might conclude from this that there is really only one object in Black's universe, the universe itself.

Ramsey sentences not only help us be clear about Black's universe, but allow us to get clear on precisely what Garcia must avoid. Black's universe is so simply defined that it can be easily axiomatised in first-order logic. Call the two spheres a and b, and let's say that they are six feet from one another. Where 'Sx' means that x is a sphere and '6xy' means that x and y are six feet from one another we can characterise the universe thus:

1. Sa
2. Sb
3. 6ab
4. $\neg(a = b)$

These say: (1) a is a sphere, (2) b is a sphere, (3) a and b are six feet from one another, and (4) a and b are not identical. One might think that this is enough, but in fact the sentences are consistent with there being more than two things. So let's add an axiom that expresses that there are exactly two things in the universe.

5. $\exists x \exists y (\neg(x = y) \wedge \forall z (x = z \vee y = z))$

This says that some x and y are such that they are not identical to one another (so there are at least two things) and that for all z, x is equal to z or y is equal to z (and so there are at most two things). There being at least two things and no more than two things is equivalent to there being exactly two things.

Remember that the point of Ramsifying a non-logical term is to characterise the denotation of that term entirely in terms of the relations that that denotation enters into. In the philosophy of mind, this was supposed to give us a characterisation of psychological kinds as functional roles. Thus, if we could Ramsify *all* of the non-logical terms we would reveal the relational structure of the world. Of course, such a task would be both misguided and impossible with respect to the real world, but simpler realities such as Black's can easily be so Ramsified. The first step of Ramsification is to just conjoin all of our axioms.

$$Sa \wedge Sb \wedge 6ab \wedge \neg(a = b) \wedge \exists x \exists y (\neg(x = y) \wedge \forall z(x = z \vee y = z))$$

The second step is to quantify out the non-logical vocabulary. We will start with the predicates 'S' and '6'.

$$\exists X \exists Y (Xa \wedge Xb \wedge Yab \wedge \neg(a = b) \wedge \exists x \exists y (\neg(x = y) \wedge \forall z(x = z \vee y = z)))$$

This says that there are properties X and Y such that a and b have X and a is related to b by Y. To get a universal Ramsey sentence, revealing the relational structure of Black's world, we simply Ramsify out on our names a and b.

$$\exists z' \exists z'' \exists X \exists Y (Xz' \wedge X z'' \wedge Yz'z'' \wedge \neg(z' = z'') \wedge \exists x \exists y (\neg(x = y) \wedge \forall z(x = z \vee y = z)))$$

And now we have that there are z prime and z double prime such that the relational structure holds of them. This is the relational structure of Black's world.

But we remember that z prime is the variable that replaced a, so a universal Ramsey sentence for a in Black's universe would be the following:

$$\exists z' \exists z'' \exists X \exists Y (Xz' \wedge X z'' \wedge Yz'z'' \wedge \neg(z' = z'') \wedge \exists x \exists y (\neg(x = y) \wedge \forall z(x = z \vee y = z)) \wedge z' = a)$$

But this proposition is equivalent to just replacing z prime with a in the universal Ramsey sentence.

$$\exists z''\exists X\exists Y(Xa \wedge X\ z'' \wedge Yaz'' \wedge \neg(a = z'') \wedge \exists x\exists y(\neg(x = y) \wedge \forall z(x = z \vee y = z)))$$

And here we have characterised a entirely in terms of a's role in the relational structure that characterises Black's world. Process philosophers should be happy.

Actually, not so much. Notice that the sentence is also true if we replace z prime with b!

$$\exists z''\exists X\exists Y(Xb \wedge X\ z'' \wedge Ybz'' \wedge \neg(b = z'') \wedge \exists x\exists y(\neg(x = y) \wedge \forall z(x = z \vee y = z)))$$

Our new proposition says that b possesses a property X and that some distinct z double prime also possesses X and that some relation Y holds between b and z double prime (and that there are exactly two things in the universe).

The upshot of this is that, at least with respect to Black's universe, if things are just positions in a relational structure, then there is no way to differentiate between things. Both things just have the same property of being a node in the relational structure. Now, if one accepts the Leibnizian view that two objects must have something distinct about them, it follows that there are not two objects in Black's universe after all.

Graham Priest gets close to this interpretation but doesn't quite get there. He dismisses the relevance of Black's symmetric universe in this manner:

> The simplest reply to the objection would seem to be that the two objects *do not* have all the same properties. Thus, being distinct, they are made of different matter: so one is made of matter m_1, and the other is made of different matter, m_2. Moreover, they have different spatial locations. So, supposing that the space in which the spheres are located is three-dimensional, then for any coordinate system, their centres will be located at the distinct points <x1, y1, z1> and <x2, y2, z2>. Of course one could push the thought-experiment further. Not only are the spheres the same weight, colour, and so on, but they have the same matter, are located at the same spatial point, and so on. Now, however, the intuition pump ceases to function. The

insistence that the spheres are nonetheless distinct starts to appear incoherent.[13]

Were Priest here considering philosophies that take difference to be more fundamental than identity, and relations as prior to objects, he would have seen that this is precisely the point. Such philosophies *cannot* appeal to the difference of the matter contained or the absolute spatio-temporal positions to differentiate the objects.

Priest comes closer to realising this when he discusses the challenge that quantum physics poses to the view that distinct objects must have distinct properties.

> It has been argued that two particles may be distinct, even though any measurement on one will yield exactly the same as a measurement on the other. Given that all properties are observationally determinable, we have a counter-example. The objection is harder to get to grips with, since it cannot be disentangled from interpretations of quantum mechanics. However, I am of the view that to talk of particles in this context is misguided. Any system (of one or more 'particles') is determined by a state function, which maps points in space (and time) to complex values in a Hilbert space. (The state function determines the probabilities of the various outcomes which a measurement may produce.) The correct view, it seems to me, is to be a realist about, and only about, these state functions. They characterize what is really there. There are no particles in reality, though an observation may be described, for example, as a particle at a certain place.[14]

The object-oriented ontologist could hardly ask for a better example of overmining. The particles go the way of the state function in which they occur. Priest does not consider this to be an argument against quantum physics, because he takes it to be limited to quantum physics. However, recent analytic metaphysicians of a more thorough naturalistic bent,[15] such as James Ladyman and Don Ross, do apply this kind of reasoning more generally to argue that there are no objects whatsoever, only the relational structure taken to be posited by some physicists.[16]

Priest's suggestion about Black's *Gedankenexperiment*, when put together with his meditations on quantum physics, is potentially misleading. For one might think that the only thing the process philosopher must do at this point in the dialectic is show that the actual world does not contain indiscernible objects. Perhaps the only candidates for indiscernible things where this strategy doesn't work come from quantum physics. But those entities are so weird that we are better off eliminating them from our ontology in favour of the structures that we originally took to give rise to them.

This would be a good thing to hold, were it not the case that the Ramsification strategy I pursued above also holds of non-symmetric universes. Let us consider a universe just like Black's, except that one of the spheres is red and the other green. To denote this, we just add four axioms to those that describe Black's universe:

6. Ra
7. Gb
8. ¬Ga
9. ¬Rb

The first two say that a is red and b is green. Since nothing in logic prohibits two objects from simultaneously bearing two incompatible colours, we need the next two, which state that a is not green and b is not red. Conjoining all of our axioms then yields,

$$Sa \land Sb \land 6ab \land \lnot(a = b) \land \exists x \exists y (\lnot(x = y) \land$$
$$\forall z(x = z \lor y = z) \land Ra \land Gb \land \lnot Ga \land \lnot Rb$$

And the corresponding universal Ramsey sentence is

$$\exists z' \exists z'' \exists X \exists Y \exists Z \ \exists Z' (Xz' \land Xz'' \land Yz'z'' \land \lnot (z' = z'') \land$$
$$\exists x \exists y (\lnot(x = y) \land \forall z(x = z \lor y = z)) \ Zz' \land Z'z'' \land \lnot Z'z' \land \lnot Z$$
$$z'')$$

Since z prime is doing service for a, the universal Ramsey sentence for a is thus

$$\exists z' \exists z'' \exists X \exists Y \exists Z \ \exists Z' (Xz' \land Xz'' \land Yz'z'' \land \lnot(z' = z'') \land$$
$$\exists x \exists y (\lnot(x = y) \land \forall z(x = z \lor y = z)) \land Zz' \land Z'z'' \land \lnot Z'z' \land \lnot Z$$
$$z'' \land z'=a)$$

Which is logically equivalent to

$$\exists z''\exists X\exists Y\exists Z\,\exists Z'(Xa \wedge Xz'' \wedge Yaz'' \wedge \neg(a = z'') \wedge$$
$$\exists x\exists y(\neg(x = y) \wedge''z(x = z \vee y = z)) \wedge Za \wedge Z'z'' \wedge \neg\, Z'a \wedge$$
$$\neg Z\, z'')$$

This says that a has the property of being such that there exists an object z double prime and properties X, Y, Z, and Z prime such that a and z double prime have the property X, a is the relation Y to z double prime, a is not equal to z double prime, there are exactly two things, a has the property Z, z double prime has the property Z prime, a does not have the property Z prime, and z double prime does not have the property Z. And our world straightforwardly makes this true with the intended interpretation of the non-logical vocabulary. If b instantiates z double prime, X is the property of being a sphere, Y is the relational property of being six feet apart, Z is the property of being red and Z prime is the property of being green, everything fits perfectly. Our universal Ramsey sentence fully characterises the structure in which a finds itself.

And here is our point: even though our imagined universe is such that a and b do *not* have all of the same properties, it is *still* the case that a's universal Ramsey sentence applies to b! That is, the sentence arrived at by existentially quantifying out every non-logical expression except for 'a' remains true when we replace 'a' with 'b'. Consider this sentence, true of b.

$$Sb \wedge Sa \wedge 6ba \wedge \neg(b = a) \wedge \exists x\exists y(\neg(x = y) \wedge$$
$$\forall z(x = z \vee y = z) \wedge \neg Rb \wedge \neg Ga \wedge \neg\neg Gb \wedge \neg\neg Ra$$

This says that b is a sphere, a is a sphere, b and a are not equal, there are exactly two things, b is not red, a is not green, it is not the case that b is not green, and it is not the case that a is not red. Our universe, where a is a red sphere and b a green one, makes this sentence true as well.

But if we let our properties be the property of *not* being red and green we get the same universal Ramsey sentence. Let us Ramsify everything except for b in the sentence.

$$\exists z''\exists X\exists Y\exists Z\,\exists Z'(Xb \wedge Xz'' \wedge Ybz'' \wedge \neg(b = z'') \wedge$$
$$\exists x\exists y(\neg(x = y) \wedge''z(x = z \vee y = z)) \wedge Zb \wedge Z'z'' \wedge \neg\, Z'b \wedge$$
$$\neg Z\, z'')$$

The property that instantiates the existential quantifier involving Z here is the property of not being green and Z prime that of not being red. And this sentence is true in the intended interpretation of our original model. Some object z double prime (a), and properties X (being a sphere), Y (being six feet from), Z (not being red), Z prime (not being green) are such that b and z double prime have the property X (are spheres), b and z double prime are in relation Y, b is not equal to z double prime, there are exactly two things, b has the property Z (is not green), z double prime has the property Z prime (is not red), it is not the case that b has the property Z prime (b is not not red), and it is not the case that z double prime has the property Z (z double prime is not green). Our non-symmetric universe makes this sentence true.

But now let us consider the logically equivalent universal Ramsey sentence for b that we can construct from this.

$$\exists z' \exists z'' \exists X \exists Y \exists Z \; \exists Z'(Xz' \wedge Xz'' \wedge Yz'z'' \wedge \neg(z' = z'') \wedge \\ \exists x \exists y(\neg(x = y) \wedge ``z(x = z \vee y = z)) \wedge Zz' \wedge Z'z'' \wedge \neg Z'z' \wedge \neg Z \\ z'' \wedge z'=b)$$

Since this is logically equivalent to the previous sentence, it is also made true by our universe consisting of a red and green sphere. But notice that the sentence is nearly identical to a's initial universal Ramsey sentence.

$$\exists z' \exists z'' \exists X \exists Y \exists Z \; \exists Z'(Xz' \wedge Xz'' \wedge Yz'z'' \wedge \neg(z' = z'') \wedge \\ \exists x \exists y(\neg(x = y) \wedge ``z(x = z \vee y = z)) \wedge Zz' \wedge Z'z'' \wedge \neg Z'z' \wedge \neg Z \\ z'' \wedge z'=a)$$

We have exactly the same result that we had for Black's symmetric universe. A proper name for any object in the universe can sub in for any of the variables in the universal Ramsey sentence.[17] But this then means that from the perspective of structures that characterise a world, the identity of objects is irrelevant. All objects do in fact have the same property, that of instantiating the relational structure. In fact, the only thing that behaves at all like an ordinary object, with properties that characterise it, is the structure itself. If relations are primary, and objects must be defined in terms of them, then Priest's analysis of Black's universe becomes universal. It is no longer just strange quantum particles that are realised to be indistinct from one another. Now it is the case that any two objects are in fact indistinct, just indiscernible placeholders in the overarching structure which is strictly speaking the only object.

Even more so than Priest, *Reason, Truth, and History* era's Hilary Putnam came very close to making the argument we have made here. He does not employ universal Ramsey sentences but, rather, standard permutation arguments from model theory to argue for the following.

> I shall extend previous 'indeterminacy' results in a very strong way. I shall argue that even if we have constraints of whatever nature which determine the truth-value of every sentence in a language *in every possible world*, still the reference of individual terms remains indeterminate. In fact, it is possible to interpret the entire language in violently different ways, each of them compatible with the requirement that the truth-value of each sentence in each possible world be the one specified. In short, not only does the received view [that the interpretation of linguistic units is determinate] not work; *no view which only fixes the truth-values of whole sentences can fix reference*, even if it specifies truth-values for sentences *in every possible world*.[18]

Putnam's argument that such a reinterpretation is possible is similar to our argument involving the Ramsification of the theory describing Black's symmetrical and my non-symmetrical universe above. Just as I showed that a's universal Ramsey sentence was true of b by taking the properties Ramsified out by the sentence to be whatever is denoted by the negations of the original predicates in question, Putnam basically reinterprets 'on the mat' and 'on a tree' so that a particular cherry being on a tree makes true the sentence 'A cat is on a mat.'[19] The permissibility of this follows from a standard permutation type result which he exploits to prove this theorem at the end of the book:

> *Theorem* Let L be a language with predicates F_1, F_2, ... , F_k (not necessarily monadic). Let I be an interpretation, in the sense of an assignment of an intension to every predicate of l. Then if I is non-trivial in the sense that at least one predicate has an extension which is neither empty nor universal in at least one possible world, there exists a second interpretation J which disagrees with I, but which makes the same sentences true in every possible world as I does.[20]

The permutation will be an interpretation of the language that makes the same sentences come out true, but which gives the parts of the sentence (such as 'on the mat') and proper names ('Fluffy') different interpretations.[21]

During the period during which *Reason, Truth, and History* was composed, Putnam saw his indeterminacy argument as lending credence to his Internal Realism, a view that was to split the difference between realism and anti-realism. In the Preface to the book he writes:

> In short, I shall advance a view in which the mind does not simply 'copy' a world which admits of description by One True Theory. But my view is not a view in which the mind *makes up* the world, either (or makes it up subject to constraints imposed by 'methodological canons' and mind-independent 'sense-data'). If one must use metaphorical language, then let the metaphor be this: the mind and the world jointly make up the mind and the world.[22]

For Putnam, the denial of the claim that there is One True Theory is supposed to be supported by the fact that 'A cat is on the mat' (and all of the other true sentences of English) can be made true with a model where 'cat' picks out cherries, 'mat' picks out trees, and 'on the' picks out whatever relation fruits have to the trees from which they hang. The picture one gets is a neo-Kantian one, where our conceptual schemes apply like a net to an unconceptualised reality.[23] If one equates a conceptual scheme with the set of true sentences not involving reference, then the fact that the same conceptual scheme can apply so many different ways suggests that there could be different ways of carving up the same content. If one includes statements about what refers to what, then Putnam takes himself to have established that the same reality admits wildly different conceptual schemes. This isn't facile relativism, because there may be better and worse ways of carving up nature.

But my discussion of universal Ramsey sentences suggests a completely different moral from the one Putnam once drew. Rather than seeing formal semantics as an instance of a conceptual scheme that can be applied in variant ways to reality, why not see it as a picture of the structure that is constituted by a set of canonical relations between linguistic units and between linguistic units and bits of the world? Then what Putnam has shown is that this relational structure can be instantiated in variant ways. Nothing very interesting follows from this unless one takes it to be the case, with the process philosopher, that the relational facts are in some sense all the facts there are. Only then could one say that each instantiation of the structure is as good as any other instantiation.

First, so put, Putnam's argument is simply another version of the argument I made earlier involving universal Ramsey sentences and a non-symmetric Black universe. If objects are nothing more than placeholders in the relational structures, then nothing outside of the structure itself individuates separate objects. The content underlying Putnam's various schemes starts to assume the form of an amorphous blob. Second, any cursory reader of Heidegger will reject this. My concept of a screwdriver has very little to do with the fact that the word 'screwdriver' refers to screwdrivers, and a lot to do with a characteristic turning motion of my wrist, which is not linguistic. Again, Putnam-type arguments might apply if we thought the underlying facts were the relational facts presupposed by our grasp of language, but they aren't. Finally, one need not embrace the neo-Kantian view of reality as passive content waiting to be organised by human conceptual schemes to join the Hilary Putnam of *Reason, Truth, and History* in his rejection of scientism and the hegemony of One True Theory. Object-oriented philosophers such as Harman and Garcia try to provide a theory of what reality is like such that it resists being captured by One True Theory. For Garcia, the key step is the understanding of objects as differentiators between that which they contain and that which contains them. But unless the Putnam/Parmenides argument can be blocked, Garcia's differential structure will be voided of objects. In the next chapter we turn to his audacious solution to this problem.

Notes

1. Whitehead, *Process and Reality*, p. 39.
2. Robinson, 'Substance'.
3. The use of quotes here is not meant to signal mention versus use. Treat the two phrases with the quotes as separate variables.
4. Harman, 'Tristan Garcia and the Thing-in-itself', p. 29.
5. These are subtle points about which scholars disagree. In 'The Assemblage Theory of Society', p. 193, Harman provides an important corrective to the above.

   In passing, I would like to argue against all attempts to identify figures such as Bergson or DeLanda with a completely different current containing figures such as Latour and Whitehead. Sometimes the phrase 'process philosophy' is used loosely to encompass all such figures, who are joined by their rejection of old-fashioned substance and perhaps by little else. Notice that substance is rejected for opposite reasons in these two traditions. For the school of dynamic becoming, the problem with substance is its excessive rigidity and fixity. Substance is always too specific for someone like DeLanda. But for a relational philosopher such as Latour, the problem with substance is its *insufficient* rigidity: it pretends to hide behind all specific determinations and endure through shifting states of affairs, when in fact it should be thoroughly defined by them. If Bergson rejects any isolated instant, the thoroughly relational thought of Latour and Whitehead *requires* entities to be fully articulated in an instant, even if this occasion must immediately perish.

Also see Johanna Seibt's excellent *Stanford Encyclopedia of Philosophy* article on process philosophy.

6. Working title of the paper that develops this argument, 'One of Everything Please: How to Putnam/Parmenides a Process Philosophy'.

7. Harman, 'Tristan Garcia and the Thing-in-itself', pp. 31–2.

8. See my *Notre Dame Philosophical Review* of de Boever et al.'s *Gilbert Simondon: Being and Technology*. In his rich article 'The Assemblage Theory of Society', Harman makes this criticism against middle-period Delanda.

9. Harman, 'The Assemblage Theory of Society', p. 179.

10. Harman, 'Bruno Latour, King of Networks', p. 87.

11. A complete discussion would compare the argument I am going on to present, as well as Garcia's position, with that of Jonathan Schaffer's revival of the neo-Hegelian case for monism in 'The Internal Relatedness of all Things'. See also Schaffer's *Stanford Encyclopedia of Philosophy* article on monism.

12. From Black's 'The Identity of Indiscernibles'.

13. Priest, *One*, p. 23.

14. Priest, *One*, pp. 23–4.

15. According to Jeffrey Roland (for example, in 'On Naturalizing the Epistemology of Mathematics'), thoroughgoing naturalism has both a metaphysical and an epistemic dimension. One might use Roland's typology of naturalism to argue that contemporary ontic structural realism only qualifies as metaphysically naturalistic.

16. See Ladyman and Ross's *Every Thing Must Go: Metaphysics Naturalized* as well as Steven French's slightly more ecumenical *The Structure of the World: Metaphysics and Representation*. As far as I know, nobody has done a close examination of the connections between the process philosophy tradition and Ladyman, Ross, and French's ontic structural realism, which is a process philosophy in the sense I have characterised.

17. This example is mine, though Jeffrey Roland and I are extending it and tying it to standard permutation results in model theory as well as Quinean literature about ontological relativity.

18. Putnam, *Reason, Truth, and History*, pp. 32–3.

19. I've simplified this a little bit, treating 'on the mat' as a unary predicate and 'a cat' as a proper name to make the comparison clearer. If this offends, just replace Putnam's sample sentence with 'Fluffy is on the mat'. Nothing is lost in doing so.

20. Putnam, *Reason, Truth, and History*, p. 217.

21. There are a lot of logical and philosophical connections between standard permutation results, the upshots of universal Ramsey sentences, and Massey-type (for example, his 'The Indeterminacy of Translation: A Study in Philosophical Exegesis') embedding/ translation theorems. Jeffrey Roland and I are working through some of these. In this context, it is particularly interesting that Ramsey himself thought of objects as being nothing more than roles played in structures described by the theories of those objects, and that such a view fits well with the views of Quine, whom Putnam takes himself to be extending.

22. Putnam, *Reason, Truth, and History*, p. xi.

23. Putnam abandoned the view both because he came to doubt that scheme-content could do this philosophical work, and because he realised it didn't need to. See, for example, his *The Threefold Cord: Mind, Body, and World*.

6

Neither Matter Nor World: Thing

We are now in a position to begin a rigorous explication of Garcia's Janus-faced ontology. As we shall (and have) see(n), Garcia's anti-reductionism leads him to take entities to be in some sense constituted by their relations to other entities. Yet he wants to resist Graham Harman's principal worry about process ontologies, which is that privileging of relations over substance leads to the Schellengian (according to Hegel) night in which all cows are black. The danger is clear.

> Since being is a certain sense of the relation between things, every thing is enmeshed in a dyadic relation with being: that which is this thing (that which enters into this thing); and that which this thing is (that into which this thing on its own enters). (FO 113)

But if everything is defined by its relation to everything else, then what really differentiates two entities? Within a given structure, objects are differentiated by the relations that are part of that structure. But, if process philosophy is correct, from an external perspective it is a matter of complete ontological indifference which objects fit into the various parts of the structures. Putnam's Internal Realism and John McDowell's quietism are both attempts to prevent us from adopting what McDowell[1] calls the 'sideways view', where we are in a position to ask about how the structure fits reality. But (pace Putnam at least) to even talk about how objects are parasitic on the relational structures in which they occur, as the process philosopher does, is already to adopt the sideways view. And one might (as Graham Priest does) argue that even enunciating the prohibition on adopting the sideways view involves discussing the structure as a totality, which is also to adopt a perspective outside of that totality.

One way to block the process-philosophical deconstruction of objects is to revive the idea of substance.[2] Perhaps there are two objects in Black's universe as well as our non-symmetric version because the properties possessed by the object do not determine the numerical identity of an object. Instead, what individuates an object is the fact that the object itself is a distinct bearer of properties. Objects-qua-property-bearers are currently referred to as 'bare particulars'.[3] But Garcia cannot embrace this because, as we have seen, he also rejects substance.

But what if bare particulars were themselves relationally individuated? To the extent that such a suggestion is coherent, it might allow one to affirm a relational view of entities without committing to the metaphysically holistic view that the only individual is the world. Garcia attempts to accomplish this by insisting that an entity must be considered in two modes: objective (the entity-qua- object) and formal (the entity-qua-thing). The entity-qua-object's existence and numerical identity are dependent upon the objects that comprehend it (for numerical identity, its sortal properties). And this does entail the massive proliferation of relationally determined objects. And were this the whole story, it might (via the Putnam/ Parmenides argument) entail that there is a strong sense in which there is only one self-identical entity, the world.

The entity-qua-thing is *not* like Bruno Latour's actant though. The entity-qua-thing is not dependent upon the *objects* that it comprehends and that comprehend it, as in fact the only entity it comprehends is 'matter'. And the only entity that comprehends it is 'world'. Garcia arrives at the entity-qua-thing by *de-determination*, the process of considering what is left when all of the properties are removed from the object. But he doesn't arrive at substance after this process is complete. For Garcia, things are also individuated by relations. However, once objects are de-determined, being in their austere formal mode, we see that a thing is simply that which differentiates matter from world. Like bare particulars, there is nothing one can say about two things to differentiate them from one another (this is the upshot of Garcia's insistence that each thing is solitary, discussed below). But unlike bare particulars, their being is still determined by that which they contain (matter) and that which contains them (world).

Where 'that which is an *x*' denotes what is contained/comprehended by *x* and 'that which an *x* is' corresponds to those things which contain/comprehend *x*, Garcia describes his two modes thus:

Formally, 'that which is a thing' corresponds to its matter, and 'that which a thing is' to its form, that is, to the world. From the formal point of view, all things have the same form, since they all enter alone into the world.

Objectively, 'that which is a thing' are objects – things which are in this thing and which compose this thing; 'that which the thing is' can be the big thing into which this thing enters among other objects. (FO 113)

This gambit is audacious and weird, albeit one of his four central conceits (along with the differential model itself, the embrace of paradox, and his treatment of intensity as metaphysically basic). I don't think it's an exaggeration to claim that by creating this new area of dialectical space, Garcia has secured his place in the history of metaphysics.

From Objects to Things

Part of what makes the early chapters of *Form and Object* difficult reading is that Garcia's order of presentation is the reverse of the proper dialectical ordering of his ideas. He characterises the odd properties of his things *prior* to describing what it is about objects that would lead one to embrace his view of things. It is only midway through Book I that objects start to crop up in aphorisms such as the following:

4. Each thing is in other things which are in other things. The membership relations between some things and other things are knowable. They are the subject of intuitive and common sense propositions, and they are the subject of well-formed, scientific propositions. They are objective.
5. If a thing is in another thing, then it is an *object*. An object is a thing with form that is another thing. An object is a thing limited by other things and conditioned by one or several things.
6. To consider, handle, and know some things in other things consists in proving that they are *objective*. (FO 78)

And this only really makes sense to the extent that one is already going along with his claim that the (formal) world is a world of things whose only role is to differentiate matter from world.

Even more confusingly, Garcia sometimes gives the impression that things and objects are different entities, with some of the things being objects but many of them not being objects. And this usage licenses even more confusion in contexts where he uses the term 'things' to refer to what can only be by his theory entities-qua-objects. For example, a central passage of the book begins thus:

> 15. Is a human being a certain 'something', a thing, as a result of its organic unity, its logical unity, or its arithmetical unity?
>
> Unquestionably, a coherence exists – a series of relations that connect this human being's bodily limbs, tissues, and functions to a biological and physical interdependence identifying this material thing as an organism. But a finger, a hand, and each cell of this body are neither something more nor something less than this organism. In other words, if it is certainly the *organic* unity of this body that makes it an *organic* thing, it is not this *organic* unity that makes it a thing *tout court*. (FO 53)

But, strictly speaking, there are no organic *things*, only organic *objects*. Each organic object is simultaneously a de-determined thing, but qua thing the entity has no properties other than being in the world.

Garcia's loose speaking here must not confuse the essential point that he goes on to make about entities-qua-objects in this passage. Garcia continues:

> So, a minimal logical unity exists that guarantees the consistency of this non-contradictory body. If this being is something, it is primarily because what composes it is not logically contradictory. Nevertheless, we have admitted that 'two equals three', a squared circle, and some white which is not white, although not concepts or logically viable entities, are not *no-matter-what*, and are therefore equally something.
>
> Thus, we will limit ourselves to counted unity. Perhaps, quite simply, if a human being is *one* human being, just as a hand is a thing since it is *one* hand, and two hands are something since they form *one* set of two hands, just as a hot-cold thing is something if it is the impossible unity of hot and cold? (FO 53–4)

This idea he is countenancing is the Quinean requirement that there is no entity without a criterion of numerical identity.

In this context, the anti-Quinean animadversion in footnote 3 of

Form and Object's Introduction shows just how important is the point he is going to go on to make. In reference to his own book, Garcia writes,

> [This] entire treatise strives to refute W. V. O. Quine's famous slogan, 'no entity without identity' (W. V. O. Quine, *Ontological Relativity and Other Essays*, p. 23). It also seeks to refute Leibniz's claim in his letter to Arnauld that 'what is not truly *one* being is not truly one *being* either' (G. W. Leibniz, *Philosophical Essays*, p. 86). The aim of this book is to actively demonstrate, through the construction of a coherent model, that there can and must be something less determined than such an *identifiable* entity or than being *one*: each 'thing' as it is 'alone in the world', and not comparable or compared with other things. Therefore, we maintain that solitude is less than unity and identity, and that it does not imply acceptance (any more than refusal) of the law of non-contradiction. (*FO* 15–16)

Garcia is here saying that things proper, entities-qua-things, lack numerical identity. They cannot be counted. But why say this? Doesn't my use of 'they' presuppose that there is more than one thing? Aren't we hereby counting them?

If we continue to read the previous passage it becomes clear why being is prior to numerical identity for Garcia. Garcia takes it to be the case that numerical identity is determined by the sort of object we are talking about.

> But a human being is *one* human being only insofar as it counts among human beings. Unity is primarily the possibility of being counted, of entering into the count. To be one is to be capable of being one of two, three, ten, and so on. To be one is to be capable of acting as a unity in the counting of that which one is, since one is one *something*.
>
> Now, something is not primarily defined as 'something' because it is in another thing, entering into another thing or a series of other things. To be a thing, not merely this or that thing, a human or a hand, is to not be a thing among other things, it is not to count for a thing among other things. Among other things, a thing is always a determined thing, a thing which matters and which is countable. And this is not what makes it a thing, but rather what makes it *such a* thing.
>
> A human being is a *human being* since it can count for *one* human being among two, three, or four human beings. A hand is a hand since it can count as *one* hand among two, three, or a thousand hands. (*FO* 54)

One human being is composed of around (depending on how one counts) seventy-eight organs; one human brain contains around one hundred billion neurons, the same number of stars in one galaxy, vastly dwarfed by the roughly thirty-seven trillion cells in one human body, in turn dwarfed by the one hundred octillion stars in one universe (ours). For Garcia, we can never simply point and ask 'how many?' The answer must always be another question: how many whats? One must know the kind of thing being picked out to know how many. And this does not work in the opposite direction. Numerosity does not entail kind. One lump of clay may be spatially coincident with one statue, and several with a diorama.

Garcia's position about numerical identity is closely related to a view that has a proud heritage in analytic philosophy. The thesis that two objects can be the same of one kind of thing and distinct from one another with respect to some other kind of thing is standardly called 'relative identity'.[4] Myself at the age of six and myself now are the same human being, but a quite distinct collections of cells. According to relative identity, it makes no sense to ask of two things *simpliciter* whether they are identical. One must ask if they are the same person, the same collection of cells, the same lump of matter, and so on. But this is precisely what Garcia says about numerosity. These views provide a unified solution to a wide variety of paradoxes concerning identity, including (as Max Deutsch shows in his *Stanford Encyclopedia* article on relative identity) the Paradox of Change, Chrysippus' Paradox, the Paradox of 101 Dalmations, the Paradox of Constitution, the Ship of Theseus' Paradox, and Church's Paradox. The price to pay is that relative identity ends up lacking some combination of the key properties true of mathematical identity: reflexivity ($a = a$), symmetry (if $a = b$, then $b = a$), transitivity (if $a = b$ and $b = c$, then $a = c$), and the substitutivity of identicals (if a has the property P, and $a = b$, then b has the property P). In standard classical logic, symmetry and transitivity follow from the substitutivity of identicals and reflexivity, and the substitutivity of identicals follows from Leibniz's Law ($a = b$ if and only if a and b have all of the same properties in common). Some, like Graham Priest, whose identity relation is non-transitive, take this as a mark against classical logic. Garcia, on the other hand, has his irreflexive and anti-symmetric comprehension relation do much of the work that has traditionally been done by identity.

Garcia's own position is clearest if we re-examine Aristotle's notions of substance. In the last chapter we saw how Garcia rejected what scholars call Aristotle's *primary* substance. However, his doctrine of relative numerosity, that the singularity of an object is determined by the properties that comprehend that object, can be seen as a generalisation of Aristotle's notion of *secondary* substance. Graham Priest marks the distinction between primary and secondary substance in this manner:

> Aristotle operates with two notions of substance, often called 'primary' and 'secondary'. A primary substance, the substance of the *Categories*, is something like Aristotle and the Sun: a stand-alone entity which can be the bearer of properties. Secondary substance, the substance of the *Metaphysics*, is, by contrast, the substance *of* something. It is whatever it is that makes the thing the (kind of) thing it is. So the [secondary] substance of Aristotle is being a person, and the substance of the Sun is to be a star.[5]

This is very close to Garcia's view about the role that properties play with respect to determining an object's unity. For Garcia, it is always either enthymematic or a non sequitur to say that there is one object. Rather, one can say (or mean with the enthymematic assertion) that there is one brain, person, or universe.

And just as readers find two notions of substance in Aristotle, there is a sense in which Garcia has two notions of being, depending upon whether we are talking about the being of entities-qua- things (which does not entail numerosity) or entities-qua-objects (which does). The role of determining the numerosity of an object is, as with Aristotle's secondary substance, determined by the latter sense of being. It is worth reproducing an earlier quote to stress this point here.

> In its other sense, the verb 'to be' (in a 'passive' sense, if you will) corresponds to the fact of comprehending. 'Being been' is comprehending. When I say that 'the wall is white', I am aware that I am claiming something about the wall. But in fact, I primarily express my judgment about whiteness. I say that the wall is comprehended in whiteness, is among white things. I am not expressing a quality of the wall, being white. If that were the case, the wall would comprehend, among other qualities, the fact of being white, as if this quality were

hung to the coat rack of the thing. No, rather, I express a quality of whiteness. This whiteness can comprehend the wall. The wall can count within the set of what is white. In the sentence 'the wall is white', the *thing* is not primarily the wall, but whiteness. Otherwise, I ought to say that whiteness is the wall – that is, that the wall comprehends the whiteness in the things which compose this wall. Likewise, I often say 'I am a person'. I think that I am expressing one of my determinations, namely, personhood. No, I am expressing one determination of the set of humanity which is able to contain and comprehend me. (*FO* 109)

To be clear, being is always being comprehended for Garcia. To be comprehended is to be a part of, which (as the above quote makes clear) for Garcia includes being the bearer of a property. What is distinctive about the kind of being that determines numerosity is that it is the comprehension of entities-qua-objects by other entities-qua-objects. But an entity-qua-thing is always only comprehended by the world.

Priest also ties the notion of secondary substance to the theory that to be is to be the bearer of a property, a view he associates with Heidegger.

Something is an object if it has properties. For if it has properties, it is certainly an object; and if it is an object, it has properties – a least the property of being an object. Hence, being, in this sense, is equivalent to having *Sosein*, in Meinong's terms. This is quite different from what it means to exist, which, I take it, is the ability to enter into causal interactions.

This is essentially Heidegger's understanding of being, too. Coming from the phenomenological tradition, Heidegger takes it that everything one can think about has being, not just what exists.[6]

Both Priest and Garcia thus affirm that to be is to be the bearer of a property, and differentiate being from existing.

However, unlike Priest, Garcia's characterisations of an object/thing as that which differentiates that which comprehends the object/thing from that which the object/thing comprehends forces him to depart radically from Aristotle's doctrine that being and unity come to the same thing. Aristotle wrote:

If, now, being and unity are the same and are one thing in the sense that they are implied in one another as principle and cause are, not in the sense that they are explained by the same formula (though it makes no difference even if we interpret them similarly – in fact this would strengthen our case); for one man and a man are the same thing and existent man and a man are the same thing, and the doubling of the words in 'one man' and 'one existent man' does not give any new meaning (it is clear that they are not separated either in coming to be or in ceasing to be); and similarly with 'one', so that it is obvious that the addition in these cases means the same thing, and unity is nothing apart from being.[7]

Garcia is happy to affirm this with respect to the being of entities-qua-objects, but not with respect to entities-qua-things. Again, this is because the differential model of objecthood combined with the theory that unity and being are one would, for Garcia, destroy the individuality of objects, collapsing into a variety of process ontology. For Garcia, objects only have unity because of their place in the relational structure of various comprehensions. But if unity and being were the same ('to be is to be the value of a bound variable'), then they would only have being because of their place in the relational structure of comprehension. But this is process philosophy.

Priest is also moved to account for unity in terms of more than relations that objects enter into. But since he is not committed to the Garcian view that objects are differentiators between that which they comprehend and that which comprehends them, he is able to posit another non-relational constituent of objects that accounts for their unity, gluons.

> Let us now put all these thoughts together. The being of something is that in virtue of which it is. To be is to be one. So the being of something is that in virtue of which it is one. And what is it in virtue of which something is one? By definition, its gluon, g. The being of something is therefore its gluon. We have answered Heidegger's question as to the nature of being.[8]

Such a solution is not open to Garcia, for it violates his anti-undermining account of objects as differentiators. Garcia instead rejects the view that to be is to be one. To be *an object* is to be one, since the properties that comprehend an object determine the number of the object in question. But when we consider that same object without its properties it is revealed as a *thing*, which has no numerosity. For entitities-qua-things, being and unity are thus not the same.

Thing

Now we are in a place to begin to explicate one of Garcia's main conceits.

> This book's central claim is that no classical determination – including the property of being non-contradictory, of being individuated, or of having identity or unity – is contained in our concept of the most unrestricted, emptiest thing and in the most formal possibility of a 'thing'. We consider as inessential all that may characterise a thing until we have properly identified what defines it as a thing, a thing and not as a *consistent* thing, *individual* thing, or *one* thing. We thus aim at neither the being of unconditioned things, nor at that of undetermined things, but rather at the being of *de-determined* things. (FO 5)

Why the primacy of things? Why must these things be de-determined?

In the concluding section of Chapter 1, we considered Garcia's first set of arguments for why everything is a thing. He takes it to be the case that the very act of differentiating something is to treat it as a thing. Thus, one cannot successfully differentiate entities from things. As differentiated entities, they become things. And this is the main route to Garcia's ontological liberalism:

> One will ask if this 'no-matter-what' is real, a mental construction, a mere extrapolation of the possible from what actually is, or some misleading linguistic effect. No-matter-what is neither real nor abstract nor both of these at once. No-matter-what is quite simply the plane of *equality* of what is real, possible, nonexistent, past, impossible, true, false, or bad. It doesn't matter. It concerns the possibility of being *either* real *or* possible, *or* real and possible, *or* neither real nor possible, *either* constructed *or* given, *either* natural *or* artificial *or* natural and artificial, *either* true *or* illusory, of not being all of these at once, but of equally being able to come under (or not) one of these determinations, any determination. (FO 30)

For Garcia, to see all of these as things is to see them on a plane of equality, abstracted from their particular qualities and from our parochial interests in them.

Garcia here agrees with the Heideggerian idea that we only gain epistemic access to this plane by abstracting from the properties we associate with objects, but unlike Heideggerians, he thinks that this does not entail that these de-determined things are *mere* abstractions from the worlds described by phenomenologists (either the lifeworld where things are experienced in terms of how they might serve our human interests, or the world described by science) in which the objects occur. Rather, the world of things is what we presuppose when we compare objects:

> This world is not the 'foundation' of things insofar as they matter to us, but, as it were, their 'gauge' or datum line in relation to which it must be possible that some things matter and that they matter to us more than others. In order for some things to matter more than others, whether they are more beautiful (for us or in relation to some idea that we have of them) or more ugly, more true or more false, better or worse, it is necessary that a plane exists on which no thing is either more or less a thing than another. This plane is situated neither beyond nor below our values which we could disregard, ought to attack with a hammer, or completely deconstruct. This plane is nothing other than the plane of reference of what matters to us.
>
> The flat world, where no thing is more important than another, supposes neither an abstraction nor a reduction, neither asceticism nor critique, neither genealogy nor deconstruction, but a simple *levelling*. The flat world is neither more nor less real than the planes on which what matters to us plays out, where things are exchanged, where we give them or receive them, where there are so many variable intensities.
>
> This is the flat world of the *no-matter-what*. (FO 31–2)

Remember that nothing is no-matter-what, but that no-matter-what can be anything. Garcia recognises that nothing is in common to all of the various kinds of determined objects in the world (including musical melodies, Gödel's second incompleteness theorem, happiness, tables, hurricanes, itches, monetary unions, dogs, and children). What is it that makes these different objects all things? For Garcia, answering this question requires thinking of them without the properties and constituents by which we might differentiate them. And, given Garcia's anti-reductionist differential model of entities, after doing this we see that, qua things, they are all differences between matter and world. The flat world of the no-matter-what is the world of de-determined objects, the world of things.

In the very next section of the book ('Thing') Garcia argues that his flat plane of things is not only needed to make sense of the view that no-matter-what is something, but also to block the metaphysical holism that besets process philosophers.

> Many things exist, and we cannot do without the concept of 'thing'. In the absence of things, the world becomes undifferentiated: the world is a self-saturated whole in itself which knows no differentiation.
>
> It is very strange to claim that, in reality, only a continuous, homogeneous world exists, traversed by various intensities, but undifferentiated by themselves, and that the existence of things would only be the reflection of a division through perception, thought, and knowledge. (FO 37)

After arguing against the view that human consciousness somehow introduces the division of reality into different objects (which would only be possible were human consciousnesses already different objects), Garcia argues that things must be in some sense metaphysically basic:

> One never accounts for the fact that there are things other than by things. A 'thing' cannot derive from anything other than another thing. No philosophical magic trick will ever give us the appearance of things from a more fundamental principle of a non-differentiation or super-difference of things. Indeed, when something is, nothing can precede a thing but another thing. If one wants to redirect the *something* of an undifferentiated totality, an immanence, an in-itself, or anything that one claims is not a product of the thingly division, this principle will retroactively and immediately be reduced to the thing's status as another thing. Nature, God, the One, the All, and Ground have never avoided and will never avoid the reduction to a thing's status. (FO 37–8)

Again we see Garcia's central conceit that the very act of differentiating entities from the realm of things is to treat them as things.

But, like the process philosopher, Garcia holds that all entities' being and unity derive from the relations that the entities enter into:

> In other words, being implies being in a relation with something. This something is in a relation with a thing that one is not oneself in a

relation with. Being *in* something is entering into the membership of a thing that comprehends us, that is, includes us *among other things*. Being in a room is being in a spatial relation with a thing (the room) that has a relation to us. This thing (the room) also maintains a relation with other things, though we do not ourselves have this relation. What does it mean for the room to comprehend us or to be greater than us, other than that there are things in the room which are not in us? A bouquet of flowers, a rug, a washbasin, and a certain density of air are in the room but are not in me. The spatial relation between the room and me is such that the room extends beyond me, for this room has the same relation to me (capacity) as to some things that I do not relate to (I do not contain them, therefore the room is greater than me).

Being is being comprehended in any modality. Being is being in a relation to a thing that maintains this same relation to some things. What is being red, for this peony? Here we do not seek to define the 'red' of 'being red', but the 'being' of 'being red'. Being red is being in a relation with a thing (redness, a colour, a quality, a part of the electromagnetic spectrum, and so on) that maintains an identical relation to other things (a table, flag, or dress) that the peony does not itself relate to. (*FO* 111)

Here Garcia is using 'thing' to interchangeably refer to entities-qua-objects and entities-qua-things, and in a context where he was initially talking about the being of a person. This makes the passage potentially misleading, as it is not true for Garcia that entities-qua-things are 'in a relation to a thing'. Rather, they are in a relation to 'something-other-than-a-thing', Garcia's world, which we have already argued is not a thing because it is not comprehended by anything (while simultaneously inconsistently being comprehended by the properties we attribute to it, such as the property of not being comprehended by anything).

When Garcia differentiates entities-qua-objects from entities-qua-things, it is clear that the fact that entities-qua-things are comprehended only by something-other-than-a-thing (the world) is what differentiates them from entities-qua-objects:

12. A thing can be in other things – be an object – since a thing always remains in something other than a thing.
13. If there were nothing *except* objects, then there would be no objects.

14. A thing can be in another thing since these two things – comprehending and comprehended – are equally but separately in the world.

15. Objects are *unequal*. A thing that comprehends another thing is objectively more than the thing that it comprehends. A thing comprehended by another thing is objectively less than the thing that comprehends it.

Things are *equal*. Each thing is equally in something-other-than-a-thing.

16. The condition of the inequality of objects is the equality of things.

17. If each thing were not alone in the world, then things could never be in each other.

For the branch to be in the tree, to be a part of the tree, this branch must be in the world *neither more nor less* than the tree. As a 'thing', the branch is in the world – that is, in everything except itself, in everything that surrounds it, in everything that begins infinitely where the branch ends. As an 'object', the branch is in the tree. (*FO* 79)

So we see both that entities-qua-things are also differentiators and that the difference between entities-qua-things and entities-qua-objects is that the latter, and not the former, differentiate themselves from other objects. Entities-qua-things differentiate themselves between matter and world.

Remember that the point of de-determination is to see what, if anything, is in common to the incomprehensible variety of objects (a cutting of acacia, peace, Beethoven's Seventh, all performances of Beethoven's Seventh after the year 2020, the square root of negative one, and so on) in which we find ourselves engulfed. We achieve this by considering these objects independently of the objects that they constitutively differentiate themselves from, those that comprehend them and that they comprehend. After de-determination, all that is left is a thing differentiating the world that comprehends it and the matter it contains. To understand how this is to work we must understand the sense in which formal matter is the inverse of world:

1. It is fruitless to define *that which is* the matter of things. Matter is what is ultimately in things.

Matter is what is, but that nothing is. Matter is the buffer inside things.

2. The physical sciences, fundamental physics, must establish a minimal determinate picture of what matter is. They present the primary image, the 'first light', to each era, of what the matter of things is.

Matter is never defined scientifically. What is defined is *that which* matter *is* minimally: atoms, elementary particles, forces, and fields. Physical science determines the primary objects of matter. These objects are then comprehended in the things that they compose, and so on.

Due to changes in observational techniques and theoretical modelling, the primary objects of matter later become secondary and composed by more primary components.

3. Matter is not itself material.

Matter is not composed of components of matter. Matter is what composes the primary components, without being itself composed.

Nothing is less material than matter. (*FO* 135)

Formally, matter is simply that which comprehends nothing yet is comprehended by things. Although he never says so, matter is necessitated by two of Garcia's commitments, the method of de-determination plus the transitivity of comprehension. Assume that some chunk of matter comprehended other entities. Then, by transitivity, any thing that comprehended matter would also comprehend those entities. But then that thing would not be fully de-determined.

Astute readers will have already noticed that formal matter and no-matter-what seem to come to the same thing. They both are comprehended by things but do not comprehend anything. In fact, Garcia uses the terms interchangeably. Sometimes, for example in the initial set of aphorisms concerning world, we find no-matter-what playing the role of formal matter:

12. A thing begins with no-matter-what and ends with its negative.

No-matter-what is what ends as a thing, and what does not begin. I cannot define *what is* no-matter-what, since no-matter-what is precisely what no thing is. 'No-matter-what' is defined by one of its limits: that which it is. It is a definition with return and without departure.

13. A thing is defined by its two limits. I can define *that which is* something ('no-matter-what') and *that which* something *is* ('something other than something'). I can define that through which a thing begins and that through which it ends. But I cannot define a thing as a whole, unless I make it compact. There is no unilateral definition of a thing; there is only a departing definition *and* a returning definition. (*FO* 71)

The fact that formal matter and no-matter-what possibly come to the same thing should not obscure the main point, however, which is that entities-qua-objects are both, for Garcia, differentiators of the objects that comprehend them and that which they comprehend, and that entities-qua-objects are (in their de-determined mode) also entities-qua-things, which merely differentiate matter/no-matter-what from world.

Solitude

Let us back up and reiterate some of our main themes. Entities-qua-things are supposed to play one of the main roles that Aristotle's primary substance plays, serving as anchors that tie the relational structure of the world to the entities that fill the roles in that structure. In addition, entities-qua-things are arrived at by de-determination. For Garcia, this allows entities-qua-things not only to prevent the Putnam/Parmenides argument's conclusion that there is only one thing, but also to articulate the formal properties of objects, those properties in common to all different kinds of objects. The world thus denuded is Garcia's flat plane of equality:

> Some will think that only this clementine really exists; others that only a clementine in general [the Platonic form of the clementine] exists absolutely. But how are they equal, other than in that they are *something*, anything (existent, nonexistent, real, abstract, constructed, true, or false)?
>
> On this plane of equality not only are this clementine and the concept of clementine comparable, but a material part of a clementine and a whole clementine are just as comparable. Let us consider a segment of this clementine, a tenth of it. A tenth of a clementine is objectively less than a whole clementine, ten-tenths of a clementine. However, a tenth of a clementine, a segment of a clementine is not only less than the thing of which it is the part. It is also *something*. Let us consider equally part and whole, the slice which has been removed from a clementine and the orange peel which happens to be removable from a clementine. (*FO* 50)

This leads to a slightly paradoxical situation, however. On the one hand, entities-qua-things (like bare particulars) are part of the explanation of how diversity exists in the world. But on the other hand (again, like bare particulars), every entity-qua-thing is exactly like every other entity-qua-thing, for there is nothing to differentiate them.

Unlike bare particulars, entities-qua-things are *not* the subjects of entities-qua-objects' predications. Entities-qua-objects are. And Garcia's entities-qua-things do *not* form an exception to the claim that to be is to be comprehended. Entities-qua-things are comprehended by the world. Neither do they form an exception to the differential model of objects/things, as entities-qua-things constitutively differentiate matter from world. Entities-qua-things have a third difference from bare particulars in that bare particulars are supposed to account for objects' numerical identity, their unity. And Garcia rejects this. Again:

> That which is *one* is generally defined as being a *thing*. Unity, logical unity or counted unity, appears as the decisive property allowing us to distinguish *one thing*.
>
> But to say that a thing 'is that which is one' is also to limit considerably the import of the thing.
>
> We will not claim that a thing cannot be one, but rather that it is not because a thing is *one* that a thing is defined as a *thing*. (FO 53)

Entities-qua-objects are one, but entities-qua-things are prior to numerosity.

But even given these radical differences from traditional bare particulars, entities-qua-things share the standard problem that they generate difference while themselves not being differentiated from one another. Garcia is aware of this issue, which he marks by saying that things are *solitary*. This is *also* the sense in which it is a category error to attribute number (even oneness) to an entity-qua-thing.

> 16. A thing in another thing [an entity-qua-object] counts as *one*, but it is not *solitary*, because it is *one* thing in *another* thing: one hand in one body, one individual in one society, and so on.
>
> Embedded in some something, a thing is *some* thing, but it is not one *thing*.
>
> In 'something other than a thing', only this or that which can be solitary can be something.
>
> A thing is a *thing* only embedded in its relation to that which is not *another* thing.
>
> 17. To be incapable of entering into a count is to be solitary.
>
> 18. Solitude makes the thing.

19. The unity of a thing is its possibility of being among other things. The thinghood of a thing is its possibility of being a solitary thing.

One is a thing only insofar as it is solitary. By being *one*, one is one *such*.

20. It is precisely because I am not *one* that I am *thing*, and that I can therefore be a thing, that is, potentially count as one. (FO 55)

The picture we get is that once all of the determinations of an object are removed, what is left is a thing absolutely withdrawn, stranded in its own reality, comprehended by the world and comprehending no-matter-what/formal matter. I use this word 'withdrawn' deliberately, for here is one of the major points of comparison between Harman and Garcia, Harman's withdrawn real object, discussed in Chapters 1 and 3 above, versus Garcia's solitary thing.

Looking at the reasons Garcia gives for holding that entities-qua-things are solitary helps understand the content of that claim:

For there to be objective systems of knowledge, thought, action, memory, will, intention, perception, proprioception, desire, or any other active relation to objects, it is necessary that these objects also be solitary things; their manifold is impossible without the exclusive solitude of each one. If each thing were not exclusively alone, then there would either be a manifold of nothing, or a compact manifold of everything. In order for manifolds – given or constructed by objects (material objects, historical objects, linguistic objects, ideal objects) – to exist, it is necessary that these objects be distinct enough to be together. Solitude in the world is the condition of distinction for belonging to an aggregate. (FO 59)

The first premise is the upshot of the Putnam/Parmenides argument. Relational properties cannot in the end account for diversity because, when considered separately, a relational structure is indifferent to its non-relational occupants, which are at best placeholders in the structure. But for Garcia, as with the process philosopher, *all* properties are relational, since entities (including properties) are differentiators between the entities that contain them and that they contain. In addition, for Garcia, numerosity itself only holds in virtue of relations, possession of the relevant secondary properties that determine the relevant kind in question. But from this it follows that there are only ever two (or more) entities to the extent that they are both counted as two (or more) of the same kind of entity (e.g. two brains versus two hundred billion neurons). Thus, whenever we talk about two (or more) entities, we are considering them as objects, mere elements in the vast relational structure of comprehension. But the structure itself is indifferent to which objects fit into its structural roles, so there would be nothing after all to distinguish the two (or more) entities.

When the object is completely de-determined, the entity-qua-thing is itself completely isolated, not only from the objects it comprehends and that comprehend it, but also completely isolated from the other de-determined objects:

> If things were not solitary, then they would never be together.
>
> Solitude is equal and not shared. This coat's blue colour is something (whether it is something for me, for someone else, for the coat itself, it doesn't matter) as much as the blue of the sky and the sky are something. The coat's blue colour as a thing is alone in the world, that is to say, on the background of everything which is not this coat's blue, including the blue of the sky and the sky. But these three things are not alone together. Each one is exclusively solitary. When the coat's blue is something, the blue of the sky cannot be something, no more than the sky, this table, or the idea of war. When the sky is something, since it is something, nothing else is something. In other words, in order for the sky to be something, it is necessary that nothing else can be something. Only one thing exists at a time. The existence of a thing as a thing destroys the possibility of the existence of another thing: only this thing exists, since this thing is in everything except this thing, in that which is not a thing, which we call the world. (FO 58)

In this manner, for Garcia, just as much as for Harman, entities are simultaneously enmeshed in relations with one another (when wearing their object *chapeau*) and (qua things) entirely withdrawn.[9]

For Garcia, the solitude of things is what prevents them from being objects. Even though things too are relationally individuated (since a thing is that which differentiates formal matter from world), they are utterly removed from the web of comprehension that constitutes the objective plane. And it is only because of this removal that they can serve as anchors to the objects in that plane.

As I noted at the beginning of the chapter, and hope to have established in the discussion above, Garcia's vision of the flat, formal plane of equality is one of the most audacious gambits in the history of metaphysics. But, as with any truly brave philosophical act, there are attendant problems. Even though entities-qua-things are of necessity entirely solitary, not related to one another, we cannot help but relate them to one another. In the paragraphs above Garcia *does* relate several entities-qua-things: the clementine-qua-thing, the Platonic-form-of-clementine-qua-thing, the coat's-blue-colour-qua-thing, the sky-qua-thing, the sky's-blue-colour-qua-thing, the table-qua-thing, and the idea-of-war-qua-thing. All of these things are related in the minimal sense that they are mentioned on page 58 of *Form and Object*. And this is entirely general; to be absolutely unrelated to one another is, after all, a distinct way of relating to one another.

Perhaps the problem is merely epistemic. Perhaps in the same sense that we cannot help but treat our world as if it were a universe, we cannot help but treat things as objects. But is this *merely* epistemic? In Chapter 3, I envisioned our inability to refrain from treating the world as a universe as the speculative moment for Garcia. What seems to be our own inability is actually reflective of the paradoxical nature of reality. Should Garcia make the same admission at the bottom of the world, no-matter-what/formal matter, as he does at the top? Is matter as paradoxical an entity as world? It is to this question that we now turn.[10]

Notes

1. McDowell, *Mind and World*. I saw Putnam lecture once in the late 1990s and he kept mistakenly referring to his own *Words and Life* as *Mind and World*. During the question and answers, it was clear how profoundly Putnam had been moved by McDowell's critique of the scheme/content distinction to see his earlier internal realism as rebarbatively neo-Kantian. On the other hand, one could argue that McDowell's quietism is important precisely because it is the last gasp of even remotely plausible neo-Kantianism in Western philosophy.

2. One can read the early sections of Hegel's *Phenomenology of Spirit* in exactly this manner. In fact, I would argue that *every* time Hegel uses a cognate of the word *verkehrte* (standardly rendered 'topsy-turvy' in English translations), something like this is going on. Certain conceptual resources are unable to differentiate two things that should be differentiated. The topsy-turvy world is simply the world where

they are seen as mirror images of one another. Dialectics, according to this interpretation, is simply adding conceptual resources by which the differentiation can be made. Further dialectical progress happens when the new resources are shown to fail to distinguish other distinct things, necessitating the addition of further conceptual resources. This is a non-trivial interpretive claim and defending it would eat up the entire chapter, if not the book. In lieu of that, I would like to baldly assert that one of the advantages of seeing Garcia as responding to Hegel is that one begins to read Hegel in interesting new ways.

3. We should be clear that Aristotle would have rejected bare particulars as substance, and in fact seems to give an argument against them and the process of de-determination in Book Zeta of *Metaphysics*. The basic thought is that if we have to strip away all of the properties to consider a bare particular itself, then we have an object with no properties. But then we could say nothing whatsoever about the object. I suspect that Garcia has a decided advantage over the bare particularist here, since his things do have properties. They comprehend their matter and are comprehended by the world. Nonetheless, Garcia's admonition that things are solitary is a concession to Aristotle's point.

4. See Harry Deutsch's 'Relative Identity' for a dialectical overview.

5. Priest, *One*, p. 40.

6. Priest, *One*, p. 49. Priest does not note that this equation of being and property possession is in tension with his characterisation of none-ism and characterisation of the quantifiers of his free-logic as presented in the Introduction of the same book! 'It [the relevant free logic quantifier] is not to be read as "there *exists* an x such that Px" – not even as "there *is* an x such that Px", being (in this sense) and existence coming to the same thing' (p. xxii). The parenthetical renders the passage consistent with the view that to be is to possess a property, but perhaps not with the Heidegger quotes on the univocity of being that follow Priest's enunciation of that view.

7. Aristotle, *Metaphysics*, p. 1585.

8. Priest, *One*, p. 51.

9. Harman sees this tension as both bug and feature. It's enough of a bug to necessitate his theory of vicarious causation, but the intrinsic philosophical interest of that theory ends up rendering it a feature. A fuller discussion would attempt to discern a proto-theory of causation from Garcia's account of intensity and then enter that into dialogue with Harman's account.

10. If space limitations were not so pressing, I would at this point compare Garcia's things with Graham Priest's gluons. Garcia and Priest both hold that there is a basic inconsistency in things, but articulate it in different ways. Priest's gluons are what account for the unity of objects. They both are and are not constituents of objects and are identical with all of their objects' parts, even when those parts are not identical with one another. This leads him to give up transitivity for identity (as mentioned above, giving up transitivity is already well motivated by several paradoxes) while keeping symmetry and reflexivity. Garcia's notion of comprehension is a mirror image of Priest's identity, as it is transitive, *anti*-symmetric, and *ir*reflexive. The difference between them derives, I think, from the fact that Priest *and* Garcia see property instantiation and composition to be more closely related than most philosophers, Garcia privileging composition and Priest instantiation. Priest's non-transitive relation is intuitively sensible when talking about the sense in which a property can be fully present in the distinct things that instantiate it. He then generalises this to some constituents of objects (the gluons). Garcia's transitive, anti-symmetric, and irreflexive comprehension relationship is intuitively sensible when talking about the sense in which a constituent is comprehended by the object in which it occurs. Garcia then goes in the opposite direction to Priest, modelling instantiation with a relation that more intuitively fits constitution. Also Priest's gluons are answering third-man-type arguments applied to hylomorphism, while Garcia is primarily motivated by the Putnam/Parmenides argument. I think Garcia would take the third-man arguments to be only a problem for those who equate identity and unity. I don't have any intuitions about what Priest would say with respect to the Putnam/Parmenides argument.

7

Neither Discovered Nor Created I: Universe and Matter

In *Quentin Meillassoux: Philosophy in the Making*, Graham Harman presents Speculative Realism in terms of the rejection of one or both of the following Kantian propositions:

a. The human–world relation stands at the center of philosophy, since we cannot think something without thinking it.
b. All knowledge is finite, unable to grasp reality in its own right.
Meillassoux rejects (b)[1] while affirming (a). But readers of my own books know that my reaction to Kant is the exact opposite, rejecting (a) while affirming (b), since in my philosophy the human–world relation does not stand at the center. Even inanimate objects fail to grasp each other as they are in themselves; finitude is not just a local specter haunting the human subject, but a structural feature of relations in general including non-human ones.[2]

On the interpretation of Garcia that I have developed thus far, he joins Graham Priest in rejecting *both* (a) and (b), with the price to pay being the cost of characterising reality as a contradictory whole.

For Garcia, metaphysics is perhaps best seen as a species of what Derrideans call the necessary impossible. We cannot help but to treat the world as if were an object in the world, which it is not. Yet in thus treating it we see that it simultaneously is an object, for in truthfully predicating of the world the property of not being an object we are simultaneously seeing a property (the property of not being an object) which comprehends the world. But the fact that the world has a property then makes it at object. The world is an inconsistent object.

What is perhaps most fascinating about Garcia is the way

that, for him, formal categories such as world, matter, and thing both are and are not objective categories. For each category, the contradiction arises as a result of the thing in question being a limiting case of the way objects become more and less compact. Garcia's discussion of relativism and absolutism at the beginning of Book II describes one of the key ways in which objects become more and less compact, and then Book II itself is a comprehensive view of reality as the battleground in which kinds of entities fight back against their own relativisation or absolutisation, which amounts to their resistance to their overmining and undermining.

Relativism versus Absolutism

Perhaps the most important section at the opening of Book II of *Form and Object* is Garcia's discussion of absolutism versus relativism. He sums up his substantive discussion in this manner:

> The relativist grasps the formal system according to which each thing is equally in the world, neither more nor less than another, in order to universalise it; each object is equivalent to another object, and nothing comprehends something without being objectively comprehended in turn by what it comprehends. The absolutist grasps the universal system according to which an object comprehends other objects, but they assimilate differences into the maximal object, the universe, in order to formalise it; an object that comprehends other objects is formally superior to these other objects, thus determining them and prescribing its identity absolutely on their differences. (*FO* 160)

For Garcia, the relativist is the stock overminer and the absolutist the stock underminer. By carefully examining this discussion, we will thus be in a position both to understand Book II and to better see how Garcia's own system is paradoxically a limit case of both absolutism and relativism.

Even though Garcia discusses relativism first, we will start with absolutism, since we have already covered some of this material in Chapter 3. To understand what Garcia means when he says that the absolutist 'assimilate[s] differences into the maximal object, the universe, in order to formalise it', we must understand the connection between the universe and universality:

The universality of laws, values, and rights concerns the accumulation and order from the comprehended to the comprehending; a
physical, social, or symbolic object which comprehends other objects
relates the differences of what it comprehends to the identity of its
comprehension. It is always possible to establish an order of objects
in objects, which leads to a universe – namely, to 'the biggest possible
thing' – manifesting the maximal comprehension of differences. From
individuals to communities, from communities to societies, from societies to humanity, from humanity to nature, to God, or to an idea, from
protons and electrons to atoms, from atoms to molecules, from molecules to bodies, from bodies to stellar systems, from stellar systems to
galaxies – this objective order is processual, since it always depends on
the capacity to arrange from the comprehended to the comprehending,
by relating differences to a thing's identity, itself different from other
possible things, and assimilated into a bigger thing. The universal
is processual and antagonistic, for it is negotiated at each scale. But
the universal is *possible* and corresponds to the capacity to organise
worldly things into universal objects. (FO 158)

Much of this is fairly standard metaphysics. A universal divides up
objects in the world into those objects which instantiate the universal
(for Garcia, those which are comprehended by it) and those which
do not. A universe as a 'maximal comprehension of differences' is
a projected totality where each distinct object is differentiated from
every other object in terms of the universals which comprehend
objects. For any two distinct objects in a universe, it must be the
case that one of them is comprehended by at least one universal that
does not comprehend the other. For example, in our non-symmetric
universe considered in the presentation of the Putnam/Parmenides
argument, each object instantiated a different colour universal from
the other. Graham Priest argued that in Max Black's symmetric
universe, the two objects possess different spatial properties. For
Priest, quantum objects that possess all of the same properties are in
virtue of that not really different objects. The manner in which the
'objective order is processual' will be discussed in the next section of
this chapter. What is important here is that Garcia takes it to be the
case that when we posit a universe, we posit a universal order that
is sufficient to differentiate objects in the universe from one another.

   In the subsequent section of *Form and Object*, Garcia describes
how we come to typically know a universe as being a unity (there is
one universe), being the container of parts that interest us (such as

the Earth), and as having privileged scales that have an explanatory priority (typically the very small among reductionist thinkers). This leads us to think of a universe as the biggest possible thing that contains everything, and that is in some sense only really composed of entities at some particular scale. To be clear, none of this is absolutism for Garcia. One can talk about 'the universe' in the same way one can talk about a dog in the room using the locution 'the dog', without meaning to rule out the existence of other dogs. Context always restricts domains of quantification in this manner. Absolutism only occurs when one confuses a universe with the (the! unrestricted) world. For Garcia, one's universe is always a provisional thing. Consider the issue of fundamental scale.

> Every scalar knowledge of an atomic or subatomic universal level may lead to the illusory existence of basic, ultimate components of matter, objects smaller than everything, primary objects or universal elements of all objects and all scales. (FO 163)

This is at least reminiscent of the undermining reductionist view that Garcia contrasts with his theory of objects as differentiators. For Garcia, if objects were nothing more than their ultimate components, then there wouldn't really be anything other than those ultimate components. In the next section we will consider Garcia's particular view about the privileging of individual scales.

Now that we are reasonably clear about what a universe is for Garcia, we can characterise 'formalising' as forgetting Garcia's injunction that 'The world of this universe, its whole and its place, like the things that ultimately compose it, is only the object not of a universal knowledge, but of a strictly formal knowledge' (FO 167). The formalist tries to undermine all universals, characterising objects as different from one another without doing so in terms of universals (those things in common to different objects). Garcia argues that this is a chimerical hope.

The 'absolutist', on the other hand, falls into error by taking the universe to be the world, that which comprehends everything but is not comprehended. But for Garcia, the universe itself is an object, a differentiator between that which it comprehends and that which comprehends it. While a Garcian universe is 'processual', an actor in the antagonistic struggle not to be undermined or overmined, Garcia's world is a universal form, the non-changing inverse of each individual thing.

To obtain a very approximate representation of the way in which form connects together the singularity of each thing and a common place, one could imagine a space containing three forms of geometric objects: a square, a circle, and a triangle. By observing each one of these objects as if it were surrounded by a stencil negatively defining its form, it is possible to imagine covering up the triangle with an infinite space pierced solely by a triangular cut, the square with an infinite space pierced solely by a squared zone, and the circle with a similarly infinite space from which one could remove a corresponding circular section. Let us consider each one of these stencils with infinite extension. They are only bordered by the *inside*, an empty triangular, square or circular *inside*. Their beginning is therefore always of a different form. But their infinity (the external edge that they will never join), the space that they define entirely around this emptiness is certainly the same. Their external infinity, on the *outside*, is always identical.

They begin differently and (do not) end identically.

Such are the forms, and such is form. *Some* forms exist by the beginning and *one* form exists by the end, which never ends. (*FO* 144–5)

The argument as stated is likely to strike most as fallacious. All of the natural numbers greater than one form an infinite set, as do all of the natural numbers greater than two, yet these are not the same set. But we must remember that in Garcia's case we are talking about that which contains de-determined things. The form of the triangle-qua-thing and the form of the circle-qua-thing would be indistinguishable, because nothing differentiates the two things. And for Garcia, a universe-qua-thing is no exception. Nothing differentiates it from our triangle or circle.

This being said, in Chapter 3 I showed that Garcia himself admits that the world that he presents is also just a universe.

In other words, the fact that the world is not something makes the local progress in the knowledge of objects possible, while ultimately precluding it. Since the world is not something, a faint colour of failure always stains all human, artistic, scientific, religious, and metaphysical pictures of the world, including the one in this book. (*FO* 85)

Form and Object's metaphysical picture of the world cannot but predicate things of the world. To say of the world that nothing is predicable of it is to predicate something of it. Garcia's most audacious act, then, is to present a limiting case of absolutism. Scientific

naturalists posit their universes as the world, but they are doomed
to failure because science involves eliding the fact that every
universe (qua thing or qua object) ultimately resists that which
it contains and that which contains it. The 'world' of *Form and
Object* is the most maximal universe because it is posited as that
which ultimately resists comprehension, in that its distinguishing
feature is that nothing comprehends it. But this is a distinguishing feature, and hence a property that comprehends it. Garcia is
making of a universe a world just as the reductionist is, but his
universe is a contradictory limit of the necessary impossibility of
metaphysics. It both is and isn't the world.

Now let us examine the relativist, who 'grasps the formal system
according to which each thing is equally in the world, neither more
nor less than another, in order to universalise it' (*FO* 160). This is
the mirror image of the absolutist's formalising the universe, and
just as interesting:

> The relativist's mistake consists in confounding the universal and the
> formal, by attributing a universal character to the formal: each thing
> could *objectively* comprehend what comprehends it, thus each culture
> could comprehend its nature in the same way that nature compre-
> hends each culture. But two very distinct orders of things exist: an
> *objective* order and a *formal* order. Humanity *objectively* compre-
> hends different human cultures, while a human culture can *formally*
> comprehend humanity. The relativist aims at compactness by suppos-
> ing that what is particular does to what is universal exactly what the
> universal does to the particular. For the relativist, a universal right
> is immediately a particular right like any other, since the relativist
> considers that a particular community can prescribe a universal right
> as *one* right in the same way that a universal right can be prescribed
> to a particular community as a *universal* right. The relativist strikes
> back. (*FO* 158–9)

Defenders of universal human rights intend them to hold for all
humans and to dictate the special way that human beings ought to
be treated. Relativists strike back by first trying to argue that different particular human communities have different views about
rights, and then arguing that there is nothing that makes one community's view better than another.

The categories of Garcia's system yield an interesting explanation
of the challenge that relativistic thinking poses to universalism:

Nonetheless, what permits the universal is also what precludes it; the formal is both the condition of universality and the dissolution of the universe. At each stage of universalisation, formalisation makes possible the problem of one object's comprehension by another. For example, a social class is comprehended in a society, can comprehend this society, contain it entirely and determine it. In this way, the order from the comprehended to the comprehending is formally short-circuited. Human nature comprehends different cultures, but each culture comprehends human nature and fashions it in turn. Formal equality may thus potentially block the order of universality at each stage. (*FO* 158)

If this is understood as a challenge to the universal in question, the short-circuiting is not a mistake. Human nature as a universal is supposed to be true of all humans. But an anthropological account of how human nature is standardly understood differently in different cultures invalidates the idea that there is a universal human nature if it is the case that each different culture correctly understands (successfully comprehends) human culture. If two parties to a disagreement are both correct, then no one is.

Garcia's 'short circuit' is when comprehension becomes symmetric (when A comprehends B and B also comprehends A). Note that since comprehension is transitive (if A comprehends B and B comprehends C, then A comprehends C) any 'loop' in comprehension entails symmetry. Say there is a chain of A_1, A_2 ... A_n where each A_i comprehends A_{i-1} and the chain loops with A_1 comprehending A_n. Then consider some arbitrary A_i which, by assumption, comprehends A_{i-1}, which by assumption also comprehends A_{i-2}. Since comprehension is transitive, A_{i-1} also comprehends A_{i-3}, A_{i-4} ... all the way to A_1. But since A_1 also comprehends A_n it follows that A_{i-1} also comprehends A_{n-1}, A_{n-2}, A_{n-3} ... all the way back to A_i. So we have that if A_i comprehends A_{i-1} then A_{i-1} also comprehends A_i. Symmetry. This kind of reasoning is perfectly general (in the presence of a loop), and will work for any A that comprehends any B.

Note also that transitivity and symmetry together entail reflexivity for any entity that is in the relation to something else. By symmetry we have that if A comprehends B, then B comprehends A. But by transitivity, if A comprehends B and B comprehends A, it follows that A comprehends A. This wouldn't work for no-matter-what or formal matter, since they don't comprehend anything in the first place. But every other kind of entity does for Garcia. This is why Garcia will mention compactness, self-comprehension, in cases where comprehension short-circuits. The relativist 'aims at compactness' by pushing the universal in question into something that would have to be self-comprehending. Earlier in the text, Garcia marks the connection between the relativist's short circuit and compactness by writing, 'Compactness short-circuits the very *meaning* of things' (FO 120).

As noted earlier, much of the drama in Book II is between different attempts to naturalistically explain phenomena such as death, gender, or adolescence in terms of the preferred scale of the naturalist's universe (absolutist undermining) and attempts to explain those same phenomena in terms of the cultural role played by them (relativistic overmining). For Garcia, the manner in which objects resist the objects that comprehend them and that they comprehend leads to their ability to resist being explained in terms of these other objects. More striking is the manner in which the object itself can change in response to our attempts to subject it to such short-circuiting. Our very understanding of adolescence as a liminal moment between youth and adulthood produces more liminal moments between youth and adolescence and adolescence and adulthood. But then adolescence is no longer a liminal moment but rather itself a stage on life's way.

For Garcia, 'formalisation' is simply the process of realising that objects exist as things on his flat plane of equality. Formalisation 'makes possible' the short circuit of comprehension simply because it guarantees that the comprehended is a distinct object. But to the extent that formalisation succeeds, the object in question tends towards the compact. Because of this, Garcia argues that a consistent, complete relativism is impossible. 'The relativist's mistake' is thinking that universality could be completely eschewed. But the only way to do that would be to universalise the relativism, which is not to eschew universals.

> Some universals exist for the relativist, since they need a *plane* to 'place on the same plane' things that they make equal. This plane of equality, this plate on which the relativist places what they make relative, is the formal world, the flat world where each thing is equal to another. But the relativist makes this world (where each thing is *solitary*) a universe where things are *together* equal to, and comparable with, each other. Thus, the relativist universalises the formal. (FO 159)

The relativist initially wants to stress differences that are elided by universals. A genuine notion of universal human rights only works if differences between groups of people are ignored. The relativist tries to undermine the universal in favour of the particular. But the limit case of this would simply be the flat plane of equality where no universals exist to differentiate things.

But what in fact happens, what must happen, is that the relativist ends up enforcing new universals. The relativist's motivation to respect cultural difference cannot rest with cultural practices that do not respect difference. The queer theorist who tries to short-circuit gender by seeing it as a cultural imposition ends up placing the normative requirement on people that they should be iconoclastic and independent with respect to their own manifestations of gender. But this is merely another universalising gender role! The universal is in fact a paradigmatic Garcian object. It will not be overmined away.

Since relativism mirrors absolutism, we must also ask whether Garcia's own system is a limiting case of formalising the universe (treating it as world is also a limiting case of universalising the formal). Remember that Garcia admits to his own system being of necessity another failed case of absolutism. He doesn't make such an admission with respect to formalism. But nonetheless, he does constantly discuss things in ways that are prohibited by his injunction that things are solitary. For example:

> Formally, more and more things quite simply are, since what begins to be possible never stops being possible. More and more things can only be insofar as nothing stops being possible, nothing ever stops being something, though new things ceaselessly begin to be. Things always begin to be and always end in the world.
>
> Things do not go outside the world or stop beginning to be in the world.
>
> *Formally*, things accumulate since more and more things are between things. However, more things are never in the world (since only one thing is in the world at one time). (FO 93–4)

In the same passage, he says that there are more things and that things are solitary. The solitude of a thing is supposed to prevent us from counting it, since counting is only possible relative to the kind of properties comprehending an object. But he continually talks of the formal flat plane of equality consisting of things, things in the plural, meaning more than one of them.

This is a big problem for Garcia. If each thing is a de-determined object, then there should be at least as many things as there are objects. But this means that there is a plurality of things. If, in addition, there are no things that are not simultaneously objects, it should be the case that there are *exactly as many* things as objects.

Garcia would retort that 'the number of objects' makes no sense. One can have a number of some kind of thing, such as heads or neurons, but not a number of objects. Likewise, we should not automatically assume that he accepts the manner in which most contemporary mathematicians currently define 'equinumerosity' (the same number as) in terms of a function uniquely pairing entities in two collections, even when the collections are infinite. But I think Garcia's presumed responses would be beside the point. We can start with a finite number of a certain kind of object, such as five heads. If each of them is simultaneously a de-determined thing, then we would seem to have five things. Or perhaps more to the point, if things are supposed to be the glue that connects the relational structure of comprehensions to the placeholders in that structure, there should be more than one of them. If they all were glued to the same object, then the proponent of the Putnam/ Parmenides argument has won. There would be just one thing after all.

When Garcia articulates the bottom part of his metaphysics, things comprehending no-matter-what/formal matter, he has to violate his own doctrines about what one can say about things. In presenting a picture of a flat world of de-determined things presupposed by the objective universe, he must present those things together as the collection of de-determined objects (and an entity-qua-thing is just a de-determined entity-qua-object). But to present them as a collection of objects, determined or otherwise, is to somehow think of them as possessing different properties from one another. We think of them as being lined up in a row, occupying different spaces, or made out of different matter. But to do that is to universalise them!

Thus, we see Garcia's own system as consisting of contradictory limit cases of absolutism and relativism. The universal cannot be formalised and the formal cannot be universalised, except in the case where the property in question is that of having no properties. In this case the embrace of failure is what guarantees the success.

The objective realm of comprehended and comprehending is the battlefield between universalism and relativism, neither of which wins:

> Far from concluding with a description of a formal world where differences between things have been reduced to zero, this book aims to assemble this description of a flat world of things that can match the antagonistic reconstruction – between universalism and relativism – of the magnitudes, values, depths, variations, and interests of present objects, accumulated endlessly, and contested by several methodological approaches. (FO 6)

But at the furthest limit of this realm, the world as universal container and matter as the universal contained, absolutism and relativism are both true and false.

Of course, accumulation and contestation are processes that take place in time and involve relations of more or less, as victory is partially secured and squandered. So making sense of Garcia's antagonistic realm requires making sense of his theories of temporality and of the intensive world of more and less. I will present these in the next chapter. But first I want to explore an additional worry about Garcia's views of objective matter and the universe.

Objective Matter

The most philosophically substantive claim that Garcia makes about matter is offered in passing:

> It is an obvious fact that there is an infinite (but not indefinite) progress in the scientific investigation of the 'matter' region. Of course, fundamental physics does not aim to discover the simple and primary absolute, but to transform – and to describe how to effect the transformation – the fundamental into a composite, matter into an object. The aim of a science of matter, and of its multiple subdivisions, is not to study matter in itself, but rather to understand how matter can take on the appearance of objects, how what appeared as a buffer to the *fundamental* is always a result. Therefore, there is something in what we believed was nothing knowable. (FO 132–3)

The process which Garcia baldly asserts to be infinite is the process of explaining the dispositional properties of objects at one spatial scale in terms of the behaviour of objects at a smaller spatial scale. We understand chemicals in terms of the behaviour of their atoms, then understand the behaviour of atoms in terms of the behaviour of subatomic particles, and perhaps understand the behaviour of subatomic particles in terms of something even smaller.

Although taking this process to be infinite is quite a metaphysical commitment, Garcia's description of it is not antecedently implausible:

> A science of matter is a science of the way in which the matter of objects proves to be a complex of objects. This very matter must in turn become a complex of smaller, more fundamental objects. (*FO* 133)

This objective (as opposed to formal) matter is just the undifferentiated stuff one talks about as constituting the objects at the smallest scale of objects one is talking about. The history of physics is the history of successively differentiating objective matter, and making the scale at which objects are differentiated from objective matter smaller and smaller.

Formal matter is in some respects the undifferentiated stuff still there after the objects have been scaled down to the infinitely small: 'matter is to particles what form [world] is to the universe'. Formal matter, the matter that is comprehended by entities-qua-things, comprehends nothing. Thus, unlike objective matter, it cannot be differentiated into smaller sets of objects.

There are different ways one could articulate the connection between formal and objective matter, depending upon how one articulates the infinite progress of smaller and smaller objective scales to which Garcia is committed. If one thinks of the infinity as in some sense already there, then formal matter is in some sense that which is still undifferentiated upon the completion of the infinite set of differentiations. On the other hand, if one thinks of the infinite progress as merely a potential infinity, then one might think of formal matter as that which we problematically objectify when we treat it as the undifferentiated stuff at the smallest scale humans have achieved. Garcia himself suggests the latter course in a rather, given his other commitments, surprising way.

> A science is the establishment of properties specific to the way in which a higher-level object comprehends lower-level objects: for instance,

how protons, neutrons, and electrons make up the atom, how atoms make up the molecule, and, possibly, how the graviton may be the effect of a string with wave amplitude zero, generated by a closed string, and so on. In a scalar knowledge like that of contemporary physics, these properties only make sense step by step, from one level of comprehension to a higher or lower level. In this way, an atom may be inside a molecule, a proton inside the nucleus of an atom, and quarks inside a proton, even though quarks did not exist *as such* in a molecule; it is necessary to pass through the atomic division for quarks to be.

Imagine a straight line. On this straight line, we divide a line segment AB. Then we point to the middle of this line segment called C. The location of point C already existed on the straight line, but point C could only be determined, *as the midpoint between A and B*, once A and B were established on the straight line. In the same way, the midpoint D between C and B did not exist *as such* on the line segment AB; its properties only appear once the line segment BC was divided within the line segment AB. (*FO* 164–5)

Garcia is trying to somehow split the difference between anti-realist and realist views of theoretical posits in the sciences of the very small. Objects such as photons do not 'exist *as such*' prior to our ability to theorise about them and manipulate them. But this doesn't mean they are mere fictions.

Therefore, particle science discovers neither objects nor particles, which absolutely preexist particle science's examination of them. It does not invent or project these objects in nature. A science divides these objects in the universe step by step. (*FO* 164)

Somehow, when the matter/form distinction is renegotiated at another scale, the new entities informing the matter (and to be clear, for Garcia what we take to be geometric form will be a constituent and hence an object constituting part of the matter) are neither discovered nor invented or projected.

As far as I can make sense of what Garcia is saying in passages such as this, he is articulating a *very* Kantian view. He seems to be simply taking Kant's view of the divisibility of space (articulated in response to one of the antinomies in the *Critique of Pure Reason*'s Dialectic) as *potentially* infinite and applying it not just to spatial divisibility, but to the very objects we find at the smaller and smaller spatial scales. This being said, Priest shows in *Beyond the Limits of Thought* that the Kantian account of potential infinity is inconsistent with the very limit arguments that Garcia uses to establish that no-matter-what is something. The Domain Principle, discussed in Chapter 3 above, straightforwardly entails that anyone who talks about a potential infinity is committed to a completed infinity. Consider:

Priest's Domain Principle:
For any claim of the form 'all *x*s are so and so' to have determinate sense, there must be a determinate totality over which the quantifier ranges. We refer to this totality and so must include it to the group of objects over which we might quantify.

If this is true, then anyone who makes the claim that for any number there is a greater number (something to which defenders of potential infinity are committed) is also committed to the existence of the infinite totality of numbers.

I cannot possibly solve substantive debates about the nature of infinity here. However, Garcia's picture of objective reality as that which gives rise to, and preserves itself in the face of, an unending antagonistic battle between overmining/relativism and undermining/absolutism remains unaffected, as does the picture of limit contradictions at both the top and bottom of the universe. The only reason I present the worry about a potential versus a completed infinity is because honesty compels me to do so. Garcia's hints of neo-Kantianism fly in the face of my general interpretation of him as a radical post-Hegelian thinker. While this problem is not dispositive here, we will see in Chapter 9 that his attempt to split the difference between discovery and creation does raise serious issues with respect to his account of values. First, however, we must consider Garcia's account of intensity.

Notes

1. In 'Meillassoux's Dilemma', Joshua Heller and I argue that Meillassoux does not really succeed in abandoning finitude. When trying to make sense of the distinction between primary and secondary qualities as well as the way we can have knowledge of the distant past, he does reject finitude in the usual speculative manner by considering the totality of all human world correlates as a totality. However, his argument

for universal contingency relies on the inadmissibility of this very manoeuvre when applied to the totality of the possible. As Heller and I show, Meillassoux tries to motivate the restriction by noting how it blocks paradoxes of totality. But his critique of dialetheist approaches to paradoxes already assumes universal contingency. Meillassoux's argument is thus a perfect circle. At least as things stand, Priest and Garcia as philosophers of the infinite, on the one hand, and Harman as a speculative philosopher of finitude, on the other, have the decided advantage.

2. Harman, *Quentin Meillassoux*, p. 4.

8

Neither Substance Nor Process III: Events, Time, and Life

Thus far we have focused on four key Garcian tropes, his anti-reductionist, differential model of objects; embrace of limit contradictions; divorce of unity and being; and the related understanding of reality as bifurcating into formal (entities-qua-things) and objective (entities-qua-objects) modes. Garcia's fifth fundamental idea does not enter the book until his discussion of events in Chapter II of *Form and Object*'s Book II, where he introduces the notion of intensity. In both his flat formal world and the infinitely nested matryoshka-doll objective world, there is no room for gradations of more or less. Entities-qua-objects have numerosity and thus give rise to cardinality facts about whether one collection contains more of some kind of object than another. But greater or lesser cardinality is not the same thing as possessing more or less of some quality. When Garcia talks of 'intensity', he always means the latter.[1]

Garcia's account of intensity is just as bold and innovative as the other key planks of his system. For Garcia, intensity finds its metaphysical home in the comprehension relation itself. Events are instances of comprehension (some object comprehending another) that are *present*. The ordering of events into time is a by-product of varying intensities of presence. The difference between living things and non-living things is grounded in the intensity of the differentiation between that which is comprehended and that which comprehends. Below, I explain how each of these things work for Garcia. Even though I am not producing a detailed commentary on Book II of *Form and Object*, I think the reader will get an idea from my discussion of events, time, and the living of how Garcia's world of events fits with his world of things/objects.

Before beginning this discussion, I must be very clear about two important Garcian tropes. First, Garcia sometimes uses event language to mark vagueness. For example, in his discussion of animal species in Chapter V of Book II he writes: 'But we must understand that the present-day objective conditions of defining living things lead us to consider living things as a set of events, and not as a set of objects' (FO 206). According to evolutionary theory, speciation takes place over several generations. There is no clear place, for example, where God could look down at the evolutionary history leading up to *homo sapiens* and in a reasonable way determine that the children all of a sudden start getting souls while the creatures of their parents' generation didn't.[2] Each generation of offspring is the same species as its parents.

Garcia responds to vagueness by asserting that the phenomenon in question (such as evolution) concerns events rather than objects because events are the primary locus of intensity for Garcia, and paradigm cases of vagueness involve indeterminacy in the degree to which an object must possess an intensive property for us to categorise it as possessing that property. One object can be hotter than another without either of them being hot. But how much hotness is required for something to be hot? The existence of borderline cases, one of the key markers for vagueness, often holds in virtue of the fact that possessing the property is a function of crossing some vague threshold of possessing an intensive property.

A full account would compare Garcia's accounts of intensive phenomena with recent analytic work[3] on 'ontic vagueness', vagueness that is taken to exist in some sense in the world, not merely with respect to our language, concepts, or knowledge (as if those things are not in the world). Garcia's remarks on vagueness are particularly interesting in this context because there is a sense in which he supports an ontological theory of vagueness without supporting an ontic one. Being/comprehension or their presence is what gets intensified. Entities-qua-things are never intensified. But, on the other hand, since entities-qua-objects themselves are mere differentiators from the objects they comprehend and those that comprehend them, entities-qua-objects (as we will see, in the case of living things) can intensify themselves.

The other, much more dominant, Garcian trope is the manner in which almost all of the chapters in Book II contain histories of the way we have understood the kind of object discussed in that chapter. We must of necessity elide much of this here, in part because Garcia's vision is so synoptic, yet simultaneously detailed. In each case, the dialectical progress (and lack thereof) leads to the kind of perverse speculative moment where our inability to generate a certain kind of satisfying explanation reflects something about the phenomena in question. In my final chapter, the discussion of gender, adolescence, and death, enough will be on the table to fairly interpret some of Garcia's genealogies. In this chapter, I merely focus on how intensity works, and in the next I will interpret and critique Garcia's statements about value. One of the nice results of my discussion of intensity is that we will finally be in a position to fully sketch a strategy for how Garcia might respond to Harman's critique. For, as I interpret him, Harman is not merely worried that Garcia might fall into metaphysical holism, but also that Garcia's system lacks the resources to differentiate what most of us would take to be genuine objects from ersatz ones.

Events (Presence)

Continental philosophers talking about 'the problem of the event' tend to focus on how humans can make sense of extreme novelty. A canonical example of this is Badiou's *Being and Event*. Those who translate Heidegger's *ereignis* as an event of something or other (appropriation, truth, becoming, and so on) often mean something different, dating back to 'the affection argument' posed by early German idealists against Kant. It goes like this: To solve Hume's sceptical attack on causality, Kant took causality to be the result of the human mind structuring its realm of appearances. But then it makes no sense to talk (as Kant does) about the realm of appearances itself as being caused by the admixture of the human mind and external reality. One might think of the Heideggerian/German idealist problem of the event as a limiting case of the Badiouian one. What could be more novel than the uncaused pseudo-genesis of the world of appearances? Adrian Johnston's animadversions against 'negative theology', quoted in Chapter 1 above, are aimed at philosophers inhabiting this problem space.

Garcia quickly works to distance the second chapter of *Form and Object*'s Book II from the Badiouian and Heideggerian problematics:

> Let's consider an event such as a murder. Suppose a person kills another person. In a policed society, a murder may be an exceptional event, or during wartime a common event. But the properties of an

event are not affected by one claiming that an event is an exception or a rule. We must not conflate an event with an exception. (*FO* 172)

Garcia does not take it upon himself to dissolve attempts to philosophise about how the human mind can make sense of radical novelty. He just thinks it is misleading to label such projects philosophies of events.

In analytic philosophy, there are four interrelated problems that get covered by philosophies of events: (1) differentiating events from, or assimilating them to, other ontological types such as objects, facts, properties, and times;[4] (2) characterising principles and entities by which individual events and event types are individuated (for Donald Davidson, events are differentiated by their role as causes, and for Jaegwon Kim, who takes events to be facts, they are differentiated in terms of the objects or properties composing them and the time of their occurrence); (3) determining how best to logically represent parts of language, such as verbs and adverbs in English, that are implicated in events; and (4) dividing up the set of events into significant subsets, such as (traditionally) activities, accomplishments, achievements, and states.

Comparing Garcia's view of events with various doctrines offered by participants in the four analytic debates just mentioned would probably be a fruitful exercise, albeit not one that I shall attempt here. For our purposes, what is most important is the way Garcia uses his discussion of events to introduce presence as an intensive concept, something of which entities can possess more or less. Intensive presence turns out to be a core component of his theories of time, life, and animality.

For Garcia, reality consists of both objects and events. A universe consisting merely of objects would be one where 'everything is equally present':

> Imagine a universe that would only comprehend objects. In this universe, the deed exists, the murderer killed their victim; the murderer, the victim, the motive, the weapon, the armchair bathed in blood, and so on, also exist. Everything exists in the form of objects, which are present, like wax figurines of a macabre tale. Even the moment when the murderer strikes their victim and the moment when the victim collapses exist. It is not that nothing moves, that nothing comes to life in this world of objects; it is that everything is equally present. In a world of objects, everything is certainly in the world, but nothing is *either*

more or less in the world. What has been and what will be are equal, and equally objects.

Yet, even in the eyes of a god, the universe is never a series of objects, such that all is a deed, is accomplished, and that nothing becomes. A universe of objects is a universe of presentless presence. In, prior to, and subsequent to this universe, one obtains objects that are before or after other objects, in a fixed, eternal causal series, but never past, future, or present. (*FO* 173)

Such a world is the world of the eternalist about time, whom Garcia discusses in the subsequent chapter ('Time'). Garcia criticises such views for not distinguishing the present from past in intuitive ways. He provocatively poses the question of how we currently know that we are not mistaken about it being the present, that we are in fact not really in a past moment? If we do know that something is privileged and different about the present moment, there must be some difference between present and past. But Garcia thinks that we will only be able to make such differentiations if the universe comprehends not only objects but events, which can possess more or less presence.

Garcia also criticises the view that there are only really events, which is one way to interpret process philosophers, since events of change are the primary kinds of differences that make up their relational metaphysics:

In this [the process philosopher's] universe, a doing exists; the murderer kills the victim. But prior to the doing, something like 'a murderer', 'a victim', or 'a weapon' did not exist. The murderer was born, grew up, and one day encountered her victim. We separate these many events by producing substances or objects, identities such as the identity of the 'murderer', which blocks the path of all that took place in the stable and objective person. In this universe, a person tightens their arm, but neither the person nor arm exist, since people and arms are effects of a series of events. The brief tightening of the arm, all that happens and takes place exists. But nothing resembling an object – what can be present or absent – exists. Only modes of absence and presence, ways of being present and becoming present, exist, but nothing exists to be these modes. Action is primary and exclusive, rather than the acted or the acting. In this universe, a murdererless and victimless murder that one commits exists; merely the murderer's action and the victim's death exist.

> An evential universe is a universe that dissolves the consistency of objects into objective modes of presence, gradually reduced to being mere changing effects of presence. Some present ultimately exists in this universe, but nothing exists to be present. (*FO* 174)

This is the conclusion of the Putnam/Parmenides argument we considered in Chapter 5.

If we accept that we need another category of entities in the universe, we must immediately ask how to characterise these entities and how they relate to entities to which we are already committed. From an analytical perspective, Garcia talks very little about the first question, and a fair amount about the second. Remember that the world of objects is primordially structured by the comprehension relationship. Of any two objects, either one comprehends the other or it doesn't, and it is never the case that both comprehend each other. For Garcia, an event is the presence of an object being comprehended. This is very close to, if not a version of, the view in analytic philosophy that events are facts. Garcia writes:

> Whereas an object is present (or absent), an event self-presents (or self-absents): a knife is here or there, but a knife does not happen or take place. What happens is *that someone took a knife* or *that someone dropped a knife*. The taking of the knife is an object insofar as it is or is not present (is there or is there not someone in the process of taking a knife?), but its presence and the way in which it is present are an event. In this way, the red armchair is certainly an object, although the fact that the armchair is red (that it is red for only a minute, that it has always been red, that it is increasingly more or increasingly less red) is an event. (*FO* 173)

The fact that an object is comprehended by another object is an event, which can be more or less present. In Garcia's discussion of events it is not clear what he means by an event being more or less present, other than the fact that it is instances of comprehension/ being that are more or less present. But what is presence? This becomes clearer in Garcia's account of time (discussed below), if only because of the work to which he puts it there.

Early in the chapter, Garcia explicitly discusses presence and absence. Perhaps the most interesting thing he says involves making the speculative move with respect to presence itself:

> But the fact that things are present for me, or for us, is enough to assume that presence is in the universe. Since I am a part of the universe, the fact that presence is *for me* sufficiently demonstrates that presence is *for the universe*. (FO 168)

This is an important part of his critique of eternalism. If subjective time can be made sense of in terms of how the experienced present is maximally present, then there already is a time in the universe where the present has a privileged position. But then the eternalist's claim that the universe does not contain privileged present moments is false.

Garcia also distinguishes between two kinds of absence in the opening section of the chapter. The first is emptiness, where some A comprehends some B, yet B is not in A. An example of this might be the citizen of a country who is so disgusted by the hypocritical mismatch between the ideals and the realities of that country that she no longer identifies as a citizen of it, even when the country counts her as a citizen. She is comprehended by her country, yet herself does not instantiate the country. The second is exile, where some B is (in) some A, yet A does not comprehend B. Here the person identifies herself as that nationality, yet is not recognised as such by her country.

Garcia's remarks about the difference between exile and emptiness (FO 169–71) are extraordinarily sketchy. In fact it's ultimately impossible to make sense of them. If being and comprehension are simply inverses of one another, what sense does it make to say that A's being B can be more absent than B's comprehending A? If presence and absence were properties of objects, as opposed to properties of an object's comprehension, it would be easy to make the difference. An object can be absent from that which comprehends it (the citizen is absent from her country), or from that which it comprehends (the country is absent from some of its citizens). An exile is then a citizen of an absent country and the country with its absent citizen is empty. But here emptiness and exile would themselves be inverses: A is empty of B to exactly the extent that B is an exile of A, and Garcia never suggests this. Moreover, in his official account of events, which follows the discussion, objects are not more or less present. What is more or less present is the relation of comprehension between objects.

At the end of the section discussing absence, Garcia hedges substantially. Consider his example of emptiness, a non-present lover:

By accumulating the memory of my lover, which is with me, and the fact that my lover is currently elsewhere, I create the chimera of an absence, an emptiness, or a being that I comprehend within me, but which is not with me. In reality, my lover is not absent, since I must relate to her memory or to the projection that I make of her actual, distant being: her memory or image is present for me. Strictly speaking, of course, my lover is neither her memory nor her image. But since I can identify my lover with what she is in my memory or in my imagination, I can lack her, I can artificially comprehend her, contain her inside me without her being there inside me. This is what we call emptiness. (*FO* 170–1)

When philosophers differentiate strict from loose speaking, something fishy is always going on. And, indeed, Garcia amplifies this with the conclusion of the section, when he writes: 'While presence is real, absences are only subjective operations on reality. Absences exist no less than presence, although differently' (*FO* 171). But if absence is the converse of presence, it makes no sense to say that presence is real and absence is only a subjective operation. Luckily, the supposed distinction between exile and emptiness doesn't actually do any work in the other chapters (III–V) that centrally involve intensity. In those chapters the relevant entities are simply more or less. To the extent that we would talk about absence in those contexts, it is merely in terms of lack of presence.

Time (Intensive Presence)

Garcia begins his discussion of time by contrasting the two dominant positions in analytic philosophy: eternalism and presentism. As I have already noted, eternalists take the present, past, and future to all exist in the same manner. For the presentist, on the other hand, only the present really exists. Garcia dismisses both views rather quickly:

In the absence of a complete time, things are not organised into objects and events. If there were no present, but only an order of deeds, everything would merely be objects. If no past or future existed apart from the present, everything would merely be momentary events, and there would be no objects (we would never see a chair, but simply that a chair is there right now).

Since the formal system of things does not work without an objective system of objects and events, time must be both the present and some order of past events. (*FO* 178–9)

He doesn't give arguments for the claims that presentism is a form of process philosophy (that if the past and future do not exist, everything is events) and that eternalism does not make sense of the way in which events occur (that if there is no present, everything is objects). However, from his discussion it is clear that he thinks that eternalism fails what we can call the speculative test in the following way. Eternalism must differentiate subjective from objective time. Subjectively, the present is privileged, though there is no objective difference between the present, past, and future. But since the subject too is part of nature, this is just an admission that eternalism is false. Garcia's animadversions against presentism seem to stem from the conviction that it does not make sense of the way in which objects are identical over time. If the past does not exist, objects are constantly in the process of being destroyed and created *ex nihilo*.

To accommodate these desiderata, Garcia amends the Growing Block-Universe Theory (GBUT) of time first articulated by C. D. Broad in 1923:

> The past and present really exist, but the future does not exist. The universe continually grows in presence, like a perpetually expanding block: 'when an event becomes, it *comes into existence*; and it was not anything at all until it had become'.[5] The present is thus this coming into existence. The universe can only expand with presence; everything happens and nothing ever disappears. (*FO* 179)

Broad's theory combines eternalism about the past with presentism about the future. The past exists just as the present does, and the future does not exist. Interestingly, this fits with the feeling Garcia enunciates several times in *Form and Object* that 'the sum total of everything that is present ceaselessly grows' (*FO* 180).

Garcia builds on a recent criticism of Craig Bourne's[6] to amend the basic GBUT picture:

> GBUT produces two presents instead of one: the present that each moment had been and that each moment always is; and the present of these presents, the objective and punctual present. But from the present of my present moment, I will never obtain the objective

present; nothing assures me that I am not already in the past thinking that I am still 'now'. Nothing guarantees me that my present, which I live and experience as actual, is not an already dead present; nothing guarantees me that I am not *deceived* by time. And in such cases the venom of hyperbolic doubt always regains its effectiveness. (*FO* 181)

By thinking of the present as just the most recent slice of time, GBUT arguably suffers from one of the same problems as eternalism, not accommodating the manner in which the present now is different from previous nows. Since Garcia has already argued that subjective time is time, he is able to pose this in a striking way. If GBUT is true, there is absolutely no guarantee that my subjective present isn't in fact the objective past. On the assumption of GBUT, for all I know, the universe in some sense already contains several future versions of me experiencing their presents. GBUT just presents a series of eternalist universes with most of their presents not differentiated from the others.

Garcia's solution to this problem is almost deceptively simple, ordering time according to amount of presence, with events in the actual present always possessing the most presence:

> The past is not an *absolute* non-presence, but a *relative* non-presence. The past is what is less present than the present. It follows that the present is always *the maximum of presence.*
>
> What we call present is *the greatest presence*: what cannot be more present. Presence is the being and comprehension of things in each other, when one thing is in another. The present is *the maximal state of the being and comprehension of things.*
>
> Consequently, the past corresponds to the overtaken present, to the present that is not what is *more* present any more; the past is, it exists objectively, but is a lesser presence. Insofar as it is a process, the past is all that weakens in presence. The more the past passes, the less it is present. But we know, and not only because we have faculties of memory, that the past is not purely absent: it is a state of increasingly weaker presence. (*FO* 183)

Thus, Garcia is able to differentiate past from present by deploying a resource already introduced in his theory of events, the presence of comprehension, by intensifying it. Memory then becomes a kind of direct perception of the comprehension of objects by other objects, with the comprehension more absent the more past something is. For Garcia, objects contain other objects less as time passes. The difference between the current and the past pen is entirely the result of the current pen being comprehended more by its properties, such as blackness. But, with the GBUT theorist, Garcia is able to accommodate the difference between the present and the future by holding that future events are maximally absent, having zero presence.

Garcia recognises one seemingly paradoxical consequence of this view. If the future is maximally absent, and time is measured by amounts of absence, then there is less time between past events and the future and present events and the future. Consider five temporally ordered events T_1, T_2, T_3, T_4, and T_5, with T_4 being an event taking place in the present and T_5 an event taking place in the future. Let $p(x)$ denote the amount of presence of a given event (really the presence of the relevant fact's comprehension relation). Then we have $p(T_1) < p(T_2) < p(T_3) < p(T_4)$. But if $p(T_5)$ is equal to zero then $p(T_1)$ is closer to the future than the present is! Garcia explicitly denies that the future comes after the present.

> Rather, one ought to think about every present event as being at the top of an infinite stack of sheets of paper. The future is the foundation, the ground on which the stack of paper rests. The present is the sheet at the top. Each time that a new sheet covers up the prior sheet, any particular sheet in the middle of the pile, a 'past sheet', moves further from the top, which is situated higher and higher. But the distance that separates our 'past sheet' from the foundation – from the ground, however far that it may be, perhaps even infinitely far (if one assumes that time has no beginning, that no pure future or pure primordial absence had ever been) – never changes. (*FO* 185–6)

For Garcia, this is a sensible thing to hold, because 'the future' names a state of maximal possibility, with each event narrowing down the set of possibilities available to objects. When I was a child I might have grown up to be a soldier. But this future became increasingly distant the more my life experiences and choices made this less and less likely.

Garcia's own philosophy of time exists more in the realm of *possibilia* than actuality. There are at least three important issues. First, in defending the claim that the past is closer to the future than the present, Garcia ends up in fact giving us a separate account of temporal ordering. On the one hand, of two events that have presence (and so are not future), the one with less presence is temporally prior to the one with more presence. On the other hand, of two events a and b that are causally connected, if a's set of active possibilities is a proper subset of b's, then b is temporally prior to a. Garcia clearly sees a connection between the two accounts, for example:

> Recalling my birth, before I became what I am, is to extract this event from the order of the past, from the progressive weakening of its presence in relation to the present, and to consider it in relation to the future. In relation to the future, my birth has remained what it was – an event whose consequences and continuation are indeterminate. (FO 185)

Temporal order is *both* the increase of presence and the decrease of indeterminacy. But Garcia does not provide a theory of possibility and necessity (to be fair, a tall order for anyone), so the reader cannot easily evaluate this marriage. Would a worked-out theory of greater and lesser indeterminacy obviate the need to bring in intensities of presence? It is not clear.

Second, Garcia does not provide a detailed theory of how objects retain their identity through change. In Chapter 5, we focused on the role that entities-qua-things play in blocking the Putnam/Parmenides argument to metaphysical holism. But Harman's criticisms actually focused much more on the difficulty process philosophers have making sense of how the same entity exists over time. Let us reconsider part of Harman's criticism of process philosophy:

> What object-oriented philosophy rejects in this philosophical current is its tendency to treat entities as purely relational or agential. For Whitehead, entities turn out to be nothing more than their relations; for Latour, they turn out to be nothing more than the sum total of their effects on other entities. As a result, there are no enduring things for these two philosophers, but only perishing instantaneous 'actual occasions' (Whitehead) or actors that exist in one time and one place only (Latour).[7]

Garcia's ontological liberality allows him to retort[8] that his philosophy has room for perishing objects and objects that persist over time. If 'no-matter-what is something', then changing objects are something. However, Harman's problem is that he cannot see how Garcia's model of objects as differences between that which they comprehend and that which comprehends them can make room for changing objects. When a white armchair becomes red, then something that was comprehended by whiteness becomes something comprehended by redness. If entities are merely differences, then we have distinct objects, and Garcia faces the same problem that Whitehead and Latour do.

I do think Garcia has a good response. First, as I have already noted, if I could change one translational decision, it would be the decision to homophonically render the French *différence* as 'difference' in these contexts. For Garcia, objects are not mere differences, but rather differentiators. That which differentiates the armchair's constituents from its properties can continue to do so when it goes from being comprehended by whiteness to being comprehended by redness. And Garcia clearly thinks that his formal ontology of things plays a key role in making this possible:

> Objects and events never communicate between each other, but only through things; the armchair in the room and the fact that the armchair became red are only related to the fact that the armchair is 'something'. Several objects never yield an event and an event is never composed of objects; objects are among objects and events are among events, but events and objects only communicate through things. Given all the objects of a murder, I can never derive an event from the murder, the fact that the murder *happened*. I can never decompose the event, in which one person kills another, into fixed objects, but only into earlier events in some causal chain. Things connect the chains of events to the pictures of objects. Each object is a thing and each event is also a thing. Given that the armchair is red, I can infer that the armchair is some *thing*, that the redness is equally some *thing*, as is the red armchair. So, given the object that the red chair in this room is, I can obtain these same *things*. (FO 175)

Here it is clear that entities-qua-things are in some sense playing another role played by Aristotelian primary substance, that of being the same even as the object changes. On Garcia's picture, the armchair is comprehended by both red and white, but the fact of it being comprehended by red has more presence than the fact of it being comprehended by white. The armchair itself is that which differentiates that which it comprehends from those things that comprehend it. Qua object, the armchair differentiates itself from (among other objects) redness and whiteness (with different levels of intensity of comprehension), but qua thing it differentiates itself from its matter and world.

One might still be dissatisfied, thinking that Garcia owes us more of a story to differentiate genuine objects such as our armchair from ersatz ones such as the mereological sum of the redness of the armchair and the flash of the weapon. 'No-matter-what is something' seems to license both as equally objects/things and to end the story there. I suspect that Harman would retain this worry even in light of my decision to retroactively change the translation of *différence*. In the concluding paragraphs of the next section I will suggest a way out of this problem for Garcia.

A third, and final, worry concerns exactly how the ordering of the intensity of presence takes place. Do past events retain the intensity of their presence, and each new present event just becomes more and more intense, to infinity? Or do past events lose intensity as the future progresses? Garcia does not clearly differentiate, and both models present problems. The first model seems to inherit a problem related to the one Garcia levelled against GBUT. When I was thinking about Harman's criticism fifteen minutes ago it didn't seem in any way less intense at the time than me thinking about this sentence now. My remembering of earlier events is less intense than my current experience, but at the time the experience certainly didn't seem any less intense. How do I know that my current thinking is not really taking place in the past?

So let's opt for the other version, with intensity decreasing as events sink into the past. But there are dangers here too. First, it seems as if we have two timelines now, the time in which new present events are popping into existence with maximal presence and the time in which earlier events are slowly losing presence. And this causes a problem for the view that temporal ordering of two events is entirely a function of intensity of presence. I want to say that the armchair being red occurs after the armchair being white because the being of the first fact has a more intense presence, but on the declining presence model this is not true. On this model, five minutes ago the armchair being white had just as much presence as the armchair being red does now! It's just that *now* the intensity of it being white is so much less. But if this is how the model is supposed to go, we clearly cannot derive a temporal order from intensities of presence. We must already index the events to a given time and *then* compare their intensities. But this prior indexing is not explained by Garcia.

One solution might be to index time slices simply in terms of which ones contain the most events, with futurity secured by the increase, as the increase in the number of things is a constant refrain of *Form and Object*. Or perhaps one might develop a theory of necessity and possibility and index time slices in terms of the decrease in possibility, as suggested by Garcia in the quote above. In either case, one could *then* index the events in those time slices in terms of intensity of presence. This would save the interpretation of levels of presence in terms of a continual declining of comprehension of past events, while keeping Garcia's revision to GBUT. But the cost would be not having present and past be a function of those levels.

Life (Intensive Difference)

As with his account of time, Garcia's account of life is deceptively simple. For Garcia, life is self-intensification. Since intensity for Garcia just denotes being more or less, 'self-intensification' literally means something being more than itself:

> Even though living things are local events, which are mere fractions of the objective universe, living things are also events that considerably intensify the universe. Living things augment the universe more than formally (by simply adding new things). Living things give value to the universe (by adding things which are more than what they are). (*FO* 189)

I will put off making sense of the weird yet intoxicating notion that one can be more than oneself, and the idea that this adds value to the world, until the next chapter, which is devoted to Garcia's theory of value. Here we will simply return to Garcia's notion of 'self' to make sense of what it would be for a self to be intensified.

For Garcia, every object is a self, since a self is nothing other than the 'difference [differentiation] between *that which is in the thing* and *that in which this thing* is' (*FO* 191). Living objects, then, are those objects where the differentiation is intensified. The differentiation, for Garcia, is simply the sense in which neither comprehended nor comprehending reduce to one another. So objects are living to the extent that the irreducibility of their properties and environment to their constituents (and vice versa) is greater than it is for non-living things. To be clear, for Garcia the distinction between the living and the non-living is a vague one. There will be borderline cases.

Garcia makes the point that what is increased is irreducibility most clearly when he is responding to Neil Campbell's attempt to characterise life in terms of emergent (irreducible) properties that are not held by non-living things. But since for Garcia, all objects are irreducible to that which they comprehend or that which comprehends them, irreducibility alone will not mark the difference:

> Instead, the emergence of living things is the *intensification* of this irreducibility. The property of irreducibility of a thing to what is in this thing, is this thing, and composes this thing accounts for the stratification of the entire material universe into levels. The emergence of living things can be thought from the fact that this irreducibility has a particular *intensity*. (FO 192)

Garcia states that living things typically intensify their irreducibility through 'self-reproduction, self-preservation, self-maintenance, and self-evolution', and models this increase in terms of the object's resisting its own dissolution:

> A eukaryotic cell marks an accentuated difference between *that which is in it* and *that in which it is*, a certain energy resistance of this difference. A block of quartz in no way precludes the distinction between what composes it and what it is in; this difference *exists* (since the block of quartz can be 'something'), but it does not *resist*, in the sense that no energy is expended in maintaining this difference.
>
> What is living expends energy by maintaining the difference between what it comprehends and what comprehends it, spatio-temporally. The set of synthetic and degradation reactions which make up the metabolism of a cell-energy extraction through cellular respiration in carbohydrates, and the formation of the cellular metabolic network, accelerated through enzymatic processes and anabolic or catabolic pathways – marks the physico-chemical intensification of the self, both through the integration of what exists on the outside into what is on the inside and through the resistance of what is on the inside to what is on the outside. (FO 196–7)

The manner in which living things actively resist their ceasing to exist involves increasing the irreducibility between what is spatially internal to them and their environment.

Garcia's point is very clear if we focus on metabolism, which centrally involves a living being not changing along with environmental changes. External temperature may change thirty degrees in one day, but warm-blooded animals' bodies will regulate themselves so that the temperature of their internal parts does not vary nearly as much. Or consider what happens when sources of nourishment are more acidic. A slight variation of the acid/base level of mammalian bodies leads to quick death, so mammals that find themselves in environments with acidic nourishment (typically phosphoric acid in soda pop) in effect digest their own bones so that the base in the bones' calcium renders the body less acidic. Non-living objects' inability to metabolise renders them unable to actively resist changes in environment.

The other direction, where an environment can stay the same yet the inside of the object changes, is perhaps even more obvious. Living beings sustain themselves through a set of automatic processes (digestion, respiration, circulation, and so on) that involve constant changes of the inside of the being, even in relatively static environments. Living beings propel themselves, not in slavish reaction to changes in external stimuli, but as a result of their own internal workings. We often propel ourselves when nothing is going on at all. In this case, and in the case where the environment changes and the same properties of objects interior to the self do not change, we see clear cases of the irreducibility intensifying.

In Chapter IV of Book II, Garcia also has interesting things to say about the manner in which the order of life is a local universe in his technical sense. At the top is the biosphere. It comprehends all living things, yet is not itself a living thing. This is analogous to the way that Garcia's world comprehends all things, yet is not a thing. And at the bottom is the cell, which is comprehended by all living things, yet does not itself comprehend living things. This is analogous to formal matter/no-matter-what, which is comprehended by all things, yet comprehends nothing. In between various specialised cells and the biosphere are tissues, organs, and organisms.

Finally, Garcia's account of life suggests an approach to the problem that ersatz objects posed for his ability to give an account of objects' identity over time, broached at the end of the previous section. When Garcia writes that 'no-matter-what is something' he means that, for all determinations, there is something that the determination is true of. But this does not mean that for all determinations *there exists* something of which the determination is true. Living objects are those whose intensified irreducibility allows them to continue to exist in the face of hostile environments. For the living, to exist is to resist.

This perhaps teaches us something about non-living objects that continue to be the same selves over time for Garcia. The problem is that 'no-matter-what is something' grants being to every possible (and impossible) jerry-rigged object, such as the wood of my desk currently and the redness of the Tabasco sauce I consumed last night. But then how is it possible that some objects maintain their identity over time while others do not, changing into new things or being destroyed? Garcia would retort that 'no-matter-what is something' does *not* grant *existence* to every possible and impossible object. So the armchair that is comprehended by both white and red, but in the latter case more intensely, the white armchair that survived as it became red at a later moment, has both being and existence, while ersatz objects only have being. Perhaps something in this neighbourhood finally lays to rest Harman's criticisms, though much more would need to be said about what differentiates existent from non-existent things. From his discussion of the future as maximally absent, I conjecture that non-existent things are just those *all* of whose comprehensions are maximally absent, but as far as I know Garcia has not worked out a doctrine about this issue.

Notes

1. Garcia does not here intend to mark the purported basic distinction between intensive and extensive difference in the manner of Deleuzians. For Deleuzians, intensive differences (such as differences in heat, brightness, and speed) lack three properties that extensive difference (such as differences in location) possess. Objects with intensive differences are *not* such that they (1) reliably yield greater aggregate differences when combined (combining two objects with a difference in heat will not reliably produce a hotter object), (2) reliably yield lesser aggregate differences when separated, and (3) can be explained by the more intense object possessing some feature the other one lacks (the greater and lesser bright objects are both bright).

On this distinction, see the Deleuze chapter in Moore's *The Evolution of Modern Metaphysics*. Several times in conversation now I have heard Deleuzians complain (often adopting the more-in-sorrow-than-anger pose) that Garcia has no theory of intensity. But they are really objecting that he does not adopt Deleuze's metaphysics, which makes the intensive/extensive distinction basic and privileges intensive difference. Since these two moves are a key part of Deleuze's reworking of Gilbert Simondon's process philosophy, which Garcia explicitly rejects, the charge against Garcia is disingenuous.

2. See Franklin Worrell's and my 'S-Vagueness and R-vagueness: Some Results from Counterexamples to the Underlying Comparative Theory', for an argument that this example exhibits a distinctive theory of vagueness that has largely remained occluded in analytic philosophy since Bertrand Russell's on the whole unfortunate attacks on British Hegelianism. The example of God and speciation is from James Donovan.

3. See especially Ken Akiba and Ali Abasnezhad's edited book *Vague Objects and Vague Identity: New Essays on Ontic Vagueness*.

4. For this and the succeeding three, see Roberto Casati and Achille Varzi's *Stanford Encyclopedia of Philosophy* article, 'Events'.

5. Broad, *Scientific Thought*, p. 68.

6. Bourne, 'When Am I? A Tense Time for Some Tense Theorists?', p. 362.

7. Harman, 'Tristan Garcia and the Thing-in-itself', p. 29.

8. In Garcia's 'Crossing Ways of Thinking: On Graham Harman's System and My Own'.

9

Neither Discovered Nor Created II: Beauty, Truth, and Goodness

Book II, Chapter XII of *Form and Object* interweaves three types of discussions: broad theses concerning the metaphysics of value, genealogies of reigning conceptions of the three valuative kinds that Garcia recognises (beauty, truth, and goodness), and more regional ontological theses characterising what is distinct about these kinds. The main reason I am leapfrogging Garcia's discussion of animals, humans, representations, arts and rules, culture, history, and economics (all of which likewise combine metaphysics, genealogy, and regional ontology) is because his discussion of values follows naturally from the discussion of time and life. In both cases the basic metaphysical operation is the addition of intensity to a kind already thematised in Garcia's system. The time-order results from various intensities of presence of comprehension/being. Life results from the intensification of the *difference* between that which comprehends a differential object and that which the object comprehends. For Garcia, beauty is in some ways the reverse mirror image of life, as it results from the intensification of the *identity* of a differential object. Truth is the result of a characteristic intensifying of the comprehension/being of an event (not the intensifying of the *presence of* an event, which is temporality for Garcia) and the decrease in the intensity of events incompatible with that event. And goodness is the process of an object's amplifying the intensity of another object. The most general form of goodness is when a universe is intensified. Since the intensification of an object (its identity) is beauty for Garcia, it follows that for him the good is in general that which produces more beauty.

The reason Garcia's discussion of value follows his discussions of animals, humans, representations, arts and rules, culture, history, and economics is because in those chapters the genealogical accounts of these kinds typically involve the antagonistic battle between relativism and absolutism. Since beauty, truth, and goodness are in some sense our basic normative notions, the stakes over which this struggle is fought are perhaps the highest in Chapter XII. As is typical with Garcia's regional ontologies, and a key way in which he remains a Hegelian, he does not carefully distinguish between the history of how humans conceive of these kinds and the history of the kinds themselves. This is *not* because Garcia is a relativist who thinks that the kinds are nothing over and above what humans think about them. Rather, it is because, like Hegel, he rejects the Platonist conceit (more on this below) that abstract objects such as beauty exist frozen for all eternity just waiting to be instantiated by material things. With Hegel, and against Kant, he rejects the view of knowledge as paradigmatically discerning the extent to which non-abstract objects copy pre-existing forms or concepts.[1]

The trick is to affirm that beauty, truth, and goodness *have a history* without at the same time taking them to be *merely* historical (comprehended by history, in Garcia's terminology), as relativists do. Building on his earlier discussion of economics, Garcia makes it very clear that relativism is his main enemy.

> This objectivity of values is immediately made implausible by the relativity of values that the modern economy reinforces. In reality [according to the relativist], there are no *values*, but only *valuations*. The values of objects connected to an economy, to an exchange system of these objects, which we analysed in the previous chapter, would thus be dependent upon the values that one attributes to them. The source of each value is obtained through humanity's collective or individual projection of its interests onto things of the flat world. The replacement of values by economic valuations consists in combining the objective with the formal. The non-human objective universe is conceived as the flat, formal world. In contrast, human actions produce a topological interface of intensities in the universe of surrounding objects. On this view, nothing has value *in itself*. Nothing is beautiful, true, or good, except in relation to the human actions that attribute values to other objects. Beauty, one might say, is in the eye of the beholder, good in the interest of the one who defines it, truth in the mouth of the one who speaks it. This is entailed by an economic conception of objects. (FO 332)

If we think of objects as merely things that receive their value in terms of their worth in exchange, then we think of value as something that human agents grant them. In one historical epoch it might be the case that five tangerines are worth one cup of coffee. In another they might be worth two. From an economics perspective, nothing about the tangerines themselves or the coffee determines their worth relative to one another.[2]

Garcia rejects the relativist's model of values being nothing more than part of the stain left by humans in their wake:

> However, the problem with the economic *valuation* model is twofold. On the one side, this model always assumes an underlying dualism between a part of the flat universe without intensity, awaiting its valuation or devaluation, and a part of the active universe, which is the source of all intensification and evaluates or devaluates according to its potential, interests, or orientation. On the other side, this model attributes all intensity to the donor and no intensity to the receiver, so that the intensive object continues to have *replaceable* value. (FO 333)

Garcia takes the dualism of humans as value-givers and the world as valueless in itself to be obviously problematic. Perhaps most importantly, he takes the correlationist/relativist's picture of value to be unable to make sense of the manner in which objects can be uniquely valuable. When we value our family members, we are not measuring how many tangerines or spoonfuls of coffee they are worth in trade. To do this is precisely *not* to value them:

> The mirror-image of my interest or desire to find something beautiful is not what makes something beautiful. Rather, we find beautiful that which is beautiful. If one finds beautiful that which is *not* beautiful – if this value that we attribute to faces or landscapes was merely a valuation by the one who finds the faces or landscapes to suit their taste – then everything could be *equally* beautiful, since anything that I find beautiful can be replaced by another thing that I find beautiful. Valuation allows us to conceive of the *replaceable* value of things, which connects equally evaluated objects. Now, when we find something beautiful or claim that something is true, we attribute an *irreplaceable* value to it. Value makes something singular, while economic valuation yields particulars. (FO 334)

Garcia is not just pointing out that our phenomenology of norms is starkly at odds with the relativist's explanation of how such norms come about. He is also making the claim that it is part of the nature of normative concepts that humans can get them wrong. If values were ultimately just part of the human stain, then not only should nothing be irreplaceable, but everything would be as potentially valuable as everything else.

Given this critique, one would expect Garcia to embrace a strong form of realism about the normative. If values are not part of the human stain, then the beautiful, the good, the true are there waiting for humans to discover them, for us to live correctly or incorrectly to the extent that we subject ourselves to them. But Garcia does not affirm this. Rather, he affirms the seemingly contradictory position that values are *both* discovered and created:

> All value is paradoxical in this way: what I find beautiful or true or good, I 'find' beautiful, true, or good; I do not 'attribute' beauty, truth, or goodness (any more than I am 'attributed' beauty, truth, or goodness), but I discover beauty, truth, or goodness in objects even though these values are not intrinsic to the objects. (FO 335)

Not only are values paradoxically non-intrinsic yet discovered ('intensities are situated in things without those intensities being there' (FO 335), 'objective values [are] situated in the objects without these values being there' (FO 336)), they also paradoxically force us to see things as both replaceable and irreplaceable:

> The 'crisis of values' consists in the progressive compacting of the two senses of every value, as if it were a problem of opposing values: on the one side, irreplaceable values in the things themselves; on the other side, economic replaceable values in human beings' relations to things through their exchange. (FO 336)

Garcia's philosophy of value is difficult to grasp and frustrating to explicate precisely because he refuses to dialectically resolve this contradiction.

For Garcia, beauty, truth, and goodness are themselves only to the extent that they resist *both* their reductive explanation by the relativist or naturalist who wants to account for them entirely in terms of the naturalistic properties of ourselves and the things that we take to be beautiful, true, and good, *as well as* the absolutist who wants to overmine them in terms of the things that beauty, truth, and goodness are, such as a general account of abstract properties or as laws given by a God or Moses. Garcia's genealogies are simply stories of how these antagonistic struggles have worked out up to now. His differential model of objects combined with his critique of both relativism and absolutism ensures that regional ontologies could be little more. Remember that, for Garcia, *all* objects are simply differentiators between that which they comprehend and those objects that comprehend them. Nonetheless, there is some general metaphysical upshot from traversing the genealogies.

Beauty (Intensive Identity)

Garcia starts his discussion of beauty by endorsing Adorno's defence of Wilhelm von Humboldt's famed rebuke of a landscape for not containing enough trees. One initially wants to mock von Humboldt as a philistine. Haven't the Romantics taught us not to approach nature this way? And isn't the landscape just what it is anyhow? What sense does it make to rebuke it? But for Adorno, von Humboldt's response reveals something essential to aesthetic judgements:

> Aesthetic judgment appears to correspond precisely to the possibility of intuiting the difference beneath the natural mask of a thing's identity and how 'it could have been otherwise', how it *ought* to be different than what it is. Every aesthetic judgment is based on the possibility of this implicit reproach, otherwise nothing can be beautiful. We must understand that it could have been different, that it could have been what it is differently, and that it is ugly if it is insufficiently what it is. (*FO* 337)

In Garcia's model this becomes the claim that an object is beautiful to the extent that its identity is intensified. To determine this, we compare an object to plausible ways the object could be but isn't, and in doing so discern whether the actual object is more itself than these other possible objects. For the object to be more itself is for it to be more beautiful.

Garcia does not say much about what it is for an object to be more itself, but he gives a strong hint near the end of the section on beauty when he writes that 'the Beautiful is what makes any thing, distinct, original, singular' (*FO* 341). So an actual object is beautiful to the extent that the plausible other ways that it could be different result in the thing being more easily replaceable. And ugliness holds to the extent that the actual objects are more replaceable. Von Humboldt intuited that the same landscape would be more distinctive, less replaceable, were it to include some more trees.

Garcia's genealogy of beauty goes through several moments, starting with the Platonist idea that something is beautiful to the extent that it instantiates the form of Beauty, which itself is beautiful. Such a form would be compact for Garcia, since its own beauty amounts to the form comprehending itself. But the recoil from this form of compactness led to various Renaissance, Romantic, and now naturalistic conceptions of the beautiful as some form of human excrescence (or its stain). In the arts this has led to a perverse resolve to find beauty in everything:

> Romanticism's assimilation of ugliness, Victor Hugo's union of sublimity and vulgarity, the taste for monstrosity, and the beauty of ugliness are clearly symptoms of a sensibility that sought primitive values and that weakened the modern understanding of the idea of the Beautiful. But at the same time the Beautiful increased its extension. The nineteenth century carried out the reversal of what was situated outside the Beautiful: the Baudelairian eternal and ephemeral halves, and assimilation of the contingent and the ephemeral, the Rimbauldian resentment against beauty placed on its knees and insulted, Nietzsche's promotion of the Dionysian, and Oscar Wilde's denial of absolute beauty and the beautiful in itself – all these clearly contributed to the formalisation of the Beautiful. It is no longer a problem of determining the Beautiful as a self-to-self relation in and through harmony, unity, symmetry, and so on, but of understanding as Beautiful everything that can be intensely what it is. (FO 340)

But to say that everything *can become* beautiful is *not* to say that everything *is* beautiful or that becoming beautiful is simply a matter of being believed to be beautiful. The end point of formalisation would be the flat world without any distinction, where beauty is an epiphenomenon of human valuations reflected in how humans exchange goods ('the compactness of the ancient Beautiful as a substantial irreplaceable value made way for the compactness of the modern Beautiful as a formal self-replaceable value' (FO 342)). But beauty resists this too.

The meaning of the Beautiful as an objective value must be decided between the two. It is the intensification of this thing. The Beautiful is the transformation of a determined thing with greater or lesser intensities through natural, cultural, and individual processes, through which one compares the thing to what it could have been and to what it could be. A thing's beauty is its value insofar as one can find in it the potential to see another thing as what it is, and as one compares the thing to what it is not. A thing's beauty is the value that it takes when one finds or does not find in it something more and better than itself, or not more and better than itself. (*FO* 342)

Better or worse is measured here in terms of the value that beautiful things command when we exchange them for other things that are not so beautiful. But paradoxically, the very singularity we find when we discover beauty resists the economic hegemony of exchange.

As I noted, for Garcia the contradiction concerning values being both discovered and created forms an unresolvable antinomy. The nearly overwhelming philosophical desire one experiences to resolve this is really, for Garcia, the desire to explain away beauty, which itself is contradictory. I must confess here that I find this difficult to stomach, as that which is supposed to be neither creation nor discovery just looks like a form of creation to me. As with Garcia's similar claims with respect to entities to which our sciences of the very small are committed (discussed at the end of Chapter 7 above), he strikes me as in danger of collapsing into some kind of Kantianism.

The closest way to get to a non-Kantian construal is to interpret Garcia along the lines of Bertrand Russell's view of 'sense data' in *The Problems of Philosophy*. For Russell, when a human being views a table, the way the table looks pops into existence as a result of the interaction. The way the table looks, the table's sense data, is just as real as the table itself. It is not a fiction or a property of the person viewing it. It is just that its existence is dependent upon the person and the table interacting. Of course, in Russell's hands (as opposed to Graham Harman's neo-Russellianism), this model involves the invidious distinction between entities that grant sense data and those that don't. For Russell, two tables interacting do not generate sense data for one another. In the second quote provided above, Garcia clearly follows Harman in rejecting such invidious distinctions. But consider this quote I provided in the previous chapter:

Even though living things are local events, which are mere fractions of the objective universe, living things are also events that considerably intensify the universe. Living things augment the universe more than formally (by simply adding new things). Living things *give value to* the universe (by adding things which are more than what they are). (FO 189)

The picture there really does seem to be that living beings somehow make it the case that objects are more or less what they are. Garcia's animadversions against relativism then simply amount to affirming the Russellian view. The objects' identities really are more or less intense once we interact with them. And, as with Russell's view, the phenomenology of said interaction is passive, both in that we do not experience the increased intensity as popping into existence and in that we have no control over the process. But unless Garcia can specify what is special about the living such that they can plausibly be thought to have these powers, this (as well as the Russellian view of perception, for that matter) frankly strikes me as wizardry. It is far better to go with Harman's neo-Russellian view, where sensual properties and sensual objects attend the interactions of any two objects. Perhaps, analogous to Russell's account of what happens when a human perceiver interacts with an object, two tables can provoke one another to be more or less what they are.[3]

Finally, Garcia's talk of an object's identity being intensified is still too loose. Remember that, for Garcia, objects themselves are mere differentiators between that which they contain and that which contains them, and life is the result of this difference being intensified. So Garcia has to accommodate a sense in which a differentiator can be intensified while (assuming the beautiful object is non-living) the difference made by that differentiator is not intensified.[4] His comments about the comparison of actual objects with their counterfactual near doppelgängers tracks *how we make* such judgements, but (as with his comments on time's arrow decreasing possibility), barring a worked-out theory of possibility and necessity, it doesn't tell us very much about *the content of* those judgements. Again, intensification starts to look magical. Perhaps it is! But before affirming this, one wants to feel that one has exhausted alternative possibilities.

Truth (Intensive Comprehension)

We must be clear about something. In this brief section Garcia does *not* take himself to be offering a 'theory of truth' in the way that analytic philosophers of language, logicians, and metaphysicians use the terms.[5] There is no model or proof theory concerning how one should deal with truth paradoxes (for example, the one involving the sentence 'This sentence is false') or truth-relevant quantification and anaphora (for example, 'if Aristotle wrote it, then Frank believes it'). There's no attempt to make sense of the existence of different logics, no attempt to see what the characterisation of knowledge as justified, true belief might commit us to about truth, no detailed account of whether and how different standards of objectivity do or do not give rise to different kinds of truth, and no sustained attempt to adjudicate between (or dissolve) traditional characterisations of truth as some kind of correspondence, coherence, or perhaps (along a Heideggerian or Hegelian vein) something prior to either.

Instead, Garcia does three things. First, he provides some broad hints about how truth can be made sense of from within his system. Then, he sketches one of his genealogies, with truth peregrinating from a religious identification with divinity to an Aristotelian correspondence between belief and fact and then to a post-Kantian coherence with other things held true. Finally, he demonstrates how these peregrinations have permitted an unprecedented new form of scepticism characteristic of modern conspiracy theorists. Garcia's genealogy in this section is very sketchy, and it is not entirely clear how it fits with his own characterisation of truth as intensified being. Instead of focusing on the genealogy, I will sketch Garcia's own characterisation of truth and connect his account of conspiracy theories with some relevant work in analytic philosophy.

In 'On the Essence of Truth', Martin Heidegger argues that the Aristotelian view that truth is a correspondence between belief and reality cannot be the whole story. The view seems at first unproblematic because other cases of representation, such as a picture of Caesar on a coin, do not strike us as philosophically problematic. Determining whether a belief is true or false would merely be akin to checking to see if a picture is a good likeness of what it is supposed to represent. But, as Heidegger notes, beliefs are not similar to the entities in the world that lead us to accept or reject beliefs.

My belief that a table is hard in no way resembles the hardness of the table. So Heidegger's first point is that representational truth requires of us the ability to discern which facts are relevant to the truth or falsity of beliefs. His second point is that representational truth also requires us to determine whether those facts are actual.[6] As a result, representationalism about truth does not clear up problems, but rather raises them. How do we determine which facts are the ones represented by the beliefs whose truth or falsity is responsive to the existence or actuality of those facts? And (for Heidegger the really important question) what it is for those facts to be actual?

The neo-Kantian[7] tradition of trying to characterise truth in terms of how a belief coheres with other beliefs can be seen as motivated by deep scepticism about the possibility of answering Heidegger's two questions.[8] But such views themselves have notorious problems. Minimally, neo-Kantians need to specify what this 'coherence' relation comes to. This is a difficult task, as whole groups of people can (arguably, any group does) believe consistent, yet false propositions. For example, people used to believe that the sun orbited around the earth. This agreed with everything else they believed, yet we now know the belief to be false. Coherence views tend towards idealism, with believers cut off from any world that might (de)legitimate their beliefs about said world.

Garcia's suggestions about truth should be understood in this context. Heidegger himself took his problematic to entail that there was a deeper notion of truth that is more originary than correspondence platitudes (for example, 'beliefs are true if the facts they represent are actual'), and in fact explains those platitudes. Originary truth for Heidegger concerns being, the actuality of the facts that legitimate our true beliefs. Division One of *Being and Time* is centrally concerned with how our engagement with the world demonstrates a non-linguistic grasp of this originary truth and how referential language is bootstrapped from these prior abilities.

Garcia has a theory of being. Being is the inverse of comprehension, and this allows him to very quickly answer Heidegger's second question about truth:

> Truth is the possibility that the relation between two objects can be reinforced or redoubled. To say that it is true that I have stolen money from the wallet is to distinguish the fact that I have stolen money from

the wallet from the fact that I have not stolen it, by redoubling the former by a value, an intensity, which makes it *more* than the latter. However, the fact that I have not stolen the money from the wallet *is* not less: it *is* untrue, it *is* fictional, and it *is* illusory. Perhaps it is even beautiful. Formally, it is *equal*, whether I have stolen from the wallet or not. The two events are equivalent, even if they are different things (a real fact and a fictional fact). Truth is what intensifies one of the two events by redoubling its being. One fact is more than the other. Falsehood diminishes the intensity of an event's being, while truth accentuates it. (*FO* 343)

Let us parse this. The 'relation between two objects' that is reinforced is being. Remember that Garcia's model of predication is that the object picked out by a predicate of a proposition comprehends the object picked out by the subject. Also remember that being is just the inverse of comprehension for Garcia. So, the proposition that my pen is black is true for Garcia because the intensity of the comprehending of the pen by blackness is doubled. For Garcia this is intensifying an event's being because he is committed to a Kimian fact-like picture of events as involving one object comprehending another.

There is a closeness between the picture of truth and the picture of time. As we saw in the previous chapter, time for Garcia involves the presence of an event's comprehension being intensified, whereas truth involves the comprehension itself being intensified. For Garcia, 'Truth is thus what reinforces the being of an event, the relation between objects, while falsehood is what weakens it' (*FO* 343). This refers to the being/comprehension itself, not the presence of the being/comprehension. Unfortunately, Garcia doesn't remark on this closeness. Elucidation about what differentiates the intensity of comprehension from the intensity of the presence of comprehension would further clarify both his accounts of truth and of time.

Garcia's account of truth is not merely distinctive because he sides with the early Heidegger against neo-Kantians (and against perhaps most contemporary disciples of the late Heidegger). It is also distinctive in the manner in which, as I noted in the previous chapter, intensity is the way Garcia marks vagueness:

Truth is an intensity because it never has the power to reduce falsehood to nothingness. The fact that it is true that I stole money from the wallet diminishes the intensity of being false, but it does not reduce being false to nothing. The fact that I have not stolen money from the wallet is always something; in short, its falsehood weakens it. (FO 343)

This commits Garcia to what analytic philosophers call a 'fuzzy' view of truth, where propositions (the being of events, for Garcia) can be more or less true.

In the concluding paragraphs of this section, Garcia discusses a 'crisis of truth', where global scepticism about our ability to know truth threatens in a new way. Classic arguments for scepticism or relativism involve attacks on the idea that we have appropriate epistemic access to the truth-makers (those facts relevant to the determination of the truth or falsity of a claim) in question. If there is a widespread failure of such access, then we seemed to be trapped in the neo-Kantian prison, where at best we redefine truth in terms of how claims we believe to be true cohere with one another.

Garcia astutely notes that contemporary conspiracy theorists do something quite different:

It is symptomatic that the greatest contemporary scepticism is tied not to doubtful affairs, but rather to particularly well-attested events; doubts about the attacks against the World Trade Center and the Pentagon on September 11 demonstrate the weakening force of truth. The more one demonstrates the truth of a relation (that two planes struck two towers which fell and were filmed), the more the elements of this relation are doubted. What if something other than the planes caused the collapse of the towers? What if explosives caused their collapse? What if the American Secret Service, which still had some of their offices in the towers, financed or encouraged this attack? Why did the towers fall in *this* way? What if the responsible parties were not the responsible parties and the victims not the victims? (FO 347–8)

Garcia also notes that Holocaust denial often works in the same way. The denier begins by admitting that, *of course*, Jews were killed:

But by safeguarding certain relations (for example, the fact that the Nazi authorities planned and accomplished mass exterminations of Jews in World War II), one immediately weakens the relational terms.

The fact is accepted, but each object that enters into this relation is weakened. Why only mention exterminations of 'Jews'? What does one mean by 'mass'? Was there really a 'plan'? It is not falsehood that opposes truth here, but the weakening of terms in the reinforcement of relations. (FO 347)

Contemporary conspiracy theorists perform 'a flank attack' (FO 344) on truth because they start by accepting the truth of some claim but then deny the truth of claims involving key terms in the initial proposition. If they are successful, then one no longer accepts many of the key entailments initially taken to follow from the truth of the proposition in question. Garcia presents the ability of conspiracy theorists to do this as a weakening of truth itself, a push back towards neo-Kantianism. In a sense Garcia himself is doing the conspiracy theorists' work with respect to his own doctrine of truth as intensified being. Yes, of course truth is intensified being. But what can it mean for truth to be intensified when a Holocaust denier admits the truth of the claim that mass Jewish extermination was planned and accomplished in the Second World War? And, as usual, Garcia does not solve this problem, but concludes the section in *aporia*. The reader is left with an appreciation of truth as that which survives all of this explanatory batting around.

There is a deep connection between Garcia's puzzle of the conspiracy theorist and what analytic philosophers call the Quine–Duhem problem,[9] often articulated in terms of the search for a theory of correct scientific truths. One might think if your theory predicted an observation sentence that was falsified by the experiment (say you predicted that a dial in the laboratory would read 7, and it actually reads 5 when you do the experiment), then one of your scientific laws would have been falsified.[10] However, observations are only predicted via a description of the experimental setting as well as whatever mathematical approximations make the theory's equations useable. The scientific laws that were to be tested might be true, and the other theoretical apparatus involved in generating the prediction might be what went wrong. Thus, when you get a falsified prediction, you have a choice: you are only forced to reject either the scientific laws, the description of the experiment, or the mathematics used. The Quine-Duhem hypothesis concludes from this that no set of observations can ever rationally compel one to abandon a hypothesis. It is in effect a pessimistic conclusion about there being a fact of the matter about which of the three you have to do in such a situation. The thought is that if we want to hold on to a belief badly enough, we can always hold that belief true and maintain consistency by making compensatory adjustments elsewhere to explain why our observations didn't accord with our predictions. To the extent that scientific explanation is just a more rigorous model of how we rationally determine beliefs, this problem is absolutely general.

Garcia's conspiracy theorist is in the same position as the person who doggedly holds on to a scientific hypothesis that has been disconfirmed over and over again by rejecting other beliefs involving the central terms of that hypothesis (concerning how the hypothesis is to be tested). At some point, the very meaning of the hypothesis is brought into question. The person who still asserts that the Earth is the centre of the cosmos, yet also accepts all of the empirical data that leads everyone else to reject this claim, starts to look as though they must mean something different by the claim. Unfortunately, however, there is no switch that is flipped when meaning shifts. For meaning, just like truth on Garcia's model, is subject to gradations in a manner that leaves it irredeemably vague.

The upshot for us is that the challenge to truth posed by the conspiracy theorist might be taken to be the same challenge posed by the Quine-Duhem problem. If that's the case, then the future of Garcia's genealogy of truth might lead through substantial tracts of analytic philosophy, a result he would, I think, welcome.

Goodness

Garcia's genealogy of the good has several moments, starting with the classical idea of a sovereign good that is good in itself, either God or the Platonic form of the Good.

> This 'good Good' appears as the Sovereign Good in Western antiquity. The Sovereign Good is a substantial good in itself, not the Good for a thing, however big, but the Good in itself, both universal and formal. (FO 349)

Of course, Garcia rejects such a model since he rejects the idea of anything being in itself. In the tradition of Western philosophy, a 'Euthyphro dilemma'[11] arises as the result of wondering what it might mean to say that the good itself is good. If God, or a form, provides the standard for goodness, then claims that something is good become uninformative. Goodness is just whatever that object (God, Plato's form) is like. But that, then, is consistent with the goodness of any object, contingent on the nature of that creature. But our normal conception of goodness is that some acts are so wicked that they could not possibly be good.

The Thomistic response to this dilemma[12] is to block such arguments by motivating the claim that God has all of his properties essentially, and in some sense all of God's properties refer to the same thing. If that works, then one couldn't point to the possibility of an omniscient, omnipotent, non-loving creature to show that the Sovereign Good is inconsistent with our normal moral intuitions about how some acts are irredeemably wicked. And it is in the context of the Thomistic response that Garcia's critique of the Sovereign Good must be understood.

> The problem of compactness is that it tends to unify everything that self-compacts; the ancients confounded substantial values. How can one distinguish the Good, the Beautiful, and the True when they are confounded in the One, Plotinus's *apex* of value compactness? The more that the Good is compact, in itself, absolute, the more it is unified with the True and the Beautiful. The crisis of the desubstantialisation of values is nothing other than the attempt to distinguish values and to go beyond the ancient compactness of a true and beautiful Good. (FO 349–50)

This is the point the relativist always makes, that absolutising views conflate things that should be kept distinct. The relativist attacks the notion of universal human rights, because different societies configure rights in (supposedly) radically different ways. The proclamation of universal human rights is then presented as an act of violence against cultures where (again, according to the relativist) different notions of rights exist.

As we have seen, Garcia thinks that this logic becomes incoherent when pushed to its final extreme. Relativism ends up either defending a new universalist view (no one should ever judge what people in other countries get up to), hence not being relativist, or abolishing all normative judgements altogether. But this does not, for Garcia, mean that the absolutist is always right. Minimally, from what I have already said, it should be clear that Garcia does not identify the beautiful (objects being more intensely themselves) and the true (the intensification of an event's being/comprehension).

Garcia's genealogy of good goes from the Platonistic Sovereign Good through Epicurus and Diogenes Laertius through Descartes and Kierkegaard, and ends up with the form of utilitarianism presupposed by economists, which identifies good with that which people find desirable. This works for economists for two reasons. First, it allows the identification of value with exchange value. We can measure how much people desire objects and experiences by determining how much they would pay for those objects and experiences, with money being the measure of exchangeable value. And in elevating exchange value, the economist neatly sidesteps the relativist complaint, since exchange value respects the fact that people in different communities value different things.

But then value itself becomes an inconsistent entity. Monetary value is a measure of how much we value something, but at the same time to put a monetary value on some things is precisely to radically devalue them. 'Each thing receives with its value what makes it simultaneously exchangeable with another and irreplaceable' (FO 352–3).

Garcia himself differentiates the good from the beautiful in the way I have already indicated at the beginning of this chapter. His fundamental notion is 'good for', with something being good for something else if it helps that other object be more itself. Since being more oneself is Garcia's technical notion of beauty,[13] this means, for Garcia, that something is good for something else to the extent that the first thing increases the beauty of the other thing. But aren't some things just good, irrespective of how they affect other things? Garcia accommodates this intuition by noting that many kinds of objects are good for the universe.

> To do Good is to augment the objective universe, a set of objects and events, more than the mere existence of this object augments this universe. Everything that does more than bring mere existence to the universe is good. Everything that overflows from the mere fact of existing and strengthens a community of living beings, a set of objects, is good. (FO 349)

Our acts are good to the extent that they help the universe be more what it is, to the extent that they help the universe be more beautiful.

This is a radical view substantially at odds with how most of us think about beauty and goodness. It seems that Garcia is committed to denying that things we intuitively take to be beautiful, yet morally atrocious, are either not really beautiful or not really morally atrocious.[14] It is not, after all, good to help a psychopath be more himself. Perhaps every such case involves making the universe less what it is? I don't know. From what we have thus far in *Form and Object*, it is not yet clear just how revisionary Garcia takes his accounts of the good and the beautiful to be.

Notes

1. Robert Brandom's discussion of the 'two-stage' theory of conceptual application in *Reason in Philosophy: Animating Ideas* is the best contemporary reconstrual of this bit of Hegeliana, both in terms of why Hegel is right here and why it's an important thing to be right about.

2. Were their arguments worth rebutting, Garcia's discussion of the connections between correlationist views of value and the hegemony of economics would in fact decisively rebut poseur-left claims (for example, Alexander Galloway's 'The Poverty of Philosophy: Realism and Post-Fordism') that object-oriented ontology is politically rebarbative.

3. Harman's essay on Alphonso Lingis in *Towards Speculative Realism* can be read as motivating such a view.

4. Incidentally, this also shows why Mark Ohm and I should not have translated *différence* homophonically in the context of Garcia's differential model of objects. The intensification of the difference (life) is *not* the same as the intensification of the differentiator (beauty).

5. See especially Richard Kirkham's excellent *Theories of Truth* for an introduction to what analytic philosophers take to be the desiderata for a theory of truth.

6. This is my take on the upshot of Heidegger's essay. He would not have approved of this loose talk of actuality.

7. Part of why Garcia's discussion of truth is relegated to a small section of a chapter is because he covers themes about representation elsewhere in the book. A full treatment would tie this together with Garcia's implicit rebuke to Derrida's incommodious neo-Kantianism in his discussions of representation, art, and rules. Astute readers of Division One of Heidegger's *Being and Time*, or late Wittgenstein for that matter, rightfully see the Derridean dichot-

omy between an Augustinian representational account of meaning and the deconstructionist's model of infinite deferment as perhaps the most howlingly false dichotomy in the history of philosophy. See Lee Braver's *Groundless Grounds: A Study of Wittgenstein and Heidegger*.

8. The 'myth of the given' in analytic philosophy is at its heart a sceptical problem posed with respect to any attempt to answer the first question. Thinking deeply about this always involves some concessions to Hegel, as the idea that normativity is in nature is one way to make sense of how natural facts could exert normative force on beliefs. Hannah Ginsborg's recent *The Normativity of Nature: Essays on Kant's Critique of Judgment* is fascinating in part because she very plausibly reads Kant himself as having grappled with these issues.

9. A really misleading title, since A. J. Ayer formulated it in Chapter V of *Language, Truth, and Logic* over a decade before Quine.

10. See Nancy Cartwright's *How the Laws of Physics Lie* for an account of this.

11. This is still very much a key philosophical issue with wide resonance outside of value theory. See, for example, Jeffery Roland's 'A Euthyphronic Problem for Kitcher's Epistemology of Science'.

12. For a wonderful description of how this works in Aquinas, see Eleonore Stump's 'Dante's Hell, Aquinas's Moral Theory, and the Love of God'.

13. It would be interesting to compare Garcia and Harman on beauty. As noted in Chapter 3 above, in *Guerrilla Metaphysics* Harman characterises beauty as a kind of allure that is experienced when one senses a characteristic discontinuity between the perceptual properties of something and the underlying executant reality. To appreciate Harmanian beauty requires appreciating both all of the effects of poise as well as the author of the poise. Weirdly, one might argue that Harman's is a stereotypically French notion and Garcia's account (in terms of something becoming more truly what that thing is) is a more stereotypically American one. Not that American and French academics are reliably drawn to either, but that each reflect a normative reality deeply characteristic of the other philosopher's culture.

14. My student Marylynn Smitherman first called my attention to this as a possible problem for Garcia. Debates about 'moralism' in analytic philosophy are highly relevant here. For an attempt to reconcile aesthetic moralism and immoralism, the former true of the act of

making an aesthetic judgement and the latter true with respect to the content of those judgements, see my and Graham Bounds's 'A Cheap Holiday in Other People's Misery? Yes, Indeed: Towards a Compatibilist Theory of Immoral Art'.

IO

Neither Substance Nor Process IV: Existence and Resistance

The final three chapters of Garcia's book all in their own way illustrate the manner in which his metaphysics is fundamentally tragic. For Garcia, the hope of any kind of ultimate wisdom or reconciliation is precluded by the very constitution of objects. Gender, adolescence, and death are, like everything else, paradoxically constituted at the most basic level by their irreducibility to those objects that they constitute, and that constitute them. Since we are the creatures trying to understand our own gender, ages of life, and death, the very advancements in our own understanding paradoxically change the things we sought to understand, in ways we could not have predicted. Garcia's genealogies model these changes as histories of objects subverting their own attempted under- and overmining. For Garcia, this entails that wisdom is hyper-Socratic; the only wisdom is a radical humility about the prospects of becoming wise.

Gender

Garcia's discussion of gender in Chapter XIV of *Form and Object*'s Book II provides perhaps the clearest example of an object persisting by resisting its own undermining and overmining. Gender, like all objects for Garcia, is that which differentiates between the things that comprehend it and the things that it comprehends.

In fact, gender subsists only insofar as one thinks of it in two senses, between its singular dissolution and its specific determination. Gender is the primary difference between objects or events which allows the stratification of objective accumulation. Gender is neither purely inscribed in the nature of things nor purely projected by the human mind, but exists as a minimal relation between *that which is gender* and *that which comprehends gender* – the primary relation which objects in the same thing maintain. (FO 382)

Garcia's stock characters here are the undermining naturalist, who tries to explain gender in terms of human biological facts that constitute gendered subjects, and the overmining nominalist, who tries to explain gender in terms of the cultures that include gendered subjects. Garcia demonstrates that both explanatory directions carry the risk of conflating normative and descriptive as well as the risk of misreporting the descriptive.

Normative questions are not really part of the naturalist's purview, as naturalist explanations should just be explanations of how natural systems tend to evolve when set up in various ways. However, the very fact that naturalist explanations foreclose possibilities makes it the case that naturalist explanations carry normative weight. Common sense and the Kantian[1] suggest that we do not have a moral obligation to do the impossible. We comfort one another by telling ourselves that we did all that we could. The thought is that if one really did all that one could to secure a morally desirable outcome, then one is not blameworthy for failing to secure that outcome. But then naturalist explanations will have the tendency to morally absolve everyone for the existing state of affairs, since they will tend to demonstrate how reality could not but have evolved to its present state of affairs.

Evolutionary biology provides the key step to the naturalist's ascent. The fact that females typically can produce far fewer offspring than males is taken to explain social gender roles. Given the physical difference, nature forces different reproductive strategies:

If a female primate wants to produce 'high-quality' direct descendants, it is better for her to mate with males of good quality. The ability to fight is proportional to size and to the state of health, two parameters in large part determined genetically, which appear as selective advantages for males. Numerous species, like seals, appear to essentially adopt this strategy: the female chooses the largest and healthiest male as her primary candidate. The well-nourished and cared for offspring become strong and healthy in turn. But education is as strategically important, in this perspective, as genetic determination. Therefore, a female primate may sometimes mate first and foremost with conquered and subordinate males who, losing their capacity to conquer other females, can help them raise their offspring. (FO 375)

While this is purely a description of how baboons and seals evolved, it is very easy to import it into the long history of human evolution that we know very little about and use it as a lens through which to interpret human culture.

Since seals and baboons are natural, the normative upshot would be that there is nothing one can do about the way gender is configured in contemporary human cultures. Garcia actually mocks this kind of naturalism:

> We know that this difference of reproductive possibility has conse-
> quences on sexual and non-natural selection, which has an influence
> on secondary sexual characteristics like the proverbial peacock's tail:
> the female must be seduced and the male must seduce. Here again male
> and female are conceived according to the difference between activity
> and passivity, like that projected onto the man/woman pair. (FO 375)

The mockery is clear precisely because the 'here again' refers to his earlier discussion of Aristotle's conception of the male as essentially active form and the female as essentially passive matter. And, for Aristotle and Garcia's naturalist, this makes domination inevitable, 'Aristotle claims that the female is "softer" in order to show that the female "becomes more quickly tamed" and there-fore that what she knows how to do better than the male is submit, that is, acknowledge her inferiority' (FO 372). Thus the modern naturalist recapitulates what is the canonical metaphysical defence of oppression in the Western tradition.

The nominalist descent is an attempt to fight this. In most American universities, on the first day of a women and gender studies class students are taught that 'sex' refers to a biological difference determined by chromosomes, hormones, and genitals, while 'gender' refers to the various ways cultures construct femin-ity and masculinity. The Kantian thesis that one only has an obli-gation to the extent that one can fulfil that obligation is also tacitly accepted, as much of the course will then trace different ways that feminity and masculinity are treated in different cultures so as to instil in the student a heightened sense of contingency about gender. This is all taken to be vaguely empowering because the nominalist shares with the oppressive naturalist the Kantian thesis that ought implies can. Contingency shows us that it is not the case that social structures cannot be changed. So it doesn't follow that we have no obligation to work to change them.

However, Garcia notes that the nominalist's programme too can recapitulate the Aristotelian dichotomy:

> One can imagine a nominalist starting from singular differences to construct their masculine or feminine or other gender, which would deconstruct the objective gendered differences all the while leading back to a form of domination. For instance, they would consider 'active' gendered individuals superior to those who 'passively' accept their function. The nominalist is sometimes compelled to consider the individual who falls under a gendered category (who claims to naturally, normatively, or 'properly' be a woman or man) as being *lesser*, since this individual does not singularly adopt the singular, but singularly espouses the non-singular. For this reason, the nominalist reintroduces a value judgment and a *more* or a *less*. On their view, all singular individuals are equal, but some are more equal than others, insofar as they realise and adopt this singularity (they are queer), in relation to those who 'banally' express it generically (they are straight). (*FO* 380–1)

The nominalist wants to deconstruct all gender, but ends up just saying that we should all be male in the Aristotelian sense of maleness. And it is not clear that this is any more emancipatory than the naturalist's evolutionary story. Perhaps the biggest debate in contemporary American feminism, alluded to by Garcia, concerns the fact that the standard freshman level WGS story does such violence to the lived experience of, and biological knowledge about, many transgender people. For example, the standard story can do nothing but dismiss a transgender female who reports feeling that, as a child, she was forced to behave in the wrong gender.

For Garcia, neither side can win. Each time the naturalist ascends from one scale to another, exceptions pile up. At the genetic level, XX and XY chromosomal pairs are not exhaustive. Then, the epigenetic processes that produce female genitals from XX chromosome foetuses and male genitals from XY chromosome foetuses can get switched, and (at least at the time of his writing) there is no exhaustive theory of how these processes work. Then, the evolutionary story that is supposed to explain how gender roles arise out of environmental selective pressures on creatures with different reproductive systems (our story of baboons and seals) itself has massive exceptions. One can always find a living species that fits one's preferred social gender norm. But one must be circumspect about what this may or may not say about human social organisations. And nominalism can never succeed in the end for Garcia, as we cannot help but cognise the world in terms of universals. Garcia's claim that things are solitary is in part the claim that we differentiate things in terms of universals.

Garcia does not present a theory of domination, and only notes here that neither naturalist nor nominalist has a monopoly on emancipatory politics. Naturalism is in fact sometimes an important part of emancipation from domination, especially in modern societies with respect to gay and transgender people. Or it could be the opposite. For Garcia, a politics is good only to the extent that it helps people be more intensely who they are. And we determine this by comparison with other possible versions of ourselves. From this perspective, the first danger of both naturalism and nominalism is the manner in which they prescribe in advance the possible versions of ourselves. Typically the naturalist prescribes too few (we must be like most baboons) and the nominalist too many. But for Garcia, there is no alternative. Gender is that which survives and resists the antagonistic attempts to explain it. And there is no simple recipe for utopian liberation here. The best gendered subjects can do is become more what they are.

Garcia concludes with a broader metaphysical point. Universals divide the world into things that instantiate the universal and things that do not instantiate the universal. If a universal did not do this, it would become compact. 'There are always at least two objects in a thing, otherwise an object which is in a thing and a thing in which an object is would be compact' (FO 382). For example, if all of humanity were male, then there would be no distinction between maleness and humanity. The naturalist constitutively tries to explain the division created by the universal in terms of naturalistically acceptable entities, while the nominalist constitutively tries to deconstruct the universal in favour of differences that are elided by the distinction imposed by it. Again, Garcia lauds both efforts, but ultimately argues that much of the knowledge they yield is negative. We come to better understand the universal in terms of how it survives such attempts. Finally, this survival takes place in time and often results in the universal changing. Garcia notes that sex might be evolving such that there are more than two stable ones.

If Garcia's chapter on gender presents his clearest presentation of an object as resisting both nominalism/relativism/formalism on the one hand, and naturalism/absolutism on the other, then his chapter on ages of life presents his clearest presentation of the way that an abstraction like adolescence can gain a kind of monstrous agency through this process. As I will attempt to demonstrate in the next section, Garcia's technical apparatus gives him surprising insight into why and how adolescence conquered Western civilisation.

However, there is an important disanalogy between adolescence and gender. With gender, the naturalistic terms 'male' and 'female' obey a binary logic. One is either male or female, or perhaps some third (or fourth, or fifth, and so on) sex. But the more culturally laden terms 'masculine' and 'feminine' are intensive in Garcia's sense. One can be more or less masculine and feminine across an array of different culturally recognised markers. That Garcia has deconstructed this distinction of distinctions (showing sex to be more cultural and gender to be more biological than either naturalists or nominalists admit) does not undermine the point about the inferential role of the terms.

Adolescence

Interestingly, adolescence flips the inferential roles that we associate with gender vocabulary. With adolescence, the biological processes present an array of different markers, of which one can possess more or less:

> Three phenomena allow us to isolate the pubertal event, which affects *gender* in ways we saw in our discussion of 'sexual differentiation'. First, the acceleration of the speed of bodily growth begins. Second, morphological changes affect the whole person, especially in the development of secondary sexual characteristics. Third, the individual transforms into a sexually fertile being, dependent upon the genital intensification analysed above. A great inter- and intra-individual variability marks these various processes, the supposed unity of which allows us to define something like 'puberty' in general. From one individual to another and at the very core of a single individual's life, events can follow one another, overlap, shift direction, accelerate, persist, halt, vary in duration, change intensity, begin, or end. The growth of the bust, pilosity, the Adam's apple's protrusion, changes in relations between the hips and waist, and voice mutation – all these events intersect each other. (FO 388)

And mean ages at which these changes happen vary wildly across cultural groups and history. In this respect, biological development obeys a logic much more similar to that stressed by proponents of cultural studies who argue that gender is not a strict binary between male and female.

Ages of life, on the other hand, obey a discrete logic. Like sexes, there are always a finite number of ages of life and a person is either in one or the other. This is because the social organisation requires somewhat arbitrary cut-off points. It would not be possible (nor, arguably, desirable) to determine perfectly who deserves to vote and who does not, so ability to vote is granted at the same age for everyone:

> However, every division of ages is necessarily the imposition of a discontinuous order that is external to the continuity of an individual's temporal becoming. It is impossible to derive ages from the course of a life. It is always necessary to impose ages on a life when ordering what is suitable for it. (FO 393)

Some of the most interesting discussion in this chapter is Garcia's Whig history of how and why different historical moments in the West have divided up human life into different numbers of ages. The Greeks had three phases depending upon which part of the soul was to be educated during those periods. The Romans had four phases divided in terms of which civic functions one was allowed to assume (cf. our example of voting in contemporary societies). After the collapse of the Eastern Roman state the main functional distinction was between those who were dependent and those who were not, so servants and slaves were as much children as actual children. As formal education reappeared in Western civilisation, the Greek model re-emerged with six successive stages of life, depending upon the nature of appropriate education during those periods. With modern economies, these again collapse, but this time not entirely, and we are left with legal systems that make a twofold division between children, those creatures that should be protected from wage slavery and sexual exploitation, and adults, who are legally permitted to enter into contracts.

Garcia discusses the way in which traditional societies are rife with rituals by which children are more or less successfully transformed into adults. These often involve the creation of a liminal space between the two where the ceremonies take place and the child is no longer a child, yet not an adult. As such ceremonies lost their efficacy in contemporary societies, the limit between childhood and adulthood becomes a thing itself, in the manner of the logic of the limit that Garcia has already articulated in his discussions of supposed exceptions to the realm of things as well as his understanding of matter:

> The widening historical gap between the childhood-object and the adult-object led to a reinforced elasticity of the gap between the time of puberty and the departure from the household, the access to civil autonomy, legal responsibility, the right to adult sexuality, and entrance into the working world. Between the two, a no man's land extends, widens, and in turn affects the time of puberty, moves the intermediary age forward, shifts and increases a child's status through nutritional and educational concerns. Little by little, the limit between the two objects, childhood and adulthood – the former comprehended in the latter, but both increasingly separated – itself became an age.
>
> Adolescence is the limit between childhood and adulthood, reinforced until it clearly becomes *something* in turn. This is the objective consequence of the formal logic of limits that we described in the third part of Book I. (*FO* 394–5)

Strangely, as Garcia shows, Kant himself commented on this, noting that the extended period of education for humans in modern societies has created a situation where people are able to procreate yet not able to direct their own affairs in civil society. Thus, the transition between adults and humans starts to become itself a new age of life.

With the political and economic changes wrought by the success of the New Deal model of society in the post Second World War era, adolescence became stronger and stronger:

> This 'third-age' accelerated in the post-war years, in the United States, England, continental Europe, and Japan, before spreading to the whole world: the result of the democratisation of access to the university; economic prosperity; allowances; increases in individual buying power among those still dependent on the familial household; sexual maturation; cultural autonomy; economic heteronomy. The developments of the mass culture and leisure industries determined an adolescent culture, accelerated and realised in the 1960s. (*FO* 397)

But what is this adolescent culture? For Garcia it is first and foremost the culture of refusal, where people are old enough to understand their society's narrative of adulthood but who nonetheless refuse it.

As Garcia plausibly presents it, modern developmental psychology is largely a heroic (and unsuccessful) attempt to utilise dialectics to naturalise ages of life and in the process naturalise adolescence. The contradictory nature of adolescence is first recognised via G. Stanley Hall's twelve contradictions associated with puberty:

> alternation of overactivity and exhaustion; having fits of laughter and exuberant cheerfulness toward every real or imaginary object, but crying for no reason and having anxiety about death; egoism of the selfish boy who is proud of his figure and particular about his reputation, but who sees himself lacking virility and becoming effeminate or careful; altruism and a passion for noble causes, but contempt for the rights of others; oscillation between goodwill, a desire to be moral, and the basest desires, a tendency to infringe upon social constraints; a taste for solitude and natural beauty, but an incapacity to think and speak except in the company of others, in society; increase in sensitivity, but development of cruelty; successive states of curiosity and a natural or affected indifference; a bookish attitude of the spectator and the desire to act; reformist behaviour and enemy of conventional forms, but conservative when provoked; oscillation between the senses and the intellect; wisdom made of intuitions and moments of madness or imbecility (FO 399–400)

Then, a dialectical logic is imposed on these contradictory tendencies, with development into adulthood being a quasi-Hegelian traversal into a consistent final state.

Garcia discusses the most infamous pseudo-scientific approaches from developmental psychology: Kohlberg's six stages of moral development and Erikson's eight stages of development. Such approaches are interesting because they are self-conscious attempts to re-impose something like the Greek or Roman or Renaissance model of ages of life, but with (as was necessary in the twentieth century) a veneer of scientific respectability hiding the fact that theories such as Kohlberg's and Erikson's are actually proposed virtue-theoretic accounts of how (developmental psychologists think) one *ought to* live one's life, not naturalistic accounts of how people actually do live their lives. And adolescence contemptuously rejects all such projects:

> But such a finalist psychological picture misses precisely what adolescence questions. Conceiving of personal life as a permanent synthesis, an experiential accumulation, directed toward the possibility of ultimate wisdom, it cannot conceive of adolescence as the denial and negation of the synthesis of ages toward wisdom. (FO 403–4)

As the limit between childhood and adulthood became itself an object in the 1700s, those inhabiting that object gained a critical distance from adulthood that rendered its promises hollow.

Kohlberg, Erikson, et al. cannot possibly compete, for there is greater wisdom to be found in the rejection of their model of human life as the progressive accumulation of wisdom:

> Unlike what all psychological models of life claim, being an adolescent implies losing all that is gained with age, and becoming an adult implies a loss equal to the consented gain. No dialectic exists between what is gained and lost from one age to another; all that I gain by growing, I lose by ageing. Music or poetry cannot be understood without grasping – quite unlike the psychological models of a life's rational progress and experiential gains – the human consciousness of the loss which accompanies the passage from one age to another. This loss is called 'nostalgia' (which we have already mentioned in its relation to history in chapter X), the price to pay for the experiential blind spot of scientific psychology. (FO 406)

Garcia notes how the rhapsodic adolescent has become a stock literary trope with an essential history: Goethe, Hölderlin, Rimbaud, József, Salinger, Plath, Dean, Elvis, Dylan, and Cobain. 'The *rhapsodic* adolescent, as opposed to psychology's adolescent in crisis, is the embodiment of the age against the stage and the moment' (FO 406). The (anti-)wisdom of adolescence is in a sense *the* wisdom of *Form and Object*,

> No *absolute experience* exists since no formal accumulative order of ages of life exists. The price that the adolescent pays is also the chance which belongs only to her, and which escapes adulthood. Adolescents provide for themselves naturally and are relieved of civil constraints by their civil status (education, family). Adolescents are not yet quite

dependent on civil constraints ('autonomy', work). Society relieves them of the constraints of autonomy at the very moment when autonomy is acquired.

Adolescents have the *chance* to be autonomous from the state of social autonomy.

Adolescents are the soothsayers of contradictions. Adolescence is the gap or contact between our cultural customs and nature. What adolescents have less of is what allows them to acquire an additional quality, which modern society stages: a non-assimilated autonomy in the social domain, disclosing everything in which we are, our life's necessities disclosed from the outside as *contingencies*. (FO 407–8)

For Garcia, adolescence's refusal is also simultaneously a recognition of tragedy. Everything brings with it a cost and there is never a point where all of the tensions and contradictions are resolved.

Death

If I were a novelist, I would write one with this plot. At the story's outset our middle-aged professor protagonist is grieving the death of a colleague and dear friend, whose unwillingness to carefully treat his own congenital illnesses hastened his death. Our protagonist has difficulty sleeping. She cries at embarrassing moments. Even though she hears her friend's voice at odd times and dreams of him in numinous ways, she begins to lose the little of her religious faith that has survived her childhood. She is furious at herself and her colleagues for not having done more to prevent her friend's death. The anger becomes misdirected and she becomes hypercritical towards her (to be fair often irritating, this being an academic novel) colleagues, who themselves have little patience with the behavioural epiphenomena attending her grief. And, as the main narrative conflict of the novel, in the midst of this overwhelming grief our protagonist is herself diagnosed with a medical condition that at best will shave decades off the lifespan she expected.

There is nothing unusual about this plot. Fiction writers set their characters up in difficult situations and then see what happens.[2] And, given the actual hegemony of death over the living, our set-up is not unrealistic. However, the evolution might be. *Most* fiction assumes that the world in which characters evolve is a fundamentally just one.[3] If the plot of my novel evolved in a just world, our protagonist would use her own illness to learn to forgive herself, her colleagues, and her self-destructive dead friend. She would discover genuine wisdom, somehow reconciling herself with a world that contains her own and her loved ones' deaths. If it were competently written, the novel would encourage readers to hope for a similar wisdom when confronting the death of themselves and those they love.

For Garcia, such hope is chimerical. At the naturalistic physical level, death does everything to evade us. As medical technology advances, making us better and better at reviving people and harvesting organs for transplants, we successively change the definition of what it is to die. Not only have we changed it from cessation of breathing, cessation of cardiac function to cessation of various brain functions, but the length of time the functions must have ceased and the conditions of their cessation become paramount. For example, if the body is cold enough, revival is possible after much more time has elapsed than if it were warm. But things are confused, unsolved, and so now it is the case that centuries-old metaphysical debates about the nature of consciousness obtrude. In the United States, some hospitals now have philosophers on call to help determine whether it is permissible to harvest organs from 'brain-dead' victims. What seems at base physical ramifies out into our deepest understandings of consciousness and its moral relevance.

As Garcia notes, there are terrible prices to pay for the advances that have forced these redefinitions and confusions. It is no accident that the zombie is a canonical fantastic figure of our age. The end result of our ability to reanimate the flesh has resulted in a vast increase in people in rich countries living years of their lives in states of advanced dementia, slowly losing everything that made them distinctive. Zombies are fictitious limit cases of our demented future:

The autonomisation of functions which were connected through the human powerlessness to modify them, to affect them (respiration, circulation, brain functioning), fragmented the living body as much as death itself. Today, various limit states of death exist, which outline a continuous field between the clearly living and the clearly dead (the decomposed corpse), a between-life-and-death causing zombies and living Dead to resurface in books and on the screen.

The more we had control over death, the less we managed to

distinguish what death could be on its own, independent of our activity as living beings who struggle against it. (*FO* 416)

In this context it is interesting to note that the zombie is the inverse of Hegel's universe. For the Hegelian, the progressive resolution of contradictions in history is also the universe becoming self-conscious, matter becoming spirit. But the zombie is the revenge of matter on spirit.

Garcia also considers newer attempts to defeat death by understanding it as ultimately caused by the finite upper limit of the number of times DNA can reproduce. If we could programme our DNA not to be so limited, we could defeat death. However, this already happens naturally when people live long enough: cancer. Dementia and cancer illustrate the irreducible tragedy of nature.

But it does not end with nature. Even our successes carry existential crises. Recent transhumanists, such as Aubrey De Grey, have tried to develop health regimes that thread the Scylla of cellular sterility and the Charybdis of cancerous reproduction. But here too there is a price to pay:

Modern humanity is relieved through medicine and the biology of a fast-approaching death, but pays the price for it. Humanity takes up an historical responsibility vis-à-vis their own mortality, and makes death something against which they think they can be active, something for which they feel responsible, since they think that they are able to change it or slow it down. But can one live by attaching an excessive value to life? (*FO* 419)

One of the truths that fiction teaches us is that eternal life would be agonising. A mind that could live through hundreds of thousands of years without devolving to a state of Lovecraftian gibber would be so alien that it would no longer strike us as being a mind. Creatures like us certainly could not manage it. Yet death too is intolerable.

In addition to zombies and cancer, we must add vampires to our bestiary. Not just because infusions of young people's blood (stemming from successful parabiosis experiments with rats) is the somewhat horrific hope *de jour* for reducing human ageing. Rather, it is also the case that speculative fiction about vampires teaches us something about death. In the world of Anne Rice's *Interview with the Vampire*, very old vampires periodically hibernate for years at a time, making themselves preternaturally still and insensate to the world around them. At some point it seems that the hibernation becomes permanent and the vampires become hardly distinguishable from statues. Those of us who can become vampires do so, because death is intolerable. Yet we already know from speculative fiction that being a vampire too is ultimately intolerable.

Finally, in addition to the *aporia* posed by physical death, Garcia notes an *aporia* between the normative requirements imposed upon us by the death of others and our own deaths. Epicurus enjoins us to not worry about our own death because when we are dead we will not experience anything. Whether this works as a metaphysical conceit, it is true that wisdom counsels stoicism in the face of one's own death. Consider the protagonist of our fictitious work of fiction. *Should* she react to her own impending death in the same manner she did to her friend's? Wisdom says no. Grieving our own impending death hinders our ability to set our affairs in order. But on the other hand, *should* she have reacted to her friend's death with the calm equanimity advised by Epicurus? Would that not be monstrous? Is love even possible without grief? No.

> The sage who does not think about death lacks wisdom about the death of others that occur in the sage's own life; this sage becomes a bastard, in the Sartrean sense of the term. But the sage who thinks about death, who experiences the death of others, lacks wisdom about her own death; this sage demonstrates the madness of considering her own death like the death of others.
>
> Sages do not exist when confronted with death. Death is thus the revelation that no ultimate wisdom exists, that is, no position, attitude, thought, or belief which would allow us to remain equal to what is equal. Faced with equal death, like the world, which is the same for every true or false, beautiful or ugly, good or bad thing, nobody is equal. Whoever is *in this way*, and not otherwise, loses what they gain and gains what they lose. No good attitude toward death exists, since nobody will die less by having this attitude; no formally better or worse thing is in the world, since nothing will ever be either more or less in the world. (*FO* 427–8)

The impossibility of wisdom is, for Garcia, also the impossibility of dialectical resolution.

One way to understand Kant's central ethical insight[4] is as a challenge to the wrongdoer to specify why she should be an exception to a rule that everyone else must follow. Certain kinds of unethical acts, paradigmatically lying, murder, and theft, only succeed to the extent that the vast majority of the wrongdoer's victims accept the normative constraint not to do that kind of activity. If everyone constantly lied, then a public language would be impossible and the wrongdoer's lie would not succeed. Even in a society where people are honest enough for there to be a public language, but there is widespread lying about what one intends to lie about (say the quality of a car one is selling), there won't be enough public trust for the lie to be successful. So we can only rationally hope for our own lies to succeed to the extent that we are committed to other people organising their lives around the principle that one should not lie. So what is special about you such that rules like 'Don't lie' should apply to others and not to you? Since there is nothing special about you in this regard, lying always involves, for the Kantian, a fundamental unreasonableness.

This is fine and right as far as it goes, but it is easy to generalise it too far. The limit of this kind of Kantian thinking would be to deny that genuinely tragic choices arise when we consider obligations concerning ourselves and others. If there is never an asymmetry between obligations concerning myself and those concerning others, then perhaps morality could be encoded in a set of binding laws. The wise would be those people whose knowledge of how to apply these normative rules in any situation not only gives them oracular power vis-à-vis the rest of us, but who are reconciled with the natural order as a result. Or perhaps one can, with Hegel, tell a story of history such that fundamental tensions such as those between the individual and the collective are progressively resolved, until nature is resolved with itself, and matter becomes fully self-conscious through humans, who participate in just and wise governments.

For Garcia, death makes a mockery of any such hope. Wisdom cannot be attained by reconciling oneself with the natural order, for the natural order cannot be reconciled with itself. The normative tension between individual and collective cannot be reconciled. And the zombie is not just a figure of science fiction or a metaphor for what happens to reanimated humans. History does not seem to lead to just and wise governments, but rather to institutional zombification, where knowledge of the true, good, and beautiful are unable to direct the lurching reactions of a reanimate state. Those who understand are the trapped souls of their nations, gazing passively out of the eyes of the lurching collective, itself shambling towards Bethlehem, or Paris (Jerusalem, Athens, Alexandria, Vienna, London), as the city cracks, reforms, and bursts, spirit progressively unwinding itself into matter. The vampires retreat to their lairs, minions rampant over the rest of us, turning on one another as their cadaverous masters grow senescent, hibernate. The walls slowly crush them, a new and virulent cancer, the very concrete with some semblance of life now, expanding pustulent as the grating sound of a thousand shrieking flutes hails the Iad Uroborus swarming across every negated horizon . . .

The only ultimate wisdom offered by *Form and Object* derives from the paradoxical way its reader might reconcile herself with irreconcilability. But this does *not* mean reconciling oneself with the reversed Hegel that one might read into Garcia at his most pessimistic (as I did in the previous paragraph), where, in a parody of the astrophysicist's collapsing universe, spirit becomes matter as consistency progressively unresolves itself. For Garcia, reality resists this narrative too.

As a fundamentally tragic philosopher, Garcia always stresses a price that must be paid. But the realisation that you cannot swallow yourself by the tail in no way precludes continuing to attempt the opposite, pulling yourself up by your own hair. For the elusive, and with Harman allusive, nature of reality also entails that individuals and collectives always have the chance to discover, create, and perhaps be something new.

Notes

1. I don't mean to dismiss by fiat the late period phenomenology tradition (coming out of Levinas and Derrida in American continental philosophy) of thinking of ethics in terms of a necessary impossible (see, for example, François Raffoul's *The Origins of Responsibility*), which involves a denial of the Kantian view that ought implies can. In this book I have focused on thinking through *Form and Object* as a work of analytic Speculative Realism. A similar endeavour from an (American) continental perspective could do much worse than take as a central conceit that Garcia extends the Derridean necessary impossible out of ethics and into metaphysics proper.

2. The latter half of my and Mark Ohm's 'Actual Properties of Imaginative Things: Notes Towards an Object-Oriented Literary Theory' sketches a theory of fiction along these lines, with there being no metaphysical difference between literary and popular fiction on the one hand, and scientists' thought experiments on the other.

3. This is one of the main ways that we gain moral knowledge from fiction. We ought to do in the actual world those things that are rewarded in those true fictions with fictional worlds where the just-world hypothesis is part of the set-up. This is not to deny that we also discover things about the moral facts in our world from reading fictions inconsistent with the just-world hypothesis. Likewise, we must confront the spectre of two indiscernible worlds: (1) the one making true a true fiction (because the actual world really would evolve that way, were the fiction's set-up incarnate), with the just-world hypothesis as part of the set-up; and (2) a false fiction where the just-world hypothesis is not part of the set-up but which evolves according to that hypothesis.

4. I *think* this is exactly what Kant is actually up to in some of the more obscure, Rorschach blottish, passages of the *Groundwork*.

Bibliography

Akiba, Ken, and Ali Abasnezhad (eds), *Vague Objects and Vague Identity: New Essays on Ontic Vagueness*, Dordrecht: Springer, 2014.

Aristotle, *Categories and De Interpretatione*, trans. and notes J. Ackrill, Oxford: Clarendon Press, 1963.

Aristotle, *Metaphysics*, in *The Complete Works of Aristotle: The Revised Oxford Translation, Volume Two*, ed. Jonathan Barnes, Princeton: Princeton University Press, 1984.

Ayer, A. J., *Language, Truth, and Logic*, New York: Dover, 1952.

Badiou, Alain, *Being and Event*, London: Bloomsbury Academic, 2013.

Bird, Alexander, *Nature's Metaphysics: Laws and Properties*, Oxford: Oxford University Press, 2007.

Black, Max, 'The Identity of Indiscernibles', *Mind* 61 (1952), pp. 153–64.

Bliss, Rick, and Kelly Trogdon, 'Metaphysical Grounding', *Stanford Encyclopedia of Philosophy* (November 2014), http://plato.stanford.edu/entries/grounding/ (last accessed 1 May 2015).

Bourne, Craig, 'When Am I? A Tense Time for Some Tense Theorists?', *Australasian Journal of Philosophy* 80:3 (2002), pp. 359–71.

Bowman, Brady, *Hegel and the Metaphysics of Absolute Negativity*, Cambridge: Cambridge University Press, 2013.

Brandom, Robert, *Tales of the Mighty Dead: Historical Essays in the Metaphysics of Intentionality*, Cambridge, MA: Harvard University Press, 2002.

Brandom, Robert, *Reason in Philosophy: Animating Ideas*, Cambridge, MA: Harvard University Press, 2013.

Braver, Lee, *A Thing of This World: A History of Continental Anti-Realism*, Chicago: Northwestern University Press, 2007.

Braver, Lee, *Groundless Grounds: A Study of Wittgenstein and Heidegger*, Cambridge, MA: MIT Press, 2014.

Broad, C. D., *Scientific Thought*, New York: Harcourt, Brace, 1923.

Brock, Stuart, and Edwin Mares, *Realism and Anti-Realism*, Montreal: McGill Queens University Press, 2007.

Bryant, Levi, *The Democracy of Objects*, Ann Arbor: Open Humanities Press, 2011.

Carnap, Rudolph, 'Überwindung der Metaphysik durch Logische Analyse der Sprache', *Erkenntnis* 2:1 (1932).

Carroll, John, 'Review of Alexander Bird's *Nature's Metaphysics: Laws and Properties*', *Notre Dame Philosophical Reviews* (June 2008), http://ndpr.nd.edu/news/23567/?id=13333 (last accessed 1 May 2015).

Cartwright, Nancy, *How the Laws of Physics Lie*, Oxford: Clarendon Press, 1983.

Cartwright, Nancy, *Nature's Capacities and Their Measurements*, Oxford: Clarendon Press, 1989.

Casati, Roberto, and Achille Varzi, 'Events', *Stanford Encyclopedia of Philosophy* (August 2014), http://plato.stanford.edu/entries/events/ (last accessed 13 October 2015).

Cogburn, Jon, 'Slouching Towards Vienna: Michael Dummett and the Epistemology of Language', PhD dissertation, Ohio State University, 1999, http://www.projectbraintrust.com/cogburn/papers/dissertation/Jdissertation.pdf (last accessed 16 September 2016).

Cogburn, Jon, 'Tonking a Theory of Content: An Inferentialist Rejoinder', *Logic and Logical Philosophy* 13 (2004), pp. 31–55.

Cogburn, Jon, 'Moore's Paradox as an Argument against Anti-Realism', in Shahid Rahman, Giuseppe Primiero, and Mathieu Marion (eds), *The Realism–Antirealism Debate in the Age of Alternative Logics*, Dordrecht: Springer, 2011, pp. 69–84.

Cogburn, Jon, 'Review of *Gilbert Simondon: Being and Technology*', *Notre Dame Philosophical Review* (July 2013), http://ndpr.nd.edu/news/41310-gilbert-simondon-being-and-technology/#_ednref (last accessed 25 August 2015).

Cogburn, Jon, *Philosophy of Mind*, http://projectbraintrust.com/cogburn/papers/9ieparticle/philosophyofmind.pdf (last accessed 9 June 2015).

Cogburn, Jon, and Graham Bounds, 'A Cheap Holiday in Other People's Misery? Yes, Indeed: Towards a Compatibilist Theory of Immoral Art', https://www.academia.edu/20122774/A_Cheap_Holiday_in_Other_People_s_Misery_Yes_Indeed_Towards_a_Compatibilist_Theory_of_Immoral_Art (last accessed 9 January 2016).

Cogburn, Jon, and Joshua Heller, 'The Bearable Inconsistency of Being: Badiou Beyond the Limits of Thought', https://www.academia.edu/18797344/THE_BEARABLE_INCONSISTENCY_OF_BEING_

BADIOU_BEYOND_THE_LIMITS_OF_THOUGHT (last accessed 22 November 2015).

Cogburn, Jon, and Mark Ohm, 'Actual Properties of Imaginative Things: Notes Towards an Object-Oriented Literary Theory', *Speculations* 5 (2015), pp. 180–224.

Cogburn, Jon, and Mark Silcox, *Philosophy Through Video Games*, London: Routledge, 2008.

Cogburn, Jon, and Mark Silcox, 'The Emergence of Emergence: Computability and Ontology', *American Philosophical Quarterly* 48:1 (2011), pp. 63–74.

Cogburn, Jon, and Franklin Worrell, 'S-Vagueness and R-Vagueness: Some Results from Counterexamples to the Underlying Comparative Theory', https://www.academia.edu/18797604/S-Vagueness_and_R--vagueness_Some_results_from_counterexamples_to_the_underlying_comparative_theory (last accessed 22 November 2015).

Cook, Roy, and Jon Cogburn, 'What Negation is Not: Intutionism and "0 = 1"', *Analysis* 60 (2000), pp. 5–12.

Crowell, Steven, and Jeff Malpas, *Transcendental Heidegger*, Stanford: Stanford University Press, 2007.

Dancy, Jonathan, *Ethics Without Principles*, Oxford: Oxford University Press, 2006.

De Boever, Arne, Alex Murray, Jon Roffe, and Ashley Woodward (eds), *Gilbert Simondon: Being and Technology*, Edinburgh: Edinburgh University Press, 2012.

Deleuze, Gilles, 'How Do We Recognise Structuralism?' (2002), in *Desert Islands and Other Texts, 1953–1974*, trans. David Lapoujade, ed. Michael Taormina, Los Angeles: Semiotext(e), 2004.

Derrida, Jacques, *Rogues: Two Essays on Reason*, trans. Pascale-Anne Brault and Michael Nass, Stanford: Stanford University Press, 2005.

Derrida, Jacques, 'Autoimmunity: Real and Symbolic Suicides: A Dialogue with Jacques Derrida', in Giovanna Borradori, *Philosophy in a Time of Terror: Dialogues with Jurgen Habermas and Jacques Derrida*, trans. Pascale-Anne Brault and Michael Naas, Chicago: University of Chicago Press, 2004.

Deutsch, Harry, 'Relative Identity', *Stanford Encyclopedia of Philosophy* (November 2007), http://plato.stanford.edu/entries/identity-relative/ (last accessed 9 September 2015).

Dickie, George, 'The Institutional Theory of Art', in Noël Carroll, *Theories of Art Today*, Madison: University of Wisconsin Press, 2000, pp. 93–8.

Divers, John, *Possible Worlds*, London: Routledge, 2002.

Downing, Lisa, 'Berkeley', *Stanford Encyclopedia of Philosophy* (January 2011), http://plato.stanford.edu/entries/berkeley (last accessed 26 May 2015).

Dummett, Michael, 'The Significance of Quine's Indeterminacy Thesis', *Synthese* 27 (1974), pp. 351–97.

Dupré, John, *The Disorder of Things. Metaphysical Foundations of the Disunity of Science*, Cambridge, MA: Harvard University Press, 1993.

Ferry, Luc, and Alain Renaut, *French Philosophy of the Sixties: An Essay on Antihumanism*, trans. Mary H. S. Cattani, Amherst: University of Massachusetts Press, 1990.

French, Steven, *The Structure of the World: Metaphysics and Representation*, Oxford: Oxford University Press, 2014.

Friedman, Michael, *A Parting of the Ways: Carnap, Cassirer, and Heidegger*, Chicago: Open Court, 2000.

Gabriel, Markus, *Why the World Does Not Exist*, Cambridge: Polity, 2014.

Gabriel, Markus, *Fields of Sense: A New Realist Ontology*, Edinburgh: Edinburgh University Press, forthcoming.

Galloway, Alexander, 'The Poverty of Philosophy: Realism and Post-Fordism', *Critical Inquiry* 39:2 (2013), pp. 347–66.

Garcia, Tristan, *Forme et objet: Un traité des choses*, Paris: Presses Universitaires de France, 2011.

Garcia, Tristan, 'Après Meinong. Un autre théorie de l'objet', lecture given at the Atelier de métaphysique et d'ontologie contemporaines (ATMOC), École Normale Supérieure, Paris (13 April 2012), http://atmoc.free.fr/resources/handout23.pdf (last accessed 9 September 2016).

Garcia, Tristan, 'Crossing Ways of Thinking: On Graham Harman's System and My Own', trans. Mark Allan Ohm, *Parrhesia: A Journal of Critical Philosophy* 16 (2013), pp. 14–25.

Garcia, Tristan, *Form and Object: A Theory of Things*, trans. Mark Allan Ohm and Jon Cogburn, Edinburgh: Edinburgh University Press, 2014.

Gendler, Tamar Szabo, and John Hawthorne (eds), *Conceivability and Possibility*, Oxford: Clarendon Press, 2002.

Ginsborg, Hanna, *The Normativity of Nature: Essays on Kant's Critique of Judgement*, Oxford: Oxford University Press, 2015.

Goodman, Nelson, 'A Genuinely Intensional Set Theory', in Stewart Shapiro (ed.), *Intensional Mathematics*, Amsterdam: Elsevier, 1985, pp. 63–77.

Gordon, Peter, *Continental Divide: Heidegger, Cassirer, Davos*, Cambridge, MA: Harvard University Press, 2010.

Grant, Iain Hamilton, *Philosophies of Nature after Schelling*, London: Bloomsbury Academic, 2008.

Harman, Graham, *Tool-Being: Heidegger and the Metaphysics of Objects*, Chicago: Open Court, 2002.

Harman, Graham, *Guerrilla Metaphysics*, Chicago: Open Court, 2005.

Harman, Graham, *Prince of Networks: Bruno Latour and Metaphysics*, Melbourne: re.press, 2009.

Harman, Graham, *Towards Speculative Realism: Essays and Lectures*, Washington, DC: Zero Books, 2010.

Harman, Graham, 'Bruno Latour, King of Networks', in *Towards Speculative Realism: Essays and Lectures*, Washington, DC: Zero Books, 2010, pp. 67–92.

Harman, Graham, 'The Assemblage Theory of Society', in *Towards Speculative Realism: Essays and Lectures*, Washington, DC: Zero Books, 2010, pp. 170–98.

Harman, Graham, *The Quadruple Object*, Washington, DC: Zero Books, 2011.

Harman, Graham, 'Object Oriented France: The Philosophy of Tristan Garcia', *continent* 2:1 (2012), pp. 6–21.

Harman, Graham, *Weird Realism: Lovecraft and Philosophy*, Washington, DC: Zero Books, 2012.

Harman, Graham, *Bells and Whistles: More Speculative Realism*, Washington, DC: Zero Books, 2013.

Harman, Graham, 'Garcia's Jungle', in *Bells and Whistles: More Speculative Realism*, Washington, DC: Zero Books, 2013, pp. 133–58.

Harman, Graham, 'Tristan Garcia and the Thing-in-itself', *Parrhesia: A Journal of Critical Philosophy* 16 (2013), pp. 26–34.

Harman, Graham, *Quentin Meillassoux: Philosophy in the Making*, 2nd edn, Edinburgh: Edinburgh University Press, 2015.

Harman, Graham, 'The Object Turn: A Conversation', interview by Todd Wiscombe, David Ruy, and Todd Gannon, *Anyone Corporation* (March 2015), http://www.anycorp.com/anycorp/article/228 (last accessed 30 May 2015).

Harman, Graham, 'An Interview with Graham Harman', interview by Jon Cogburn, *Edinburgh University Press Blog* (September 2015), http://euppublishingblog.com/2015/09/10/an-interview-with-graham-harman/ (last accessed 26 September 2015).

Hegel, G. W. F., *Science of Logic*, trans. A. V. Miller, London: George Allen and Unwin, 1969.

Hegel, G. W. F., *Phenomenology of Spirit*, trans. A. V. Miller, Oxford: Oxford University Press, 1977.

Heidegger, Martin, 'On the Essence of Truth', trans. John Sallis (1961), http://aphelis.net/wp-content/uploads/2011/02/Martin-Heidegger-On-the-Essence-of-Truth.pdf (last accessed 11 November 2015).

Heller, Joshua, and Jon Cogburn, 'Meillassoux's Dilemma', https://www.academia.edu/18797280/MEILLASSOUX_S_DILEMMA_PARADOXES_OF_TOTALITY_AFTER_THE_SPECULATIVE_TURN (last accessed 22 November 2015).

Hogan, Desmond, 'Noumenal Affection', *Philosophical Review* 118 (2009), pp. 501–32.

Hume, David, *Dialogues Concerning Natural Religion*, Indianapolis: Hackett, 1998.

James, Ian, *The New French Philosophy*, Stafford: Polity, 2012.

Johnston, Adrian, 'Phantom of Consistency: Alain Badiou and Kantian Transcendental Idealism', *Continental Philosophy Review* 41 (2008), pp. 345–66.

Johnston, Adrian, 'Points of Forced Freedom: Eleven (More) Theses on Materialism', *Speculations* IV (2013), pp. 91–8.

Jordie, Cat, 'The Unity of Science', *Stanford Encyclopedia of Philosophy* (May 2013), http://plato.stanford.edu/entries/scientific-unity/ (last accessed 30 May 2015).

Kant, Immanuel, *Critique of Pure Reason*, trans. Warner Pluhar, Indianapolis: Hackett, 1996.

Kant, Immanuel, *Groundwork of the Metaphysics of Morals*, Cambridge: Cambridge University Press, 2012.

Kim, Jaegwon, *Philosophy of Mind*, Boulder, CO: Westview Press, 1998.

Kirkham, Richard, *Theories of Truth: A Critical Introduction*, Cambridge, MA: MIT Press.

Kraut, Robert, 'Indiscernibility and Ontology', *Synthese* 44 (1980), pp. 113–35.

Ladyman, James, and Don Ross, *Every Thing Must Go: Metaphysics Naturalized*, Oxford: Oxford University Press, 2009.

Livingston, Paul, *The Politics of Logic: Badiou, Wittgenstein, and the Consequences of Formalism*, London: Routledge, 2014.

Lyotard, Jean-François, *The Postmodern Condition: A Report on Knowledge*, Minneapolis: University of Minnesota Press, 1984.

Massey, Gerald, 'The Indeterminacy of Translation: A Study in Philosophical Exegesis', *Philosophical Topics* 20 (1992), pp. 317–45.

McDowell, John, *Mind and World*, Cambridge, MA: Harvard University Press, 1996.

Meillassoux, Quentin, *After Finitude: An Essay on the Necessity of Contingency*, New York: Bloomsbury Academic, 2010.

Millière, Raphaël, 'Metaphysics Today and Tomorrow', trans. Mark Allan Ohm, Workshop on Contemporary Metaphysics and Ontology at the École Normale Supérieure, Paris (October 2011), http://atmoc. files.wordpress.com/2012/06/milliere_metaphysics_today_and_tomorrow1.pdf (last accessed 8 January 2013).

Moore, A. W., *The Evolution of Modern Metaphysics: Making Sense of Things*, Cambridge: Cambridge University Press, 2012.

Moore, G. E., *Principia Ethica*, Cambridge: Cambridge University Press, 1903.

Morton, Timothy, *Realist Magic: Objects, Ontology, Causality*, Ann Arbor: MPublishing, 2013.

Mullarky, John, *Post-Continental Philosophy*, London: Continuum, 2006.

Okrent, Mark, *Heidegger's Pragmatism*, Ithaca, NY: Cornell University Press, 1988.

Okrent, Mark, 'On Layer Cakes' (July 2006), http://www.bates. edu/philosophy/files/2010/07/onlayer.pdf (last accessed 8 January 2013).

Parsons, Josh, 'Against Advance Modalizing' (November 2011), http:// www.joshparsons.net/papers/aam/against-advanced2.pdf (last accessed 9 January 2016).

Plato, *The Republic*, in *Plato: The Collected Dialogues*, ed. Edith Hamilton and Huntington Cairns, Princeton: Princeton University Press, 1989.

Priest, Graham, *Beyond the Limits of Thought*, Oxford: Oxford University Press, 2002.

Priest, Graham, *Towards Non-Being*, Oxford: Oxford University Press, 2007.

Priest, Graham, *One: Being an Investigation into the Unity of Reality and of its Parts, including the Singular Object which is Nothingness*, Oxford: Oxford University Press, 2014.

Psillos, Stathis, 'Ramsey's *Ramsey-sentences**', *Vienna Circle Institute Yearbook [2004]* 12 (2006), pp. 67–90.

Putnam, Hilary, *Reason, Truth, and History*, Cambridge: Cambridge University Press, 1981.

Putnam, Hilary, *Words and Life*, Cambridge, MA: Harvard University Press 1995.

Putnam, Hilary, *The Threefold Cord: Mind, Body, and World*, New York: Columbia University Press, 2001.

Quine, Willard, 'On What There Is', in *From a Logical Point of View*, Cambridge, MA: Harvard University Press, 1961, pp. 1–19.

Quine, Willard, 'Two Dogmas of Empiricism', in *From a Logical Point of View*, Cambridge, MA: Harvard University Press, 1961, pp. 20–46.

Quine, Willard, *Ontological Relativity and Other Essays*, New York: Columbia University Press, 1962.

Raffoul, François, *The Origins of Responsibility*, Bloomington: Indiana University Press, 2010.

Ramsey, Frank, 'Theories', in *The Foundations of Mathematics and other Logical Essays*, ed. R. B. Braithwaite, London: Routledge and Kegan Paul, 1931, pp. 212–36.

Rice, Anne, *Interview With the Vampire*, New York: Alfred A. Knopf, 1976.

Robinson, Howard, 'Substance', *Stanford Encyclopedia of Philosophy* (February 2014), http://plato.stanford.edu/entries/substance/ (last accessed 27 July 2015).

Roland, Jeffery, 'A Euthyphronic Problem for Kitcher's Epistemology of Science', *Southern Journal of Philosophy* 47 (2009), pp. 205–23.

Roland, Jeffrey, 'On Naturalizing the Epistemology of Mathematics', *Pacific Philosophical Quarterly* 90 (2009), pp. 63–97.

Russell, Bertrand, *The Problems of Philosophy*, Oxford: Oxford University Press, 1912.

Schaffer, Jonathan, 'Monism', *Stanford Encyclopedia of Philosophy* (March 2007), http://plato.stanford.edu/entries/monism/ (last accessed 7 January 2016).

Schaffer, Jonathan, 'The Internal Relatedness of All Things', *Mind* 119 (2010), pp. 341–76.

Schelling, F. W. J., 'Ages of the World', in Slavoj Žižek and F. W. J. Schelling, *The Abyss of Freedom and Ages of the World*, Ann Arbor: University of Michigan Press, 1997, pp. 105–82.

Schufreider, Gregory, *Confessions of a Rational Mystic: Anselm's Early Writings*, West Lafayette: Purdue University Press, 1994.

Schufreider, Gregory, 'Sticking Heidegger with a Stela: Lacoue-labarthe, Art and Politics', in David Pettigrew and François Raffoul (eds), *French Interpretations of Heidegger: An Exceptional Reception*, Albany: State University of New York Press, 2008, pp. 187–214.

Sebold, Richard, *Continental Anti-Realism: A Critique*, Lanham, MD: Rowman and Littlefield, 2014.

Seibt, Johanna, 'Process Philosophy', *Stanford Encyclopedia of Philosophy* (October 2012), http://plato.stanford.edu/entries/process-philosophy/ (last accessed 22 November 2015).

Smith, Daniel, 'An Event Worthy of the Name: A Name Worthy of the Event', *The Journal of Speculative Philosophy* 29:3 (2015), pp. 387–94.

Sparrow, Tom, *The End of Phenomenology: Metaphysics and the New Realism*, Edinburgh: Edinburgh University Press, 2014.

Spencer, Lloyd, and Andrzej Krauze, *Introducing Hegel*, London: Icon Books, 2012.

Stern, Robert, *Routledge Philosophy Guidebook to Hegel and the Phenomenology of Spirit*, London: Routledge, 2002.

Stump, Eleonore, 'Dante's Hell, Aquinas's Moral Theory, and the Love of God', in *Arguing About Religion*, ed. Kevin Timpe, London: Routledge, 2009, pp. 500–11.

Tennant, Neil, 'A New Unified Account of Truth and Paradox', *Mind* 124 (2015), pp. 571–605.

Unger, Peter, *Ignorance: A Defense of Skepticism*, Oxford: Clarendon Press, 1979.

Whitehead, Alfred North, *Process and Reality: An Essay in Cosmology*, Cambridge: Cambridge University Press, 1929.

Wilson, Mark, *Wandering Significance*, Oxford: Oxford University Press, 2008.

Index

Note: 'n' indicates chapter notes.